Who Believed in You?

Dina Powell McCormick
and David McCormick

Who
Believed
in You?

HOW TRANSFORMATIVE MENTORSHIP

CHANGES THE WORLD

HarperCollins
Leadership

An Imprint of HarperCollins

Published by HarperCollins Leadership, an imprint of HarperCollins Focus LLC.

Any internet addresses, phone numbers, or company or product information printed in this book are offered as a resource and are not intended in any way to be or to imply an endorsement by HarperCollins Leadership, nor does HarperCollins Leadership vouch for the existence, content, or services of these sites, phone numbers, companies, or products beyond the life of this book.

ISBN 978-1-4002-3594-0 (eBook)
ISBN 978-1-4002-3591-9 (HC)

Library of Congress Control Number: 2023931440

Printed in the United States of America
25 26 27 28 29 LBC 6 5 4 3 2

"If I have seen further, it is by standing on the shoulders of giants."

—*Sir Isaac Newton*

CONTENTS

✦

PART I

The Four Pillars of
Transformative Mentoring

❖

PART II

Transformative
Mentoring in Practice

◆

PART III

Transformative Mentoring
for True Change

Who Believed in You?

PART I
The Four Pillars of Transformative Mentoring

Your Invitation

H ere's a true story about a powerful executive, a writer at the beginning of his career, and a bird in a wicker cage.

The name of the bird is long forgotten, but the name of the executive is Deanne Barkley. It's the late 1970s in Hollywood, and Ms. Barkley chairs NBC's entertainment division. She's described in the press as having "more economic clout than probably any other woman in television."[1]

On this particular day, a young, unknown writer has managed to wrangle an appointment with her. As he's led into her office, he pauses long enough to notice the bird in a beautiful wicker cage on the other side of the room.

Interesting, he thinks.

Knowing he only has minutes to make an impression, he sits and gets right to the pitch. He has a comedy project he wants Ms. Barkley to buy. Two projects, if things go well. Thankfully, she appears highly intrigued, laughing during all the right moments. Until right in the middle of the pitch, when they both hear a soft thump. The bird has inexplicably keeled over.

Dead.

The writer's mouth falls open. He's positive his pitch is over. This will go down as the worst meeting in the history of Hollywood!

But much to his surprise, Ms. Barkley glances at the bird with a bewildered expression, furrows her brow as if searching for an explanation, then starts to laugh. Hysterically. "This is a moment for both of us!" she roars, wiping her eyes. "Kismet. Destiny. Fate. I'm buying both your projects. We're going to do this!"

Deanne Barkley didn't just buy the young man's screenplays that day. She also became his behind-the-scenes coach and personal door-opener. She introduced him around her network, which included moguls of the entertainment industry. Fortunately for the writer, Ms. Barkley's near legendary status opened a lot of doors.

She went further, advising him to develop a signature look. To stand out in Hollywood, she said, he needed an iconic identity. How about going by the moniker "Shorty"?

He wasn't sure about that one. But heeding her advice, he decided to adopt a spiky hairstyle. That was sure to get attention, and it seemed cool and original. (Also, his four-year-old daughter immediately approved.)

The writer continued to make the rounds in Hollywood. But there was still a problem, as he told us in an in-depth interview for this book.

"The meetings would go well at first, but I often had trouble toward the end of those meetings, particularly if a meeting grew long. My ideas were good, but my pitches kept getting rejected."

Ms. Barkley observed several meetings, then pulled her protégé aside. "Here's why the meetings aren't going well," she said. "It's because you're an exaggerator. You have a good heart, but in your effort to make a sale, you push a point too far. It comes across as disingenuous."

Who was that young exaggerator? Brian Grazer. You've probably heard of him. If you haven't, you've likely seen his name in the credits of a movie. Today, he is one of the most successful movie producers in Hollywood.

"I took her words to heart," Brian told us. "Deanne Barkley was smart and judicious, and I thought, *Wow, that's some big, tough love she just gave me.* It was true: I was trying to build my life on hyperbole. This was a fatal flaw."

He decided to change things. He took to imagining an old-school light switch, the kind you can flip up or down. "From then on, whenever I went to a meeting," Brian said, "I'd visualize that light switch. If ever I felt like I was exaggerating, I'd mentally tap the switch. That rebalanced everything. I became very adept at always telling the truth."

Those who know Brian today say he's one of the most precise and honest people in the business. If he's set to shoot a movie tomorrow, and someone asks him if he's shooting a movie, Brian will say no, and clarify that the shooting hasn't yet begun.

Brian's first two movies, *Night Shift* and *Splash,* eventually emerged from those early pitches to Deanne Barkley. *Night Shift* forged his friendship with actor and director Ron Howard. Eventually, they cofounded Imagine Entertainment, which launched them together into a slew of other successful projects. *Splash* was nominated for an Oscar, became the most successful film at Disney in a decade, and launched the careers of megastars Tom Hanks, John Candy, and Daryl Hannah.

And for this Emmy and Academy Award–winning writer and producer, that was only the beginning.

WHAT ABOUT YOU?

Brian's incredibly productive alliance with Deanne Barkley captures so much of what we want to explore in the pages ahead. A seasoned professional meets a young, aspiring talent. The ensuing conversation sparks a formative relationship. In time, the relationship molds the young talent and produces a long and successful career, which in turn resonates across and benefits society.

It starts with a willingness in the heart of the seasoned professional. Helped by a very unexpected prompt (thank you, dearly departed bird), Ms. Barkley caught the spirit of the moment. She followed through with enthusiasm and a growing belief in the young man's potential, investing not just in his projects but also in the person, helping Brian become a more honest and authentic leader. She changed the trajectory of his life and ultimately through him shaped American culture for the better.

Her example shows the key takeaway of this book in action. It's important to help people develop successful careers, but even more important is the shift that can happen from that effort. A true mentor can unlock a person's capacity to be their best self. The benefits compound and help change many people and, over time, even an entire society, for good.

The young talent must do their part too. Ms. Barkley's leadership decision took courage and foresight on her part, but it required faith, humility, and a lot of nerve from Brian to trust her and to learn from her. By cultivating the relationship, laying bare his weaknesses, and being open to her guidance, he set himself up for an incredible journey. It takes the mentor and the mentee, together, to make these relationships work.

We have both been the grateful recipients of such transformative connections. As we'll get into later in the book, we found mentors in family members, coaches, teachers, and bosses. Many became our dear friends. All played an invaluable role in our lives. They challenged us, drove us to aspire to greater heights, and most of all, through their belief in us, shepherded us to a deeper understanding of who we were capable of being.

The power and promise of such relationships drive the conversations you'll find in the following pages.

For the seasoned professionals of the world, we want to know: What exactly is it that truly elevates talented, ambitious people? How can you help emerging leaders make the all-important shift from being self-serving functionaries to being selfless, trusted, and values-driven people committed to changing our society for good?

For the up-and-coming leaders of the world, we ask: How can any young person harness the potential of more senior guides? How can you truly benefit from their experience, character, and wisdom? How can you learn from your mentor, not just for the sake of your own advancement or career, but for the sake of benefiting your country too?

We believe the answers to these questions lie in a specific kind of mentoring that we'll describe throughout this book. When genuinely and skillfully implemented, it can help us find and develop the high-quality leaders America needs most.

And that gives us a lot of hope—both for ourselves and for our nation.

THE STRAIGHT LINE AND THE STEEL ROD

In the pages ahead, you'll read incredible stories of change and mentoring from some of the most remarkably accomplished leaders in America today, including more from Brian Grazer. These people have excelled in a wide range of endeavors—the corporate world, the military, haute cuisine, government, education, politics, nonprofits, and more. All of them are people who we personally know well and deeply admire. They want you to know how the "Ms. Barkleys" in their lives have made all the difference, and why you should become or benefit from such a mentor.

Before we begin, we want to be clear that we are not being political with this book. It is a leadership book. We hold our politics, views, and principles firmly, as you likely do, too, and we do not always share the political views of the individuals profiled here. We have invited people who we know and admire from across the political continuum to share their stories—not because of their politics, but because of one thing they have in common: they're all wildly successful, purpose-driven leaders full of exemplary character. We want you to learn from the best, and all of us— conservatives, progressives, and moderates alike—can admire and be inspired by a leader's character, even if we don't agree with their politics.

This book tells a tale about our nation that you've likely not heard before. Through stories, research, and key lessons, you'll see how leading lights of business, government, culture, and the military were transformed by mentors who took them under their wing, and how that experience made them better, wiser, more trustworthy leaders.

By the end, you'll have a strong picture of how you can take part in that same transformative process by helping people become their best selves, and how that action has a powerful compounding effect in our society. That's the central purpose of this book, and it forms what we call the "steel rod"—the core insight that we will reinforce throughout with stories, statistics, studies, and our own experiences and observations. In short: Transformative mentoring offers the pathway to solving the fundamental deficit of trust in the United States. This kind of mentoring helps people reach their full potential, which in turn results in significant, positive impact on our nation.

We've organized this book around eleven chapters presented in three parts.

In the first part, you'll see how there's a crisis of trust in America today, and how transformative mentoring can help fix it. These pages will build out the four pillars of this type of mentorship: 1) it encourages trustworthiness in future leaders; 2) it instills them with core values; 3) it mandates that established leaders invest time and resources into the mentoring process (an investment that must be returned by the mentee); and 4) it builds confidence in the recipients.

In the second part, you'll see what it looks like for mentoring to be put into practice. You'll discover how a grassroots institution forms the foundations of positive social capital. You'll also see how one of the important places we all spend a lot of time in each day can have a huge compounding positive effect on our society. This place can become a training ground for creating understanding, righting wrongs, and lessening gaps. You'll also see how unlikely mentors can be found in these places. A fascinating section, we promise—one that could be life-changing.

In the final part, we will describe how mentoring can bring about true and lasting change. In that section, we interviewed several high-level leaders, including one of the most powerful women in the world. We asked her about the secret of her confidence, and her answer will surprise you greatly.

Throughout the text you will find three features. The first is the results of a survey we commissioned with Jeff Sonnenfeld and his team at the Yale School of Management as well as Morning Consult, which asked thousands of recipients about their experiences with mentors. The data collected—the first of its kind—illuminates not only the importance of these relationships but how they are different across gender and race.

In addition to the data, this is a book comprised primarily of inspirational stories. Most chapters end with a "Spotlight on Mentoring," allowing today's top leaders to speak to you directly in a question-and-answer format. Imagine sitting down for coffee with them and letting these leaders pour their wisdom into your life. You'll hear about who mentored them, what that mentoring looked like, and how the influence of their mentors is still felt today. You'll discover how to unleash the same kind of positive action and influence in your own life.

Finally, we conclude each chapter with three takeaways that distill the main points of the preceding discussion. We hope these summaries help you absorb what you've read and then put it into action, and we hope that these points become fodder for discussions around workplaces, in classrooms, and in homes across the nation.

As two grateful beneficiaries of the American dream, and thankful of the mentors who helped us achieve it, we care deeply about uplifting leaders who can help meet the urgent challenges of our national moment.

If you do, too, this book is for you.

—*Dina & David*

1.

Trustworthiness

You have a superpower. But if you're like most high achievers today, there's a strong likelihood you don't know it. If you don't know the superpower exists, you also don't realize when it's been stolen from you, destroyed, or underutilized.

The United States has recently passed through a near-extinction event of historic proportions. What we lost is trust. This country's workplaces, communities, and shared institutions have been almost entirely stripped of it. Trust: the glue that holds families, communities, and democracies together and makes a great civilization possible. It's under siege, and almost wiped out.

Fortunately, your superpower gives you the ability to restore it. It's called being trustworthy, and it's the first pillar of transformative mentoring. When developed carefully and deployed strategically, trust can bring about enormous good.

It won't be easy to rebuild. The United States faces daunting odds. A recent report notes that while Americans still trust scientists and military leaders to some degree, we have lost our trust for almost every other type of leader and their institutions—including business leaders, journalists, educators, clergy, and law enforcement officials.[1] It can be strange to hear that people don't trust you or your profession anymore. But that's exactly what has happened in America today.

Some good reasons exist for this loss of trust within institutions and across society. There are too many examples of business leaders who have clawed their way to the top, overtly intent only on personal gain with little concern for the employees who have made their ascension possible, or even worse deceived employees, investors, and customers along the way. Too many journalists have discarded their mandate to report the news in an unbiased manner, and instead have led with their leanings, stirring up tensions and suspicions. University officials have mocked conventional values and raised tuition rates, while students who graduate with four-year degrees have emerged confused about their futures and the goodness of America and have struggled to land jobs on par with their educational level. Political leaders from the Left and the Right have fostered divisions, been mired in scandals, and shed their integrity, resorting to grievance peddling and fearmongering. Faith leaders have failed to acknowledge and subsequently discipline and remove predators.

No single person, party, organization, or profession is to blame. Yet this shocking decline of trust for our leaders has helped fuel much division and violence today. As citizens, we tend to model what we see, and our crisis of trust has only become more profound, emerging more intensely with each new hurdle our society faces. Columnist David Brooks has defined the problem as follows:

Social trust is a measure of the moral quality of a society—of whether the people and institutions in it are trustworthy, whether they keep their promises and work for the common good.

When people in a church lose faith or trust in God, the church collapses. When people in a society lose faith or trust in their institutions and in each other, the nation collapses.

We [have] had chance[s], in crisis, to pull together as a nation and build trust. We did not. That has left us a broken, alienated society. We are living in the age of that disappointment. It has produced a crisis of trust.[2]

A CRISIS OF TRUST

Where is this "crisis of trust" coming from? Once integrity has been shed and trustworthiness has been tarnished, the loudest voices in society have urged us to fear other Americans. They've shouted at us, claiming we're radically different. They've insisted we can't agree with others. The only way to allay this fear, they've contended, is to join ranks with increasingly polarized and insular groups.

Nationwide, we have observed and felt sharp divisions. It's gotten so bad that more than one-third of all Americans polled would support their state seceding from the union.[3] Given the implications, that's a staggering statistic; one in three Americans would be content with not being part of the United States.

As a result, America has become a nation of us against them. Red versus Blue. Rich versus poor. Urban versus rural. Vaccinated versus unvaccinated. Whatever wedge might exist between people—the loudest voices have told us to amplify that wedge and drive it in further. The wedge has done its damage. A national magazine declared that "there is no advanced industrial democracy in the world more politically divided, or politically dysfunctional, than the United States today."[4]

That's tragic. We Americans are beginning to believe that we're no longer "one nation, indivisible." That mistruth might bolster news ratings and make money, but it's also raised our levels of anxiety, loneliness, anger, and depression. Social commentator Timothy Carney has noted in his book *Alienated America* that polarization is only increasing, social connections are failing, and "much of America is mired in a recession of social capital."[5]

Think of social capital as a network of positive, trustworthy relationships, organized around common purpose. That's what we've lost, and that loss has contributed to the crisis of trust. Social capital is who you're connected to—in school or work, in your neighborhood and city, in the marketplace and soccer field. Social capital allows you to achieve what you greatly value. But when a country has "a recession of social capital," as Carney describes, any person in that country is hard-pressed to accomplish anything for good. You try to make connections at work, but your colleagues seem interested only in self-promotion. You hope to be friends with your neighbor, but she's put a sign in her front yard that makes you furious. You want to go to church, but you don't trust the authenticity of those who lead the community in worship.

It's not too late to reverse course. Cultural analyst Robert D. Putman has argued that America has been a trust-filled, hopeful, united country before, with deep wells of resources found in communities and social infrastructure, and that we can become a stronger, more united country again. Those who doubt the veracity of this statement need only to think back to the tragedy of the 9/11 attacks to be reminded of the common humanity, empathy, and community that all Americans experienced in that moment. We don't need to agree about everything. But we cannot waste or destroy the precious gift of our lives and careers on infighting, ethical scandals, and exploitive business models that purposely prey upon other people's insecurities, angers, and fears. We are all on the metaphoric playground together, so we better learn how to play well. Dr. Putman writes:

> When Tocqueville visited the United States in the early nineteenth century, he was struck by how Americans resisted the temptation to take advantage of each other and instead looked out for their neighbors, not because Americans obeyed some impossibly idealistic rule of selflessness, but rather because we pursued "self-interest rightly understood."

An effective norm of generalized reciprocity enables that reconciliation of self-interest and good neighborliness. And where such a norm prevails, its effectiveness is manifest in generalized social trust.[6]

Congruent with this analysis and hinting at solutions, Dr. John Hillen, professor at Hampden-Sydney College, notes: "Very early in career development, we need to train executives in ethics—not just smarts, but *wisdom*. . . . We need leaders to not just run institutions well, but to run *good* institutions."[7]

That's exactly what this book is about: the need to create leaders who are better trained in "wisdom," to use Hillen's word. We must train people to become their best selves, which in turn produces social capital, overturns the crisis of trust, and has a compounding positive effect on our society. The trust extinction event can be reversed.

You can regain our superpower—and together, so can *we*.

FOR THE INDIVIDUAL, FOR THE NATION

Make no mistake, we have no intention of bashing America—the opposite is true. We catalog these problems because we love this country, are deeply concerned about how the loss of trust has divided us, and are optimistic that together we can overcome that which ails us.

For all its faults, America remains rich with opportunity and promise, and there's a reason that people from all over the world continue to cross oceans and deserts to migrate here. In America, each person has value. We are free to question, to act, to protest, to disrupt, and to innovate—and that's a huge part of what makes our future very bright. In America, you have the freedom of religion, speech, press, assembly, and petition. You have these freedoms because America is still the land of opportunity, and you're invited to pursue this opportunity for yourself and your family—to live the American dream. In exchange, all this country asks for is your patriotism. It calls on you to pledge allegiance to the American flag, and you do it for a reason—because you are part of one nation, *indivisible*.

But what if we become divisible? What if the bonds that weave our national fabric fray? That's exactly what the extinction of trust threatens. The division that has already been sown will continue unless we stop it.

A new chapter of America's story needs to begin. We Americans must realize the importance of personal and institutional integrity. We must grasp the distinction between the necessary and valuable debate of and disagreement about ideas, and the hatred of each other. We must renovate America's culture to ensure it is rich with social capital and trust. It's going to take a collective effort to rebuild trust in our country. But that's what we hope this book will help to do.

The promising news is that each of us can be part of the solution. We can do our level best to be courageous, principled, and motivated to serve our entire community. In doing so, we will foster, encourage, and build wiser, more trustworthy leaders. Such leaders are vital for helping our nation navigate the treacherous waters of our time and for leading us to the distant shores of a wiser, more trustworthy America.

We can't think of a more timely and strategic way to create a better, more enduring future for our country than to build a culture of trust. As ethicist Sissela Bok put it, "Whatever matters to human beings, trust is the atmosphere in which it thrives."[8]

So, what is needed to create wiser, more trustworthy leaders?

THE TRANSFORMATIVE EXCHANGE

The specific solution we espouse is transformative mentoring. We use the word "transformative" deliberately. It means we believe in a person so much that we actually help change the course of their life. Transformative mentoring encourages a metamorphosis toward wisdom.

Traditionally, mentoring has been largely understood in *transactional* terms: An employee approaches a supervisor and asks to be mentored.

Why? Because the employee wants a promotion, a stronger résumé, access to their supervisor's network, or useful, specific feedback.

With *transformative* mentoring, the relationship is established with larger goals in mind. Career advancement, yes. Expanded networks, yes. Yet as positive and important as those outcomes may be, they are secondary to the priority business at hand. A mentor who cares about the whole person will tap into the mentee's deeper needs and values. The mentor will inspire the mentee with new possibilities, help them achieve greater clarity and confidence, and seek to instill in them a desire to reach for a higher moral purpose.[9]

A few definitions are needed here. Transformative mentoring is different from coaching, where the main goal is to improve conditioning, awareness, or performance. It's not the same as being a role model, because a role model could be someone you never meet (although role models can have a transformational effect on people). Transformative mentoring affects us at the microlevel. As a transformative mentor spends time with a mentee, instincts, performance, and character are shaped and enlarged. If done well, the emerging leader learns to live and lead with more competence and integrity. A new, wiser leader is born.

The cornerstone of transformative mentoring is the trust between the mentor and the mentee. Trustworthy mentors encourage and empower the mentee to be vulnerable and honest with them—to bear their deepest concerns and aspirations in the knowledge that their mentor will respect their confidences and is committed to their well-being. Likewise, trustworthy mentees seek guidance and friendship not for worldly gain alone but in honest pursuit of understanding, self-improvement, and wisdom. When the two meet, and a trusting relationship is formed, a new standard is set. Trustworthiness becomes the defining value of a deep and mutually beneficial relationship.

Put another way, your superpower of trust is restored with profoundly positive effects for our community. Transformative mentoring produces people who help restore social capital by infusing the mentee with values.

Wiser, more trustworthy leaders help guide and unite our communities and institutions that have become so fractured today—the family, the neighborhood, the church, the civic association, the educational institution, and the business world.[10] Transformative mentors produce leaders who are not concerned solely with their own interests, but about our country as a whole.

Imagine a time when today's despairing statistics are reversed. Envision a renewed America where we've regained our trust for our leaders and their institutions. We trust business leaders again. We trust journalists again. We trust educators again. We trust clergy again. We trust law enforcement and judges and attorneys and state officials and politicians. We trust our leaders because they have been mentored to be trustworthy, and now they display that trustworthiness in the way they lead.

That's why building more trustworthy leadership is not merely a good idea; it's also a patriotic duty. We must undertake it for the people around us, and also for our entire country. We have to reconcile the very real problems we see in America today with the faith and hope we have for America's future. This necessity to live wisely affects us all, because we are all leaders in some way. Every single one of us. Think back over your life history. You can probably see how a handful of mentors made all the difference for you. If your mentors had not existed, you would have become a very different person. Similarly, you see big opportunities before you today. If you invest in another person's life now, you can make a tremendous impact.

People today actually crave true transformative mentoring from their higher-ups. A recent survey by PwC asked people what they look for most in the workplace. It showed that the most desired benefit by employees—and one they said could boost any company's bottom line—was not more vacation days or the addition of Ping-Pong tables in the lunchroom. What they wanted was more compassionate, empathetic leadership.[11]

Metamorphosis at this level invariably happens in a series of one-to-one exchanges. The positive effects can be as magical and welcomed as compound interest. A parent passes on their hard-won values to their child.

The child apprentices to a teacher who concurs with the parent and helps instill values and skills. The youth rises up to become a community leader or a terrific parent or the school's much-admired football coach. The coach (or community leader or parent) goes on to mold the character and self-discipline of a team of students. One student, in turn, becomes an outstanding citizen. Another becomes a responsive and principled politician. A third becomes a successful and trusted businessperson. A fourth becomes a visionary entrepreneur. The positive legacy in individuals and groups deepens and spreads.

Mathematical genius Sir Isaac Newton pointed out that his scientific discoveries wouldn't have been possible without the contributions of those who went before him. He famously declared, "If I have seen further, it is by standing on the shoulders of giants."

Think of this book as your call to become a giant.

"WHO BELIEVED IN ME?"

We share a deep conviction that influencing an entire nation for the better through transformative mentoring relationships is not only possible but central to our purpose and privilege. We are two proud Americans from middle-class origins—a daughter of Egyptian parents who immigrated to Texas, and the son of educators from rural Pennsylvania—and we are privileged to have lived the American dream at the highest levels of business and government.

Although we worked hard, we did not rise to these levels unaided. In addition to strong supportive families, we were fortunate to have outstanding mentors who, at key moments, guided, inspired, taught essential principles, and helped us make smarter choices. Without them, our lives would have turned out very differently. And without them, we would certainly have missed out on what we might call the "virtuous cycle," as many of our mentees have become valued colleagues, friends, and supporters.

We've noticed that we can identify the pivotal influencers in our lives by asking a simple question: *Who believed in me?*

The following profiles show the giants on whose shoulders we stand, and for them we are deeply grateful.

WHO BELIEVED IN HER?
(DINA'S STORY)

I was raised far from Washington and Wall Street. My family emigrated from Cairo, Egypt, to Dallas, Texas, when I was just four. We spoke Arabic and were Coptic Christians, a minority religion in the Middle East. My father had been an Army captain in Egypt under Anwar Sadat and believed in Sadat's vision of peace with Israel. (In 1977, Sadat became the first Arab leader to visit Israel in a bid for lasting peace between the two countries.) My mom graduated from the American University in Cairo and eventually became a respected social worker in Dallas. But when they first arrived in Texas, my parents needed to take a humbler tack. They worked multiple jobs and eventually opened a convenience store to feed our family and earn a living.

Fully embracing the American dream, my parents were convinced that hard work, discipline, and education would bring our family a better life. My parents worked seven days a week throughout my childhood, while encouraging my younger sisters and me to pursue our dreams with all of our strength. I arrived in the United States knowing no English. My parents continued to speak Arabic at home, so I maintained fluency in Arabic while learning English. Eventually, my whole family became naturalized citizens of the United States.

One transformative chapter in my life was attending Ursuline Academy, an all girls' Catholic high school in Dallas, Texas. The motto of Ursuline is *Serviam*, Latin for "I will serve." Arguably, the most famous graduate of Ursuline is Melinda French Gates, who has described to me the profound impact Ursuline had on her. As she helped build and lead the Bill & Melinda Gates Foundation (now known as the Gates Foundation), that same *Serviam* spirit guided her to impact and save millions of lives around the globe. Today, she has stepped out on her own to invest $12.5 billion in organizations that support and empower women and girls around the world, including many organizations that mentor and support women.[12]

As for careers, my parents always told my sisters and me that in America we could become anything we wanted—"as long as it's a doctor, a lawyer, or an engineer." Those were secure professions in their eyes, and they wanted the best for us. So, it came as a shock to them when I showed an interest in politics. I worked full-time as a legislative assistant to a Texas state senator and also waited tables to help pay the tuition at the University of Texas in Austin where I was a full-time student. This was well outside my parents' wheelhouse.

Fortunately, one of my most important first mentors was my grandmother Nora. She was very open-minded for her generation and strict faith and for the subculture she'd grown up in. Tough, kind, and intelligent, she worked as a transcriber for the United Nations, and she always believed in me. At home in her kitchen, the warm smell of fresh baking in the air, she would whisper her affirmations and tell me, "God has a plan and purpose for your life." My grandmother instilled in me the confidence to proceed.

After graduation, I deferred my admission to law school, and followed my experience as a legislative assistant to Washington, DC, where I became an intern to Senator Kay Bailey Hutchison, another of my earliest mentors, and eventually a junior member of the leadership staff of House Majority Leader Dick Armey.

After four years on Capitol Hill, I joined the 2000 presidential campaign of Texas governor George W. Bush. President Bush later named me assistant to the president for Presidential Personnel, a senior White House role with thirty-five direct reports. At age twenty-nine, I was the youngest person ever to hold that position. President Bush remains a mentor and friend and included a portrait of me in his book *Out of Many, One*, about immigrants who have contributed greatly to America. Later, I became assistant secretary of state for Educational and Cultural Affairs, and later deputy undersecretary of state for Public Diplomacy and Public Affairs. Dr. Condoleezza Rice became one of my main mentors at the State Department. We talk with her in chapter 3.

After almost eight years in Washington, DC, I was recruited to Goldman Sachs in 2007 and moved to New York, becoming managing director of the firm's global impact investing business, as well as the first-ever director of its Office of Corporate Engagement and president of the Goldman Sachs Foundation. I led the team that launched was called 10,000 Women, a global initiative to foster economic growth by providing women entrepreneurs with business education, mentoring, networking, and access to capital. This was an unprecedented investment initiative for Goldman Sachs, with a projected budget of $100 million. Many people at the firm wondered whether we were on the right track. Would it really be worth our effort and capital to help women entrepreneurs around the world?

While preparing for the launch of the 10,000 Women initiative, I got to know Dr. Ruth Simmons, then a member of the Goldman Sachs board of directors and president of Brown University. During a board trip to the Middle East, Dr. Simmons and I spent time in the air discussing my role and the challenges of starting a complex initiative that was unlike anything Goldman had previously done. I confessed that I was anxious about my upcoming presentation to the board, which would be the final hurdle for getting 10,000 Women approved and funded.

At age thirty-four, I was confident in my analytical and presentation skills, but the Goldman board could be a notoriously tough audience. Since there was no precedent for 10,000 Women, I'd face challenging questions about how we would design the program, allocate the firm's resources, attract outside partners, and measure success. In the days leading up to my presentation, Dr. Simmons encouraged me, advising me on strategies to present to the board. As president of Brown University, she undertook her calling to build a new generation of leaders. She knew what an important movement this could be, and she knew the potential was huge: to have a global financial institution with the reach of Goldman saying the best investment we could make is to economically empower women around the world.

As expected, my presentation drew some sharp questions. After all, the board's number one mission was managing risks to the firm. At a key moment, Dr. Simmons spoke up with a passionate statement of support for 10,000 Women and my ability to lead it. She reminded everyone that sometimes you have to take a leap of faith and do the right thing, even if you can't be sure of the outcome. Dr. Simmons put her own credibility on the line to demonstrate her faith in me, bolstering my confidence then and in the years to come.

We got the green light for our initial budget of $100 million. As of 2020, 10,000 Women has blown past its original goals, supporting more than seventy thousand women around the world. It's spawned a relationship with the World Bank that has raised $1.5 billion in lending capital for female entrepreneurs. As of 2023, it has reached a hundred fifty thousand women with $2 billion in available capital, helping women worldwide gain access to business education, transformative mentors, potential partners, and other sources of investment that are essential to their success.

I still consider Dr. Simmons a mentor and friend. She is a giant, and I am proud to stand on her shoulders. I've also benefited greatly from many others who served as important mentors in my career, including Clay Johnson III, who preceded me as the director of the Office of Presidential Personnel at the White House; John F. W. Rogers, who serves as executive vice president, chief of staff, and secretary to the board of directors at Goldman Sachs; Lloyd Blankfein, the former CEO of Goldman Sachs; David Solomon, the current CEO of Goldman Sachs; and Lloyd Blankfein, the former CEO of Goldman Sachs. Lloyd was a boss, a mentor, and a friend. He always stood out as a mentor who gave me tough love and showed me the strength of honest and loving leadership. He and his wife remain among my closest and dearest friends to this day.

In 2017, I served on the senior staff of the White House under President Donald Trump. He was very comfortable having talented, capable, and strong women serve in his administration in important roles. He gave me an enormous amount of autonomy to work on important initiatives in the Middle East, including those that eventually led to the foundations of the Abraham Accord. In 2024, he worked hard to support David's campaign for senate in Pennsylvania.

I rejoined Goldman Sachs, where I once again became a partner and served as Global Head of Sustainability and Inclusive Growth. I was on the management committee at Goldman, and I also oversaw our firm's relationships with the sovereign institutions within key countries around the world. In March 2021, I helped launch our company's One Million Black Women initiative, which will invest $10 billion over ten years to advance racial equity and economic opportunity. Launched in partnership with Black women–led organizations, this new initiative is the largest of its kind and will drive investment in housing, health care, access to capital, education, job creation and workforce advancement, digital connectivity, and financial health.

At Goldman Sachs, I had the opportunity to build many teams over the years, which served to foster mentorships. When we launched 10,000 Women, we built an incredible leadership team for the program globally. John F. W. Rogers and Russell Horwitz helped guide us and keep us focused on impact and how we would define return on investment (ROI). We needed to explain, in the language of business, how this initiative would not only be so meaningful to do, but would make an impact for the firm.

To that end, we worked to define and measure jobs created, budgets, revenue growth, and more. Ultimately, we built a massive set of partnerships in more than fifty countries. We worked with the Bridgespan Group, under the leadership of Tom Tierney, who helped us measure the performance of the program. This independent consulting group helped us ensure we had the right metrics and were transparent in our reporting.[13]

As we constantly showed the impact of the program and how it helped the firm, one thing that struck me as remarkable was how often John, Russell, and Lloyd Blankfein would become emotional when they met graduates from the program. These amazing graduates would express their gratitude and describe how the mentoring and program had changed their lives.

Once at a board meeting, I was asked what the greatest impact of the program would be fifty years from now. Initially, I was unsure how to answer the question. Russell, who was known for only using quantitative data, whispered to me to say that if this program is as successful as we believe it will be, it will transform thousands of lives.

So far, the program has lived up to that expectation. Not only has it transformed the lives of thousands of women globally, it has transformed the lives of hundreds of people who work at the various offices of Goldman Sachs around the world. They have signed up to serve as mentors to the women. The mentors review business plans, provide lengthy video guidance sessions, and, in many instances, become close friends and confidants. Ultimately, this kind of mentoring has had a profound impact on both the mentors and the mentees. When we measured impact, we were also able to see how the graduates "paid it forward." After they graduated, some nine out of ten program participants went on to mentor at least fifteen or more budding entrepreneurs in their communities. Our team was together for more than a decade, and to this day, we still get together and express a deep sense of pride for the thousands of lives the program has impacted.

I've also seen over the years how one good way to mentor people is to highlight them and give credit where credit is due. When people work for us, we want to add value to their careers and ensure they're able to grow, reach their fullest potential, and have a strong impact. One of the greatest legacies as a leader is to be able to see over time where your mentees end up and what they are doing today. You can know with a strong satisfaction that you helped build effective, trustworthy leaders. I'll forever be grateful for the receptiveness, drive, tough love, and friendship of people who have been on my team and have helped build and lead these programs—Noa Meyer, Lisa MacDougall, Anne Black, Kara Gustafson, Jessica Lightburn, Amy Bradshaw, Joe Snodgrass, Jen Field, Sabina Ceric, Jackie Matza, Wade Lairsen, Jessica Taylor, Leigh Farris, Katherine Jollon, Charlotte Keenan, and Erin Walsh. They have all gone on to have great impact in the world, and their influence and leadership helps many people.

Today, the work of the 10,000 Women initiative continues under the leadership and guidance of Asahi Pompey and her team. And when we built the groundbreaking program called One Million Black Women,[14] an initiative to bridge the gaps that today's Black women encounter, I was in awe to partner with and watch Margaret Anadu help build the program and investment plan that she led. She, Asahi, and I pushed hard to make it a signature legacy initiative for the firm, with David Solomon and John Waldron's constant support.

Mentors can extend a lot of different directions. With 10,000 Women, we recruited amazing advisory boards who literally mentored us as we were leading mentoring initiatives ourselves. Warren Buffett and Mike Bloomberg cochaired a partner program we initiated called 10,000 Small Businesses, where we helped entrepreneurs create jobs and economic opportunity by providing access to education, capital, and support services.

At a graduation speech that Mike Bloomberg gave for our summit, he began his talk by describing how proud he was of the graduates and all the sacrifices they had made. "I know about those sacrifices," he said, "because I am a small business owner myself." Mike and Patti Harris, who leads Bloomberg Philanthropies, widely recognized as one of the greatest foundations in the world, helped expand the reach of our program in London, Baltimore, and other cities all while growing the impact of mentoring by adding hundreds of employee mentors from Bloomberg L.P. While the business education and capital provided to these entrepreneurs was highly valuable, the mentoring and business advising was often the most transformative and life-changing piece.[15]

I also believe so strongly in the power of peer mentors. One of my great honors was to become a partner at Goldman. It's a tight group of leaders who believe in excellence and a culture of teamwork. The partners can be tough—they expected all of us as peers to perform at a high level. More than one of my partners gave me strong and constructive feedback, some of the best advice I'd ever received. I was also particularly proud to be part of the special club that comprised the female partners of Goldman. These women proved to be incredibly supportive to me over the years, and I hope I've been that for them too.

Today I am vice chairman, president, and global head of client services, and a partner at BDT & MSD Partners. Mentorship is an integral part of our culture. I'm proud that in almost every meeting, no matter how sensitive the topic, our co-CEOs, Gregg Lemkau and Byron Trott, and Michael Dell, the chairman of our firm's advisory board, welcome junior partners and employees to participate so they can grow.

I recently received a note from a colleague that points to the power of transformative mentoring. This remarkable young woman worked for me for several years, then wrote this note on the brink of moving to another opportunity. I share snippets of her note not to shine a spotlight on me, but to show that transformative mentoring truly can impact people.

You have been such a huge part of my life for the past 3+ years that it's really hard for me to imagine a day-to-day where I don't continue to look to you for guidance and learn from you, as a professional and as a person.

Though I have learned a lifetime's worth of knowledge about transforming difficult problems and situations into creative solutions and successes through hard work, one of the most important lessons I have learned from you is how to harness kindness and empathy and turn it into action.

I am so proud to think of you as a friend and mentor, and I look forward to continuing to be in touch throughout the years.

WHO BELIEVED IN HIM?
(DAVID'S STORY)

I grew up in Bloomsburg, Pennsylvania, a town about fifty miles southwest of Scranton in a mostly rural part of the state. My dad was a college administrator and later became president at Bloomsburg State College. My mom began her career as a schoolteacher and later earned an EdD in early childhood education at Lehigh University, eventually becoming a school administrator. Their example and role modeling made a huge difference in my life. They were constantly encouraging me to become my best self. Even then, I needed some outside encouragement along the way too.

I loved playing football but wasn't all that good at first. In tenth grade, I mostly rode the bench on the varsity team at Bloomsburg High School. Our coach only let me play defense in the fourth quarter, usually when we were either way ahead or way behind. But I always gave it my best and made some key tackles and sacks.

That summer, the school fired our coach and hired a new one, Tom Lynn, to take over the football program. Coach Lynn pored through tapes of the previous year's games and reportedly asked a staff member, "Who's this kid who keeps coming in at the end of the game, giving his all, and making the key tackles?" He called me into his office and said, "You've got the right stuff. I think there's a place for you on the team this year. But you've got to earn it. You've got to go to training camp and bust your ass." I went to camp and gave it my all. At the end of camp, he pulled me aside with two other guys and pronounced us co-captains of the varsity team! I was only a junior. Juniors were never captains—not at our school. He wasn't picking me because I was the best, but because he saw how hard I'd worked and he thought I could lead.

The moment proved transformational for me. I was genuinely shocked by Coach Lynn's confidence in me, which far surpassed my faith in my own abilities. He saw potential that others had missed and convinced me that I could be a varsity linebacker and team captain. With his support, feedback, high expectations, and powers of persuasion, my self-doubts began to subside. It was one of my first lessons in the power of effective mentoring. Because he saw me differently, I started to think of myself differently.

Coach Lynn had the rare skill of being simultaneously encouraging and tough. Actually, that assessment is too nice. Truth is, he gave us hell. He could be ruthless, highly demanding. Yet he had his warmhearted side. He got to know each player as an individual and figured out how to coax the best performance from each of us, whether that meant giving us a kick in the butt or a pat on the back. He taught us that we shouldn't feel ashamed of losing unless the cause was lack of commitment, focus, or mental toughness—in which case, we should feel *deeply* ashamed. He was obsessed with preparation. He used to say, "The other team might outplay us, but they will never out-prepare us." By my senior year, he had turned our team around. We were regional champions for the first time in years, and I was named all-state linebacker. He never doubted me and the rest of the team, and that made a huge difference. My football achievements helped me win admission to West Point, which completely changed the trajectory of my life.

On my first day at West Point, all new students gathered in the same auditorium, and the speaker took a quick survey designed to show us the elite caliber of our fellow students. With a tough, gravelly voice, he asked, "How many of you graduated high school with a 4.0 GPA or higher?" All over the auditorium, hands raised, but I couldn't raise mine. Then he asked, "How many of you were president of your senior class?" More hands, but not mine. He asked several more questions along those lines, showing how West Point was populated with only the best of the best. Finally, "How many of you were captain of your school's varsity football team?"

My hand shot up.

That moment felt life-changing. Two years earlier, I would never have seen myself belonging in such a crowd. Yet thanks to the support and belief of Coach Lynn, I was in. I, too, belonged. In the years that followed, I wouldn't have survived West Point—or the many challenging periods of my life that ensued—without Coach Lynn's first lessons to me about discipline, consistency, preparation, and confidence.

We stayed in touch long after I graduated. When I was in Iraq with the Army during Operation Desert Storm, about seven years after high school, I wrote him a letter about how his faith in me had made all the difference—a letter that Coach Lynn's son, Roger, later told me he had treasured. When he passed away, hundreds of people came to his wake on a cold day in December. Generations of former players paid their respects because Coach Lynn had also changed their lives. I still think about him often, even two decades after his death.

After West Point, I went to the United States Army Airborne School and Ranger School, where I was named the Honor Graduate. I served in the 82nd Airborne Division and was part of the first wave of US troops sent into Iraq during the first Gulf War in 1991. I was the executive officer of a combat engineering company of 130 soldiers tasked with clearing minefields and destroying enemy munitions. After four years at West Point and five years in the Army, where I was blessed to have had a number of excellent role models and mentors, I continued my education, earning an MA and PhD at Princeton University.

One of my PhD advisors at Princeton, the famed professor Richard Ullman, became another excellent mentor to me. He had worked in McNamara's Department of Defense and had served on the *New York Times* editorial board. During the first semester of my master's degree, I wrote my first paper for Dr. Ullman. He handed it back marked with a long list of comments in soft-tipped lead. Dr. Ullman used a unique key system, tying his comments to sequential letters of the alphabet, A, B, C, and so on. When he reached the end of the alphabet, he began again with double letters, AA, BB, CC. After he returned that first paper to me, I just sighed. His list of comments and critiques was as long as my entire paper. He was unbelievably attentive, rapier-sharp with his logic. Although I improved in research and writing skills, he continued critiquing my work with that same depth for every paper. He invested as much time grading my papers as I spent writing them.

I learned to respect this man greatly. He also became a friend. At his suggestion, we started playing squash together. After I finished my master's, he encouraged me to pursue a doctorate. I had not been a great student at West Point and I did not think I had the intellectual chops to make it through a PhD. He assured me that I did, and with his help and the help of others, I completed my doctoral degree in record time.

In the years that followed, I joined and eventually ran a publicly traded technology company, FreeMarkets, which was part of Pittsburgh's renaissance, then assumed senior roles in government, including undersecretary of the Treasury during the financial crisis of 2008.

Throughout my career, in the military, government, and business, I was fortunate enough to have great mentors, many of them prominent, such as Colonel Mike Colpo, my tactical officer when I was a cadet, who later returned to West Point as the chief of staff before retiring; Ambassador Bob Kimmitt; Bob Steel, my counterpart at Treasury who went on to become deputy mayor of New York City; Treasury Secretary Hank Paulson; President George W. Bush; and Bridgewater founder Ray Dalio. Each of these individuals became valuable guides in different ways. Though Coach Lynn and Dr. Ullman weren't household names like a certain former president, they were giants in my eyes, and their mentorship made all the difference to me. They taught me how to believe in myself, to ground myself in ethics, integrity, and compassion, and to reach heights I didn't think possible. I am honored to stand on their shoulders.

I stepped down from my position as CEO of Bridgewater Associates, one of the nation's leading investment firms, and in late 2024, I'm preparing to assume my role as a United States senator from Pennsylvania, after winning a very tight race against a long term incumbent. I've also been fortunate to mentor many people over the years who are active today in high-level roles in business and government.

One of these individuals, Colonel Everett Spain, is now a professor of behavioral sciences at West Point. In a recent interview for this book, he recalled how we used to run together when we both worked at the Treasury Department. We would meet early in the morning, at five thirty, at the National Mall in Washington, DC, and run around the perimeter. Since he didn't have a parking spot downtown, he took public transportation to get there. His commute lasted more than an hour, so he got up before four o'clock on those mornings. He described how it was always worth it. As we ran, we talked, and I would share my thoughts and advice throughout the run. He described me as an "advocate," teaching him things, opening his eyes to greater possibilities, infusing integrity into his decisions, and enriching his life.

REIMAGINING A SHARED FUTURE

This book offers a tapestry of stories that can help educate, inspire, and challenge you going forward. Whatever political allegiance or ideology a person may hold, it's hard to dispute America's urgent need for more leaders with integrity and commitment to the public good. We are championing a nonpartisan, nonideological focus on mentoring great leaders that aims to seize this moment in history for the greater good. For that reason, we believe what we're advocating here is profoundly patriotic.

Good leaders must stand tall on their principles. But they need to be open-minded to other perspectives too. They must be able to bridge disagreement by seeing both sides of an argument, and by being charitable in their interactions with others who disagree.

Toward that end, we enlisted Dr. Jeffrey Sonnenfeld, the Lester Crown Professor in the Practice of Management, and Senior Associate Dean for

Leadership Studies at Yale School of Management. We tasked him and his research team with helping us develop and shape original, proprietary, data-driven content for this book. Dr. Sonnenfeld is also the founder and CEO of the Chief Executive Leadership Institute, a global nonprofit educational, research, and leadership organization that focuses on CEO leadership and corporate governance. His team designed and implemented a survey on mentorship and analyzed the results. In conjunction with Morning Consult, a global data intelligence company, the survey was taken by several thousand people, including C-suite executives, MBA students, and the general population. This research is woven throughout the book.

Our core value is a straightforward maxim: to lead is to serve. And to serve is to lead with duty, honor, strength, and humility. Above all else, we hope to promote gratitude. Our own sense of gratitude is immense for our families, our mentors, and our country for helping each of us reach our potential. That gratitude is the ultimate ethos underlying this project, and our promise to you is a greater sense of mission fulfillment in your own life.

We are not naïve to believe that transformative mentoring solves every problem we face today in the effort to rebuild trust in American society. But transformative mentoring is an important solution, part of the overall mosaic of answers, and a way we can all contribute to a better America.

Research clearly shows how relationships that develop with mentors are among life's most important experiences. Real change can, and in fact *must*, happen. The power of transformative mentoring will help lead the way.

KEY TAKEAWAYS

- America is grappling with a crisis of trust. We desperately need wiser, more trustworthy leaders to unify our nation and work toward understanding and solutions. With more trustworthy leaders, the perilous times we live in will be navigated more skillfully.

- Plenty of mentoring is *transactional* in nature, where one commodity is exchanged for another. But the solution to creating wiser, more trustworthy leaders is *transformative* mentoring, where mentors help mentees reach their full potential and lives are changed for the better.

- Transformative mentoring offers the pathway to solving the fundamental deficit of trust in the United States. This kind of mentoring helps people reach their full potential, which in turn results in significant, positive impact on our nation.

A Conversation
with Brian Grazer

You already met Brian Grazer in our opening story. He might be best known today as the spiky-haired genius behind Imagine Entertainment, the highly successful film and television production company he cofounded with Ron Howard.

Brian has written or produced a list of hit projects, including the movies *Splash*, *Apollo 13*, *Kindergarten Cop*, *My Girl*, *Far and Away*, *The Nutty Professor*, *Ransom*, *The Doors*, *8 Mile*, and *J. Edgar*, and the TV shows *Friday Night Lights*, *Arrested Development*, *24*, *Empire*, and much more.

Brian received the Producers Guild of America's David O. Selznick Lifetime Achievement Award for Theatrical Motion Pictures. He's been named one of *TIME* magazine's "100 Most Influential People in the World." He has his own star on the Hollywood Walk of Fame. He's written two nationally bestselling books—*A Curious Mind: The Secret to a Bigger Life*, and *Face to Face: The Art of Human Connection*. His film *A Beautiful Mind*, based on the life of American mathematician John Nash, won the Oscar for Best Picture. Brian's films and TV series have been nominated for a whopping 47 Oscars and 213 Emmys.

He and his wife, Veronica, are close friends of ours. They are enthusiastic, balanced people and tremendous philanthropists. They support organizations that champion global childhood education efforts, leader-ship development for people with intellectual disabilities, and opportuni-ties for unhoused people and children and families struggling with mental health and learning disorders. Brian's oldest son, Riley, was diagnosed with Asperger's syndrome at age three, which helped deepen a sense of compassion in Brian and eventually influenced him to produce *A Beautiful Mind*, which Brian has called his "most gratifying film to date—because it helped people."

But this high level of success and balance hasn't always been evident for Brian. We sat down with Brian and asked him to describe the mento-ring he received, and why it's been so vitally important in his life.

❖   ❖   ❖

1. Brian, who was the first mentor in your life, and what made this person so valuable to who you eventually became?

As a child, I suffered from undiagnosed dyslexia and received rock-bottom grades in school for several years. Literally, all Fs. I mean, I couldn't read until fifth grade. It completely broke down my ego. Whenever I looked at a word on the chalkboard or in a book, nothing made sense. All the letters were jumbled. Teachers would ask me questions, and I would look around the room and cough, pretending I had a cold, doing everything I could think of to deflect the questions.

Two positives helped save my childhood. First, I was a tough kid on the playground and good at sports, a kind of Robin Hood figure who regu-larly scrapped with bullies for the sake of my weaker classmates. This brought a measure of credibility and respect.

The second positive was my grandma Sonya, a four-feet-ten-inch dynamo who always carried herself like she was ten feet tall. She was a Russian Jew from New York who moved to Los Angeles to be closer to our family, and she absolutely exuded confidence. Wherever she went,

Grandma Sonya thought she was the best-looking person in the room—and I'm talking fiery hot good-looking. She was always full of these witty one-liners. In fact, many of the funny lines that John Candy said in *Splash* were inspired by Grandma Sonya.

Each week, when I was a kid—I'm talking nine or ten years old—Grandma Sonya drove over from Beverly Hills to visit our family. Whenever she left our house, she'd have me walk her out to the car. She'd bring me in close, slip me a ten-dollar bill to tuck away in a pocket, and whisper in my ear: "You're going to be special, kid. You're going all the way to the top!"

She didn't do this same thing with my siblings, at least that I could tell. But she convinced me that I was special, and for years of my childhood, I operated on that definition. There was no empirical evidence to support her view. I mean, absolutely zero. My report cards were dismal. I don't know why she believed in me to the degree she did. But thanks to Grandma Sonya, I felt like Superman. She gave me strength, support, and validation.

I think that's what everyone needs to succeed: one real champion to show you a better pathway, to help you see the value in you that perhaps no one else is seeing.

2. Was it primarily the encouragement she gave you that proved so valuable for your development, or did you sense a benefit beyond that?
Both. She also took me places, helping me navigate life. Week after week, she took me out to different restaurants and cafés around Los Angeles, introducing me to different foods and tastes. She often arranged for me to meet the chef.

Grandma Sonya was always curious. And we would exhaust that curiosity. She was relentless in her question-asking, and she taught me to be genuinely curious about life. From her, I learned that curiosity is a virtue. Curiosity has value.

Being curious has helped my career at every step of the way. When you're in the business of storytelling, you're looking for originality in the subject and point of view. For example, with the movie *Apollo 13*. When I started, I didn't know much about the space program.

But I was curious. I started by asking a lot of questions.

❖ ❖ ❖

She wasn't the only transformative mentor in Brian's life. After high school, Brian attended the University of Southern California on a scholarship, working on the side as a short-order cook at Howard Johnson's. He graduated from USC with a degree in psychology and worked for a production company for a short while, then decided to attend USC Gould School of Law. His father was a criminal defense attorney, and Brian wondered whether he should pursue a similar career. He landed an internship with the legal affairs department of Warner Brothers but quit law school a year later to focus more intently on his creative pursuits.

While working as a clerk, Brian began building bridges with people in the entertainment industry. His specific job was to be a gopher, running around the city, getting celebrities and executives to sign legal documents for Warner Brothers. Often, he hesitated at a secretary's desk or a front office, insisting he needed to personally hand his documents to the signers themselves. Sometimes, he succeeded in landing a face-to-face meeting with a Hollywood insider.

❖ ❖ ❖

3. You were definitely persistent in your pursuit of an introduction. Did any of these meetings pay off for you and eventually turn into mentoring relationships?

Yeah (chuckles). Once, while delivering documents, I asked for a brief meeting with Lew Wasserman, an icon and the most powerful person in the media business as the CEO of Universal. Lew was a tall man with broad shoulders who always wore a black suit. I stood in his lobby, insisting I needed to talk to him directly, wondering whether Lew would grant the meeting. I waited and waited, not knowing if my persistence would pay off.

Eventually Lew strode out of his fifteenth-floor office and looked me up and down. Nervously, I launched into this carefully crafted introduction. But before I could get very far, Lew interrupted: "You don't have much to say, do you, kid. Wait one minute."

He walked back into his office, emerged with a yellow legal tablet and a number 2 pencil, and added, "Hold these in your hand." He placed the pencil in one of my hands, and the paper in the other, then quipped: "If you put the pencil to the paper, it has greater value than it did as separate parts. Now get out of here, kid."

The message became clear to me. As I stood in the elevator on the ride down, I realized the pencil and paper were all I had. I didn't have connections. I wasn't the son of someone famous. I didn't have enough money to buy a bestselling book and turn it into a movie. So, I needed to create my own content.

That's what started it all. Stories are the things that define companies. They even define lives. To have value in the entertainment industry, you have to either buy or create your own intellectual property. As they say today, "Content is king." I had shown up to Lew Wasserman's office empty-handed. If I was ever to land another meeting with Lew Wasserman, I realized I needed to have something to offer.

You have to realize that I had never considered myself a writer. But with money tight, I started writing pitches. I bet I wrote several hundreds of pitches in those early days. Fortunately, my first two movies, *Night Shift* and *Splash*, eventually emerged from those pitches—really, from that one moment of Lew Wasserman kicking me out of his office.

4. In 2022, you became an Honorary Doctor of Fine Arts from USC along with Ron Howard. It's another great example of how far you've come. Brian, you're at the top of your game today. You can do anything you want. What drives you now?

I tell stories for two reasons today. First, because they interest me, and second, if they're good, they can have an impact on the culture. For instance, *A Beautiful Mind* helped the way we embrace and understand humanity. Movies and television shows can affect people in meaningful ways.

I don't always pull that off, but I've certainly done it to a degree—and I hope to do more of it. I want to create stories that prove that grit and character and belief are essential and have value in each person's life. I believe those important themes can still live inside the heartbeat of a movie or a TV show.

Ultimately, I want to do things that unify people and elevate them. That's what's most important to me, today.

2.

Values

At first, the boy only knew him as "Uncle Walker." The kindly gentleman was the biological uncle of the boy's best friend, and the three of them often went fishing, hunting for turtles, and waterskiing on the Bogue Falaya, a lazy, bayou-like river across from Lake Pontchartrain, in southeastern Louisiana, where the boy grew up.

The boy couldn't figure out what Uncle Walker did for a living. Although the man was trained as a medical doctor, and some folks around those parts referred to him as "Dr. Percy," he didn't practice medicine anymore. Instead, he spent most of his time at home, sipping bourbon and eating hog's head cheese. His face bore the lines of a man who had experienced pain—both in himself and in those he cared about—yet his eyes still smiled, and years after the boy had grown, he would describe Uncle Walker as having "a lightly worn grace"[1] about his countenance. Uncle Walker's daughter, Ann, referred to her father as a writer, but he hadn't published anything, at least that the boy knew about.

In 1961, a book called *The Moviegoer* was published, Uncle Walker's deeply lyrical and philosophical debut novel. The boy read a few pages and set the book aside to think. It was heady and thick-going, not written for a nine-year-old, but he grasped for the first time that a person could string words together for a career, much the same way a person could be a lawyer or fisherman, or an engineer, like the boy's father.

In 1962, Uncle Walker's book won the National Book Award for Fiction, and the boy understood this was a very big deal. Critics deemed the book an "outstanding literary work," but Uncle Walker didn't appear to let the praise go to his head. Instead, he stayed at home with his bourbon and head cheese, listening to the gentle ebb and flow of the Bogue Falaya.

One warm afternoon when they were sitting by the river, watching a turtle sunning himself on a log, the boy asked Uncle Walker, "It seems like you've got a lot of lessons in your book. What are you trying to teach?"

"Teach?" Uncle Walker said. "Nah. I'm not trying to teach anything. I'm just a storyteller."

The boy scratched his head. He was trying to figure out what he might do someday for a career, and Uncle Walker's example of being a writer intrigued him. "Tell me more," he said.

"Well, you and I are both from Louisiana," Uncle Walker explained. "There are two types of people to come out of Louisiana: preachers and storytellers." He looked hard at the boy. "For God's sake, be a storyteller. The world's got too many preachers!"

The boy laughed. He knew Uncle Walker was a devout Catholic who practiced his faith not so much by what he said, but by his deeds and with his heart. He asked, "How did you come to that conclusion?"

"Because that's the way the Bible does it," Uncle Walker said. "If you're trying to teach a moral lesson, you do it through a narrative tale. You tell the story of Adam and Eve and show the weight of free choice. Or you have Jesus telling a parable. Remember the Bible's opening sentence: 'In the beginning . . .'? You make it a chronological narrative. If you want to do some good in this world, be a writer who tells stories."

The boy considered the weight of Uncle Walker's words. Maybe in that exact moment, certainly in that season of his young life, the boy realized that he would follow the same path. He would become a writer who tells purposeful stories. His uncle was none other than Walker Percy, the great American novelist, and the mentoring wasn't finished yet.

The boy grew. He attended Isidore Newman School in New Orleans, where he became student-body president and did summer internships at the local newspaper. In 1974, he graduated from Harvard University, where he'd studied literature and history. He attended Oxford as a Rhodes Scholar and studied philosophy, politics, and economics, graduating with first-class honors.

One summer during his college years, he took a break from journalism internships and worked as a longshoreman on the Mississippi River, unloading and loading ships. Visions of Mark Twain and *Huckleberry Finn* floated through his mind, and he tried his hand at writing a novel, which he showed to Walker Percy. His mentor made a few encouraging remarks about his writing style, then gave him some pointed advice: "You're trying hard to write well, but you don't have a compelling story yet. You're not ready to do this. Go, get some life experience before you write your novel. Study the lives of real people—they can affect the course of history. Not just power, events, and forces. But people."

The boy took his mentor's words to heart. After graduation, he began a career in journalism at *The Sunday Times* in London, followed by a position with the *New Orleans Times-Picayune*. For him, journalism became a vehicle to tell stories about people who effect change. He joined *TIME* magazine in 1978 and rose to become editor in chief of *TIME* in 1996. In July 2001, he became the CEO and chair of CNN, and less than three months later, he guided the all-news network through the harrowing events of 9/11. From 2003 to 2018, he served as CEO of the Aspen Institute, a global nonprofit that promotes dialogue, leadership, and action to help solve the most important challenges facing the United States and the world.

He never did write the great American Mississippi River novel ("It's still sitting in a bottom drawer somewhere," he told us with a laugh), but he became a *New York Times* bestselling biographer, telling nonfiction stories with a moral influence, while never preaching. Included in the list of his published works are books about Benjamin Franklin; Albert Einstein; Leonardo da Vinci; Henry Kissinger; Steve Jobs; Nobel Prize winner Jennifer Doudna, whose pioneering work in biochemistry and genetics led to the development of CRISPR, a tool that edits DNA; and Elon Musk, the controversial innovator, visionary, businessman, and investor known for his leadership in Tesla, SpaceX, The Boring Company, xAI, Neuralink, OpenAI, and X Corp, formerly Twitter.

He discovered that mentors could be found in historical figures, too, and he noted how he learned something new from each person he wrote about, which he sought to pass on to readers.

His name?

Walter Isaacson.

One of the most preeminent writers, biographers, and thought-leaders of this generation.

"It's true," Walter told us. "One person can really change the course of your life and make all the difference in the world. If Walker Percy hadn't been my mentor, I would have become an engineer, like my dad. Walker Percy wasn't the only influence I had, of course, but by far he was the biggest transformative mentor in my life. Through him, I realized what it meant to be a writer. By telling stories, you can help shape the ethical, moral, and political tenor of our times."

INFLUENCING LIVES FOR THE BETTER

We saw in the previous chapter how the first pillar of transformative mentoring is trustworthiness. Mentoring doesn't simply help people gain promotions or broaden their network; it creates deep, trusting relationships, which in turn yield profound change within the person being mentored. This has a compounding positive effect on our nation.

In this chapter we see the second pillar emerging. The best kind of transformative mentoring instills values in a mentee. We saw this pillar of values emerge in Brian Grazer's life in the opening section when he learned to become precise in his truth telling. In Walter Isaacson's life, he learned the importance of helping to shape the "ethical, moral, and political tenor"—and we'll see a more detailed example of how he did that in a moment. Think of values as moral beliefs and actions. Honesty is a value. Treating people fairly is another. Integrity is a value. When a person lives with values, the person influences people positively wherever they go. Values are wisdom in action.

We developed this second principle after studying the results of the proprietary survey we developed in conjunction with Dr. Sonnenfeld. The most effective mentors not only dispensed advice and coached their mentees to do their best; they also helped develop or deepen values. One-third of our survey respondents noted that the greatest benefit they'd received from their mentors was a new professional opportunity, which they appreciated. But an even greater number—40 percent— noted that thanks to their mentors, they had made at least one large-scale life decision that had directed them toward a better and different pathway than before. Survey respondents noted that the change felt distinct and positive.

That profound positive change is what we want to foster beyond the 40 percent. Thanks to effective transformative mentors, people's lives can be changed for the better. An effective mentor doesn't simply shift or enhance a mentee's approach to their job or career. Rather, a mentor guides the course of a person's life and shapes that person's worldview. An effective transformative mentor helps a person develop honesty, fairness, and integrity.

Our respondents (more than twenty-two hundred people) were given the opportunity to write comments at the end of the survey. One person noted this increased sense of values and wrote, "My mentor provided a lasting model of integrity for me. She changed the trajectory of my life." Another noted: "My mentor made me a better person, husband, and father." These values make up the second pillar of transformative mentoring in action, and they are what we want to bolster throughout America today.

Yet the more we began to consider the pillars of mentoring and the writing of this book, the more we realized that mentoring remains a poorly defined concept for many. You may know it when you see it, but can you define it? Do you know where it comes from? We didn't know the answers to these questions, so the study of mentoring has been very much a journey of discovery for us personally. It seems that's true of society as a whole, as we learned by going back through history to root out the origins of mentoring.

WHEN ATHENA INTERVENED

The word "mentor" comes directly from Greek mythology. Unfortunately, the original mentor let his protégé down—according to Homer's story, recorded about three thousand years ago.[2]

Odysseus, king of Ithaca, left his island home to fight the Trojan War. Before departing, the king left the care of his young son, Telemachus, in the capable hands of his good friend, named Mentor, an elderly man tasked with nurturing the boy and offering him guidance. Odysseus also left his entire estate in Mentor's hands—including the welfare of the king's wife, Penelope.

Things became complicated when the king stayed away for too long (more than twenty years), and his household fell into disarray, particularly when hordes of lusty suitors developed an illicit interest in the king's wife. Telemachus, now a young man who should have fought them off, cowered in their presence while Mentor, the supposedly wise guide, watched from a distance, apparently twiddling his thumbs.

It took the strength of a woman, the Greek goddess Athena, to get young Telemachus back on track. Athena disguised herself as Mentor, appeared to Telemachus, and told him to protect his family, rebuff his mother's suitors, and go find his father and bring him home to Ithaca so he could help. Telemachus heeded the goddess's advice. Athena stayed with Telemachus on his trip, helping him along the way and becoming his new and true mentor in the process. Eventually, Telemachus found his dad. They returned to Ithaca (at different times), discovered that Queen Penelope had remained faithful, and dispatched the suitors once and for all.

A few takeaways emerge from this epic poem. We can see how not all mentoring goes according to plan, at least not at first—and we certainly see this in mentorship today as well. We understand how common it is to look up to a person, only to have that person fail you, or not provide exactly what you need. (We'll discuss the nuances of this more in chapter 9. Hint: Disappointments can offer new opportunities, and the short-comings of a mentor can actually become their own sources of learning and inspiration.)

We can also see in the myth that although one mentor may fail, another mentor can rise to take their place—and thank goodness for the ability to gather a team of effective mentors to surround your life, rather than one person bearing all the weight of this responsibility.

Mostly, it's this theme of "guidance in action" in the myth that appears brightest to us, which gets back to the heart of our second pillar of trans-formative mentoring.

Athena, the true mentor, emboldened Telemachus to act wisely. She became the agent of profound change in the young man's life. He needed to do the right thing; he couldn't just sit around watching a bunch of jerks disrespect his mother. You can almost hear Athena's voice in his ears: *Go! Do something. Rise up and fight! Go get your father and bring him home to help.* And fortunately, not only did Telemachus heed Athena's advice, but he did so for the honorable purpose of defending his mother. In this ancient myth, we can see the trajectory of change in Telemachus's life. With values instilled, his mentor helped him shed his cowardly inaction and find his true grit.

MENTORING THROUGH THE AGES

The practice of transformative mentoring—this action of prompting profound life change and encouraging increased wisdom and trustworthiness—has ebbed and flowed in both popularity and practice in the three thousand years since Homer's *Odyssey*. In our research, we saw it in varying cultural incarnations and epochs, through the guru-disciple traditions of Hinduism and Buddhism, through the elder-disciple traditions of rabbinical Judaism and Christianity, and through the master-apprentice arrangements of the medieval guild system.

The ethics of historical "world conquering" is a complex and controversial study today that is not always positive. Yet there are examples where mentorship led to more enlightened and selfless leadership. In the fourth-century BCE, for example, Alexander the Great, king of Macedon, conquered the entire known world, then wept that there were no more worlds to conquer. Yet scholars note that along with all of Alexander's controversial conquering, one positive thing resulted—the influence of Hellenistic culture. Why did it spread? Because Alexander (356–323 BCE) had been mentored by Aristotle, who had tutored him for three years in subjects ranging from physics and chemistry to morals and ethics.[3] Largely thanks to Aristotle's mentoring, Alexander went on to encourage education and literacy throughout his vast empire. Through his city-state system of government, Alexander raised levels of financial, artistic, and intellectual wealth, as well as scientific inquiry.[4]

Another example is the first-century leader known as Barnabas, a Cypriot Jew and one of the earliest Christians. He mentored a young man named John Mark, whom the Apostle Paul considered a quitter, but in whom Barnabas saw great untapped potential. Paul washed his hands of

John Mark. But under Barnabas's tutelage, John Mark eventually proved his worth and became a trusted, reliable leader. John Mark dropped the first part of his name and is today best known as the author of the Gospel of Mark,[5] a book that reflects Mark's newfound understanding of responsibility and "centers on one's personal choice to act."[6] Mark's transformation was so profound that it compelled even Paul to come around and accept his leadership.

During the Renaissance, one of the most fascinating cases of mentorship began when the young Leonardo da Vinci (1452–1519) moved from the village of Vente to the city of Florence. Tutors considered him too distractible to be a worthy charge. And because he was also left-handed, born out of wedlock, gay, and a vegetarian, he was often shunned by others in the artistic community. Before he was fifteen, he was apprenticed to Andrea del Verrocchio, a master draftsman, goldsmith, engineer, sculptor, painter, and theatrical set designer. In Verrocchio's studio, Leonardo found acceptance, affirmation, and inspiration. He started his path to greatness by sweeping floors, stoking fires, and learning the basics of the arts—how to mix paints, sketch, and sculpt. Most importantly, Verrocchio, a true Renaissance man, taught his student how to combine the various disciplines in ways that hadn't been done before. That's why Leonardo became not only the painter of the *Mona Lisa* but also a designer of flying machines, not only a sculptor of the Trivulzio monument but also an influential scientist and mathematician who filled notebooks with drawings of anatomy and mechanics.[7]

Before the turn of the twentieth century, a teacher named Anne Sullivan (1866–1936) took a new job as the governess of Helen Keller (1880–1968). Sullivan had once been blind herself, but she'd recovered part of her eyesight. She used her own experience not only to educate her famous hearing-and-sight-impaired student, but to offer insight and values. Keller went on to become a successful and inspiring writer, lecturer, and activist. And Sullivan's work with Helen Keller became the lasting blueprint for the education of blind, deaf-blind, and visually impaired children.[8]

The great Dr. Martin Luther King Jr. (1929–1968) credited Dr. Benjamin Mays, a distinguished African American minister and scholar who served as president of Morehouse College, as his "spiritual mentor." They met when King studied at Morehouse, where he would listen to Mays preach and speak to the student body. Soon, Mays became an advisor and role model to the young man. King would later write, "I could see in [his] life the ideal of what I wanted to be."[9]

More formal research into the power of mentoring began in the 1970s when businesspeople and researchers started to recognize "the vital role mentors play in the development of corporation executives."[10] From the 1970s onward, mentoring was increasingly used in the workplace—often to help and acculturate junior staff. In 1978, psychologist Dr. Daniel J. Levison described the importance of the mentor-mentee relationship as one of the most significant experiences in life. Mentors are not only a source of learning for mentees, he found, but they also play a key role in the development of mentees' identity and values. He also noted how the benefits extend both ways. When you are the mentor, you receive a greater sense of purpose or rejuvenation.[11]

Walter Isaacson told us he found this sort of subculture when he first began at *TIME* in the late 1970s.

When I became a journalist, the idea of being an apprentice was blended into the role of mentorship. Corporations would hire talented young people and help them become better at their craft, and better leaders too.

It was a training culture. Henry Gruenwald was editor in chief of *TIME* when I began. He was a great intellectual who took me under his wing, nurtured me, and helped me become a better journalist. He pushed all of us to go deeper intellectually, and he had a constant desire to make journalism more thoughtful.

I don't think he was doing it out of pure kindness. He was trying to shape a younger generation of writers. We don't see that kind of mentoring so much today, in a gig economy—especially in journalism—although it's still present in some industries.

When I became editor in chief, I tried to follow the same path by bringing a lot of very young and talented people into *TIME*, many of whom brought the much-needed sensibility of the digital revolution. I knew that we could not stay the *TIME* magazine of the 1980s and early 1990s, because we would have failed this new age.

Yet we continued to help mentor these writers into becoming serious, principled journalists who got to the truth and wrote with strength. We built into them empathy—the ability to see the world through people's eyes who are different than them. And we also worked to help them nurture the kindness within themselves and their readers, rather than stoke resentments.

Principles. Empathy. Kindness. Fairness. You can see the second pillar of transformative mentoring—*values*—clearly emerge from Isaacson's story. We are not espousing just any old sort of mentoring in this book. We are championing deliberate, transformative mentoring that produces greater trustworthiness and instills values.

Data shows how mentoring has taken off since the 1980s. Use of the word "mentor" has increased by 500 percent from 1980 to 2020, and the use of the word "mentorship" realized a 3,900 percent increase over the same period. A simple Google search of the term during those forty years yields over seventy million results—sparking more than a hundred thousand published research articles and ten times more general writings.

The idea of mentoring has seen a rise in popularity in recent decades, and we want to help redefine and elevate its importance in new and larger ways—particularly in a transformative sense. We want to establish mentorship as a basic building block of American community and culture. We hope to help refine how mentors help shape mentees, getting to the roots of what true transformative mentoring is about: creating profound life change while instilling a deep sense of wisdom and trustworthiness. We don't want to create leaders simply for the sake of having more leaders. We want to support value-driven leaders. Transformative mentoring can help people become that and change society for the better in the process.

DEPTHS OF PRINCIPLED THINKING

Walter Isaacson described to us how Walker Percy helped him experience this same sort of profound, values-instilling life change. In the early 1980s, when Walter was beginning his career as a journalist at *TIME*, he wrote an article about a controversial subject, citing surveys and statistics, describing the debates and legal issues involved, and quoting people on both sides of the argument. In Walter's mind, his article was a piece of fair journalism. He had cut through the bellicose rhetoric of zealots. He had talked to people on both sides.

But Walker Percy read the article after it was published, and he grew concerned. He wrote Walter a long letter, urging his protégé to drill down even further into the ethical issues contained in the stories he wrote about. Walter explained to us: "Walker Percy wanted to make sure that even though I was trying to be an even-handed journalist, I still needed to grapple with the depths of thinking that went into the issue. I'm not sure I had succeeded at that yet—at least to the degree that Walker pushed me."

That's true transformative mentorship. Walker Percy had already created profound life change in Walter Isaacson at a young age by initially inspiring him to become a writer. Later, he helped embed in Walter a value system where he could sort out right from wrong and live by integrity and truth. That's what true mentors help provide for mentees, throughout all time periods and subcultures. Our call as leaders at this historic point is to do similar things for other people.

COMPOUNDED LEGACY

Walker Percy died of cancer on May 10, 1990, ten days before his mentee's thirty-eighth birthday, and he had seen only a fraction of the success that his mentee would eventually achieve. Yet Walker's legacy as a transformative mentor did not die with him.

Today, Walter is in his late sixties, retired from his position at CNN and the Aspen Institute, yet he is hard at work on more writing projects. He is a professor at Tulane University, where he passes on his wisdom and experience to a next generation, which he selectively mentors. On a shelf behind his desk, Walter keeps a framed photograph of himself and his mentor, taken in the 1970s. The photo shows a young Walter Isaacson and a graying Walker Percy. The two are seated on a park bench together, talking, laughing, obviously comfortable in their discourse and friendship. Walter showed us this photo, and he spoke about his mentor with great care and fondness.

We have met plenty of hard-boiled journalists in the later stages of their careers—when the rigors of the job have worn thick calluses onto their demeanor. But this is not Walter. Today, whenever he speaks, he speaks with a smile. Undeniably, the protégé now wears about his countenance what once belonged to his mentor: the same lightly worn grace.

KEY TAKEAWAYS

- Transformative mentoring instills values that equip the mentee to be a wiser, more trustworthy leader who achieves positive change wherever that person goes. Ultimately, the mentor teaches the mentee how to be their best self, reach their full potential, and lead a meaningful and contributing life. This positively affects our nation.

- An effective transformative mentor helps guide a mentee's life and shapes that person's worldview. Like Athena did for Telemachus, a mentor helps develop mental strength and a mindset of integrity in the mentee.

- Research has shown that effective mentors can play a key role in the development of a mentee's identity and values. The benefits extend both ways, and a mentor can receive much benefit from the relationship too. As psychologist Dr. Daniel J. Levinson described, a mentor-mentee relationship can be one of the most significant experiences in life. When you are the mentor, you can experience a greater sense of purpose or rejuvenation. That's good news for the established leaders reading this book.

A Conversation with General H. R. McMaster

He's been described as a soldier's soldier, a truth teller, and a man who gets the job done.[1]

General Herbert Raymond "H. R." McMaster first saw action in 1991 during Operation Desert Storm. Then a twenty-eight-year-old captain, he led a spearhead of nine tanks, twelve Bradley fighting vehicles, and two 120mm mortars to push the enemy out of Kuwait. Hampered by a sandstorm, taking heavy fire, and in just twenty-three minutes, H. R.'s troops overpowered and destroyed a much larger enemy force of Iraqi's elite Republican Guard.[2] He received the Silver Star for the mission, and the action has been described as "one of the fiercest tank battles in military history."[3] The tactics and valor of H. R. and his troops during this battle are taught by military strategists today[4]—and that's only one piece of his highly prestigious career.

We sat down with H. R. and asked him to describe the mentoring he received and how it helped shape him to serve.

◆　◆　◆

1. The Battle of 73 Easting that you led in Desert Storm is studied today in modern history books. How did the mentoring that you had received earlier in life play a role in your decision-making for that battle?

Ours was the lead tank at the apex of a nine-tank wedge. The decisions to switch a tanks-lead formation and attack the enemy's defensive position reflected the mentorship, training, and education I had received across my career to that point.

I had studied military history at West Point and read all I could about armored warfare in North Africa in World War II, including the Rommel Papers, the Patton Papers, and General Ernest Harmon's memoir and his notes on combat action in Tunisia and North Africa. Our regiment had conducted challenging, realistic training, and mentors had taught me the importance of taking the initiative. Perhaps most important, our cavalry troop was confident in our ability to fight as a team and win.

Our troop's leaders understood our duty to ensure that no soldier died in combat because he didn't have the proper training. I have always felt that the only sensible measure of effectiveness in a combat unit is combat readiness. Then, once you're in combat, it's combat effectiveness.

We had trained extremely hard. After Saddam Hussein's invasion of Kuwait in August 1990, I was convinced that we were going to war, even before Saddam invaded Kuwait. We intensified our training and adapted our formations and battle drills to the desert. Good units are willing to learn from failure in training as they push the limits of their capabilities.

One of our tank platoon sergeants, Sergeant First Class Eddie Wallace, told me before 73 Easting that we might have been training too intensely. But then after the battle, he walked up to me and said, "You know what, you were right. It all paid off."

2. Talk to us about your earlier years. Who were some of your first mentors?

My mom, Marie "Mimi" McMaster, was an amazing schoolteacher and administrator. She infused in me a sense of right and wrong and the importance of ethical behavior. She also instilled in me a deep intellectual curiosity, in particular about history. I grew up in Philadelphia, a great place to get attuned to history. When we took vacations, we toured historical places including battlefields like Manassas, Gettysburg, and Yorktown. Her influence sparked my intellectual curiosity and my love of reading military history and biographies.

My father, Herbert McMaster Sr., was also highly influential in my life. From my youngest memory, I wanted to be an officer in the Army. My dad had served in the Korean War as an infantryman. He became a platoon sergeant by the time he finished his combat tour, then went into the reserves in Philadelphia. He served in other ways and was determined to make a difference in our community. He was a local ward president and coached Little League. He ran for Congress in 1968 during turbulent times in our nation and narrowly lost to the incumbent. He stayed in the Army Reserve, became a captain and company commander, and retired as a lieutenant colonel. My father fostered in me an understanding of the rewards of service.

Additionally, I went to a great grade school, the Norwood-Fontbonne Academy in Chestnut Hill, Pennsylvania. In my mind today, Sister St. Ignatius was seven feet tall. She was my first-grade teacher, and we had a rhyme about her: "Oh my goodness gracious, here comes Sister St. Ignatius." The nuns and lay teachers were strict but fair and compassionate, and the school helped me learn writing and composition. My football coach in grade school, Chuck Seaton, also taught geography and history. He was smart, good-natured, and fun, and he made those subjects come alive for his students. I recently got back in contact with him. The whole school was a great environment. Many other teachers and coaches come to mind as having a very positive influence—all the way through high school at Valley Forge Military Academy.

3. The military is known for its effective mentoring. Describe the mentors you had at West Point and early in your military career.

Colonel Cole Kingseed was my first history professor and sponsor at West Point, the faculty member whose house you go to over weekends. We spent a lot of time together with the other cadets he sponsored outside of the classroom. He was a relentlessly positive person with a great sense of humor who just loved life. He had a tremendous impact on me and helped deepen my love for history and look forward to serving as an officer. Later, Colonel Bill Betson, another history professor, became my sponsor. He was also a rugby coach and my professor in the History of US Foreign Policy course. He and his wife, Donna, provided a tremendous example of how a career of service in the Army can be compatible with a strong family life.

I didn't have the strongest academic record at West Point at first, because I hated calculus and engineering and there was a lot of that at West Point. I also had more than my fair share of punishment tours, which resulted in walking the area or being confined to my room on weekends. Colonels Kingseed and Betson encouraged me. And I went to them for advice and assistance across my career. For example, when I was writing my first book, Colonel Kingseed read the manuscript then asked if he could send it to Carlo D'Este, a very accomplished military historian who published with HarperCollins. Carlo D'Este contacted me and sent the manuscript to his editor. That led to my first book contract and the opportunity to work with a great editor, Buzz Wyeth.

At Fort Hood, my commander with the 1st Battalion 66th Armor Regiment was a larger-than-life guy named Billy McGowan. A tall, big-statured, African American man, he was a super positive leader who really fostered a sense of camaraderie. He had served with distinction in Vietnam as a combat leader and advisor to the South Vietnamese Army.

During challenging training exercises, he would come up to you, put his arm around your shoulders, and ask how you were doing. He cared about every soldier and had a positive impact on morale across the battalion. And we had high standards. No one wanted to let him down. That's what keeps you in the Army—when you look at leaders like McGowan and say, "I want to have a positive influence on soldiers and build a cohesive team like he did for the 'Iron Knights' battalion."

4. Did you ever have someone mentor you in an unlikely way, perhaps in a manner you didn't anticipate, or from someone from whom you didn't expect to receive mentoring?

When I left West Point, my original plan was to stay in the Army for five years, then work at a civilian company to save money for tuition to go to law school. I talked to my wife, Katie, about it, and she agreed. When the first five years were up, I bought a suit, signed up with a career headhunting firm, and got a ticket to fly to Chicago to interview with a large company there.

But I'd had all these tremendously rewarding experiences in the Army. I'd been a scout platoon leader, which is the best job as a lieutenant, and our platoon had deployed to Germany for a major training exercise. My squadron commander was a great officer named Colonel Tom Dials. He gave our platoon really cool missions. Like, infiltrate deep behind enemy lines and recon a landing zone for a brigade-sized air assault. At the end of the exercise, a British regiment hosted us and we played a rugby match. He asked me why I would ever leave this. I thought about it. I loved the experiences we were having. Tom Dials kept me in the Army doing what I loved.

My sergeants were instrumental there too. I was often mentored by noncommissioned officers. As a lieutenant, you must take responsibility for your platoon, but you learn constantly from your sergeants. They gave candid feedback and helped me become a better leader.

I was back at Fort Hood when I made the final decision to stay in the Army. They call it a "right-arm night," where you bring out your sergeants to have beers on you. Our scout platoon sergeants, section sergeants, and squad leaders were with me at the officer's club, when my platoon sergeant asked, "Why are you getting out of the Army? Don't you love this?! You're pretty good at it, we think. You should stay." That confirmed it. I canceled my trip to Chicago.

It wasn't all smooth going from there, of course. A lot of times, you go through an experience in your career that you think is terrible, or a job you hoped for does not work out. But you talk about it with people who provide you mentorship, and they help frame things for you.

I usually did not get the assignment I preferred. I got in the 2nd Armored Cavalry Regiment, which is where everybody wanted to go as a cavalry officer, but when I arrived, I got a force modernization job. I wanted to train troops, but instead I found myself in an office job where I was behind a desk, managing the integration of new tanks with new Bradleys [infantry fighting vehicles] and Black Hawk helicopters. Interesting, but not what I'd envisioned. I heard that I was going to be stuck in an office for two years, and I thought, *Man, that's a long time to be doing something like this.*

So I talked to the regimental executive officer, who encouraged me to stay in the regiment but look for another job within the regiment. I went to visit 1/3/5 Armor Battalion and talked to Lieutenant Colonel Dave McKiernan, who later became a four-star general and a commander in Afghanistan. It was a Thursday, and after I explained my position, I asked, "Do you think there might be space for me over here?" He said, "You can take command on Monday." He'd just relieved a company commander and needed somebody ASAP.

I had to go back and see my regimental commander, Colonel Jim Steele, a swashbuckling guy who rode a motorcycle. He'd fought in Vietnam and trained counterinsurgency commandos in Central America. I said, "Sir, there's nothing I would rather do than command a cavalry troop in this regiment, but I've heard I won't be able to command for two years. I'd rather command a shower and bath unit than do what I'm doing right now." He said, "Okay, McMaster. Go see the adjutant. You'll have a new job tomorrow, and you'll be in command of a cavalry troop within a year. Now get the hell out of my office." Long story short, I ended up becoming Colonel Steele's plans officer, which was great. I stayed in that regiment, became a commander within a year, and that was the command I took into 73 Easting.

❖   ❖   ❖

During his career, H. R. also taught at West Point, led a multinational task force in Kabul, Afghanistan, helped design and shape the Army's future, and advised General David Petraeus when he oversaw all coalition forces in Iraq.

Along the way, H. R. completed an Army War College research fellowship at Stanford University's Hoover Institution, earned a PhD in American history from the University of North Carolina at Chapel Hill, and wrote two bestselling books: *Dereliction of Duty* and *Battlegrounds: The Fight to Defend the Free World*, effectively passing on his expertise in mentoring a new generation of soldier's soldiers.

From 2018 to 2019, he served as the twenty-sixth national security advisor of United States, while he was still on active duty in the military. The three-star general briefed the US president on all security issues, coordinated multiple departments and agencies, and explained the president's policies on national and international security to the public.

Now retired from the military and his role at the White House, H. R. lectures at the Hoover Institution, the Freeman Spogli Institute for International Studies, and Stanford University's Graduate School of Business.

❖ ❖ ❖

5. You have a legendary following, and the number of military personnel you've mentored is staggering. Why do you think you've stood out so strongly over the years as somebody who people wanted to work for?
By building winning teams. Soldiers are attracted to the Army because they know it's hard but they want a challenge.

I also made it a point to provide developmental counseling and assistance. Some leaders only focus on performance counseling. But throughout my career, I'd always take time to talk with my sergeants or officers who needed assistance or advice. I think that helped keep some good people in the Army.

When we came back from a year's combat mission in Iraq, we were exhausted as a unit. I think nineteen captains put in their separation paperwork to get out of the Army. I met with them as a group and then individually and helped provide context, saying, "Hey, your whole career won't be this intense." I worked to get them other assignments. Some wanted more stability for their families, so I helped arrange for that. I called their spouses and talked through various options with them. The majority of those captains pulled back their resignation paperwork. They've gone on to become battalion commanders. They're on their way to brigade command.

Overall, to succeed as a leader, you have to be a good listener. If you're going to succeed in any complex endeavor, listening skills are super important. You want to create meaningful, thoughtful discussions, even with people you don't agree with. As a way of beginning those discussions, I'd often start with open-ended questions, just to frame the challenges and apply design-thinking to the challenges.

That's a step that's often skipped. It takes longer, that's for sure. In Iraq, you have to eat a lot of goats. Literally, you have to sit down with village elders and eat whatever food they prepare for you first before you can continue with a meeting. Sometimes I'd spend the first thirty minutes of a meeting listening. I would ask the Iraqis about the solutions they had. It takes time to achieve a common understanding of the challenges. Common understanding brings people together. The understanding leads to unity of effort and common action.

You've got to understand other people's priorities and perspective. Too often, we think of empathy as a soft skill, but it's a position of strength. If you're going to achieve anything worthwhile, you have to be able to persuade people to work together. You have to convince people to bring the tools and capabilities to bear on an opportunity. It's in their best interest to participate in a contributing way. To get that kind of buy-in, you have to build bridges and achieve a common commitment.

3.

Commitment

The odds were stacked against her from the start.

At least, that's what some people thought.

Female and Black, she was born in 1954 in the racially charged city of Birmingham, Alabama. Her great-grandmother on her father's side had carried the last name of her slave owner.

As a child in the late 1950s and early 1960s, she experienced firsthand the injustices of the era's discriminatory laws and attitudes. Once, when trying on clothes in a department store, she was ordered to use an old storage closet rather than the dressing room. Her mother insisted she use the dressing room, and the clerk gave in. Throughout Birmingham, people of color were forced to use separate restrooms, water fountains, and lunch counters, although her parents insisted on never using segregated restrooms. She never learned to swim as a child because the Birmingham commissioner of public safety decided to close the city's pools rather than give Black kids access. (She eventually learned to swim when she was twenty-five and living in California.) When she was young, city ordinances in Birmingham even forbade a White person and a Black person to play checkers together.[1]

At age eight, she had a good friend and schoolmate named Denise McNair, who was eleven. On September 15, 1963, Denise attended Sunday school at the Sixteenth Street Baptist Church as usual. It was Youth Sunday, when a special "children's message" was to be given, and the children's choir was set to sing. Denise's fourteen-year-old friends Cynthia Wesley, Carole Robertson, and Addie Mae Collins were getting ready to sing in the choir and serve as ushers. But at 10:20 a.m., nineteen sticks of dynamite planted underneath the church steps by Ku Klux Klansmen exploded in a huge, fiery blast. Denise, Cynthia, Carole, and Addie were killed, and more than twenty other people were hospitalized with injuries.

When the blast occurred, she was only a few blocks away at her father's Presbyterian church. Many years later, she would recall: "I remember the bombing. . . . I did not see it happen, but I heard it happen, and I felt it happen. . . . It is a sound that I will never forget, that will forever reverberate in my ears. The crime was calculated . . . to suck the hope out of young lives, bury their aspirations. . . . But those fears were not propelled forward. Those terrorists failed."

Her community helped her and many others to weather the storm. Collectively they lamented the tragedy, then vowed to continue the fight to end discrimination and violence. One of their biggest weapons was education. She lived in the Titusville area of Birmingham, a historically Black, middle-class neighborhood where most adults—both male and female—had college degrees and were mostly educators or teachers. She explained to us the impact this had on the youths of her community:

> The expectations for professional Black America were profound in Titusville. Our community expected all their young people to succeed. And you weren't allowed to consider yourself a victim either. My father opened his church on Tuesday nights for algebra and chemistry tutoring, and you needed to go. All the other parents felt the same way about education, too.

They had this mantra: "You have to be twice as good." I don't think they ever imagined we'd live in a world without prejudice. So, being twice as good was the way to overcome injustices. They taught me determination against adversity.

That same community produced judges and architects, lawyers, doctors, nurses, and many educators. It produced the recently retired president of the University of Maryland, Baltimore County, Freeman Hrabowski III. It produced Mary Bush—a Treasury Department and International Monetary Fund official in the Reagan administration. It produced Birmingham mayor William Bell. It produced Pulitzer-winning journalist Harold Jackson. It's amazing, when you think about it. So many successful leaders came out of one community.

Her parents invested their strength and resolve in her, again and again. Her mother taught high school science, music, and oration. Her father was a high school guidance counselor, football coach, and Presbyterian minister who later became dean of students at Stillman College, a historically Black college in Tuscaloosa, about an hour from Birmingham.

The family lived in campus housing at Stillman, and her parents never made much money during their careers, yet they enrolled her in ballet classes, piano lessons at the conservatory, and French-language lessons. When she was twelve, the family moved to Denver, Colorado, where they paid for her to attend St. Mary's Academy, a private, academically rigorous high school. They also paid for figure skating lessons.

Once, at private school, she came home upset. A classmate hadn't wanted to sit next to her because she was Black.

Her dad said, "That's fine. As long as they move."

She understood what her father meant. She had dignity and she had strength—and she was unmovable. It was the other girl's problem, not hers.

Those who know her best say she grew up reflecting the values of her community and her parents. She was raised to be strong and to keep a calm demeanor. She always applied herself academically, graduating from high school when she was only sixteen. She told us:

> The piece that I understood only when I became older is how much my parents sacrificed for me. They had a sense of limitlessness for me. They saw things in me that I didn't see in myself. So they spent extra time with me, and they invested in me financially too.
>
> One of my father's bosses along the way was Dr. John Blackburn. Long after my parents were gone, Dr. Blackburn related to me how when my parents first moved to Denver, he said to my father, "You really should buy a house now." My father shook his head and responded, "Our daughter is our house. We can't afford both a house and giving her opportunity."
>
> My parents spent resources on me, even when they didn't have them. They did everything they could to make sure I was going to succeed. Only later did I come to understand their level of sacrifice, and I hope this could be better understood by everybody—that the people who inspire you and push you along make sacrifices to do it.

Her mother had created a first name especially for their daughter, derived from the music-related term *con dolcezza*. It Italian it means "to play with sweetness." Her name?

Dr. Condoleezza Rice.

RECIPROCAL INVESTMENT IS NECESSARY

How did Condoleezza Rice traverse from there to here—from that little girl in Birmingham who wasn't allowed to use the department store dressing room to "the most powerful woman in the world,"[2] according to *Forbes*? Someone who in 1992 at age thirty-eight was the youngest provost in Stanford University's history? Someone who from 2001 to 2005 served as the nineteenth national security advisor, and who from 2005 to 2009 worked as the sixty-sixth US secretary of state?

Along the way, Condoleezza Rice broke through significant racial and gender barriers, as the first woman to serve as national security advisor, and the first female Black secretary of state. Until Barack Obama became president, Condoleezza Rice and her predecessor, Colin Powell, were the highest-ranking Black Americans in the history of the federal executive branch.

Her work has proven incredibly strategic and impactful. During the course of her service, she was tasked to help oversee the collapse of communism in Europe and to protect the United States in the aftermath of 9/11. Today, Dr. Rice's political journey is mostly behind her, although not her influence. She's a tenured political science professor at Stanford University and director of the Hoover Institution, a public policy think tank based out of Stanford.

Her journey points to the heart of what transformative mentoring is all about, and it epitomizes the third pillar of this movement. The first pillar, as we saw in chapter 1, is trustworthiness. The second pillar, seen in chapter 2, is the instilling of values. The third pillar is what we call "the investment mandate." In one word: commitment.

Good mentoring always costs something. It costs the mentor, who must provide time, wisdom, focus, and attention. And it costs the mentee, who must respond to the guidance and apply the rigors of the course. Both the mentor and the mentee must commit to paying this cost. They must both invest in the process.

As we study the multifaceted nuances of mentoring, keep in mind the steel rod of this book. Transformative mentoring fundamentally alters a person's capacity to be their best self, and it also has a compounding positive effect on society. The third pillar goes hand in glove with this definition. To be an effective mentor, an investment must be made. The same is true if you want to be mentored well. You must commit to making that investment and embodying in everyday life the values of trustworthiness that transformative mentoring instills. If only one party is committed, the relationship falls short.

What Dr. Rice's larger story shows so powerfully is that when a person has been mentored well, that's tantamount to saying they have been invested in. The mentor initially sees the mentee as a worthy investment, someone who has strong potential, and expects that person to show worthwhile returns. Equally so, the mentee recognizes that investment is being made and does their best to live up to the expectation. Both parties have responsibility, and when this mutual mandate is recognized, the best mentoring occurs.

In the aftermath of the tragic Birmingham church bombings in 1963, a community rallied together by lamenting the loss, then by continuing to spur its youths toward success and equal opportunities. The community invested in the lives of its young people by setting high standards, providing opportunities for education, then holding those youths to those high standards. *Yes, we expect you to go to college. Yes, we expect you to be twice as good. Yes, we expect you to succeed.*

Similarly, Dr. Rice's parents valued their daughter's growth and success more than they valued owning a house. Not every mentor-mentee relationship will require that level of sacrifice, yet the principle holds true. With transformative mentoring, great benefits come both to the mentee and the mentor—but they always come with a cost.

If you want to be a successful mentor, you cannot overlook the investment mandate. Your investment will be felt in the transfer of skills, your output of wisdom and time, and the innumerable conversations you will have with your mentee over the course of a year to several years. Not all mentoring is easy or problem-free. Part of your investment means traversing the frustrations that come with your mentee's growth. You must go into the relationship with that commitment in mind.

Mentees can't ignore their responsibility either. Mentees must apply themselves to learn what their mentors are teaching them. Initially, it's a mentor's duty to provide the assets. Then, as the relationship develops, it's up to the mentee to value the relationship so much that they internalize the guidance and improve because of it. A mentee must commit to being adaptable. That takes study, work, an open mindset, and effort. The mentor must realize that growth is seldom comfortable or easy. Regardless, they must be committed to the process. The mentor must be invested in the process, too, or else the process will not work.

Dr. Kathy Kram of Boston University, a longtime researcher on mentoring, has described how a mentoring relationship passes through phases, with each phase presenting challenges. In the first phase, a mentor initiates a connection with a mentee, or vice versa. The mentor works to develop rapport and clarify goals. Next, the mentor offers guidance. This can happen over a shorter or longer time frame. Next, both the mentor and the mentee reflect on the guidance given. And finally, the relationship becomes a mutually supportive, peer-like friendship with ongoing opportunities to interact. Gratitude is expressed, and the relationship has the opportunity to continue in both professional and friendship contexts.[3] All of that takes time, energy, and attention.

The word "gratitude" is also key. Dr. Kram spent a lot of time examining the vital role of psychosocial support in mentoring. She combed through the interpersonal aspects of a mentoring relationship and helped delineate "those aspects of a relationship that enhance an individual's sense of competence, identity, and effectiveness in a professional role."[4] Underscore in your mind the word "enhance." That signifies the transfer of values. A mentor works to enhance a mentee's life. A mentee must respond to the enhancement being offered. That's the investment mandate at work. The commitment must come from both people.

Dr. Kram later revised and augmented some of her views, noting that mentoring can follow multiple models. She came to advocate a sequence of programs and organizational practices that support (rather than force) any mentoring process—a change we like. Yet that emphasis on gratitude never changed in her research. Dr. Kram always pointed mentors and mentees toward the benefit of an *enhanced* life. The investment mandate cannot be ignored.

Similarly, we are grateful to Dr. James MacGregor Burns and his pioneering research on transforming leadership. When a world is overwhelmed by crises, he notes, change happens only after voices begin to call out for the vision and force of transformative leaders. That's our present-day cry as well, and our reason for writing this book. Dr. Burns writes, "Quantitative changes are not enough; they must be qualitative too. It means alterations so comprehensive and pervasive, and perhaps accelerated, that new cultures and value systems take the places of the old. Continual transactions over a long period can produce transformation."[5]

That's also the investment mandate at work. Take a careful look at Dr. Burns's teaching. The investment of mentoring produces not only quantitative results but *qualitative* results. Harmful value systems—those mired by selfishness, injustices, or dishonesty—are replaced by beneficial systems, those characterized by honesty, fairness, and integrity. That's what we are hoping to promote through transformative mentoring in America today.

We saw this investment mandate show up in our own commissioned survey. The mentoring system does work—and our goal is to bolster it anew—but the mentor must recognize that the exchange will come with a cost, and the mentee must equally recognize and respond to that expenditure.

Our data from Morning Consult showed that a whopping 78 percent of respondents felt that their mentors had challenged them to do their best "to a great extent"; 19 percent felt that their mentors challenged them to do their best only sometimes; and a mere 3 percent had not experienced their mentors challenging them to do their best.

In other words, when mentoring went right, there were indeed trans-formative impacts as a consequence of the relationship for the mentee, as well as profound outcomes. Ultimately, the mentoring mission was accomplished when the investment was realized. The mentee saw the values and then responded to them—and the mentee soared higher than before. The commitments indeed produced results. The mentor invested in the mentee, and the mentee in turn invested in receiving guidance from the mentor. When it all came together, it worked.

WITHOUT MISSING A BEAT

Condoleezza Rice had been mentored well to respond to adverse situa-tions with both strength and poise. She was taught to provide educated responses and to do so with dignity. She was taught not to lose her com-posure, fly off the handle, or respond unprofessionally. Frankly, we could use a whole lot more of this kind of action and attitude in America today.

I (Dina) spent six years working with Dr. Rice at the White House, and she became a key mentor for me. I had the amazing opportunity of trav-eling across the world with her, which facilitated many mentoring conver-sations. Immediately after 9/11, we were intensely focused on the Middle East, and Dr. Rice and I often traveled there together. We were frequently in tough, adverse situations where tensions ran high. We were often the only women in a room filled with international male leaders, many from countries with laws that did not permit us to own property, much less recognize our ability to lead.

Once, during a high-stakes global meeting about the abuse of human rights (the exact whereabouts and personalities are classified), the coun-try's leader spoke tersely to Dr. Rice, saying, "Don't come here and preach democracy to us!"

Without missing a beat, she answered, "Your highness. My ancestors were slaves, and it wasn't that long ago that my own country considered my value as only three-fifths that of a man's. So in no way can I preach to you, because I come to you with great humility in acknowledgment that my own nation has been on a human rights journey and has undergone enormous challenges. Yet, in America, we possess strength because our strength comes from our people. We desire to build a more perfect union by giving our people a voice. Perhaps you would consider the value of that kind of strength as you lead your country too."

Dr. Rice spoke those words with poise, calmness, dignity, and zeal. I was right there in the room with her. We'll never know exactly what affect her words had on that world leader. Yet you can bet he thought about her response later, as did every person in that room. I know I did.

Personally, she showed me how to turn a difficult situation around for good, and to do so with high standards and a controlled response. She continues to be the epitome of tenacity and professionalism, and this was a lesson I'll never forget.

While I was working with Secretary Rice, editor and journalist Pattie Sellers partnered with us to build a historic mentoring program at the State Department. Called the Fortune-U.S. Department of State Global Women's Mentoring Partnership, it was the first public-private partnership of its kind.[6]

Ms. Sellers created the annual Fortune Most Powerful Women List and Summit and led in its expansion. The State Department, through its ambassadors, would nominate businesswomen from around the world. Women travel from all over and shadow high-profile businesswomen from companies that were part of Fortune's Most Powerful Women's network. Over the years, the program has reached hundreds of women. Many indicated that through their participation, and from the mentoring they received from amazing women a world away, the program not only helped them with their business, it impacted their communities too. I really believe that more than one of these participants could go on to become president of her respective country, due in part to the mentoring she received. Mentoring can not only create trustworthy business leaders but trustworthy global leaders too.

Ms. Sellers and journalist Nina Easton went on to create a program focused on the next generation of mentorship for women. David and I have invested in this program too. Called "Journey to Lead," the program welcomes and connects private-sector female leaders who are tackling critical societal challenges, have overcome major obstacles, and show the skills and resilience to reach the top.[7]

WHO BELIEVED IN
CONDOLEEZZA RICE?

The investment mandate was seen in other mentors besides her community and parents. Back in high school, Condoleezza Rice had one educator who really stood out to her: the school's Latin teacher, Mrs. Winters. This teacher had her kind side, yet what Dr. Rice remembers most vividly today is the level to which Mrs. Winters pushed her students, coupled with the investment mandate of taking extra time for students.

"She was really quiet, and she had these piercing blue eyes, and very red hair," Dr. Rice told us. "She was also very demanding. I mean, incredibly demanding. St. Mary's Academy is a highly regarded college prep school, and the academic standards are high. I knew that I needed to be diligent. I needed to apply myself to her lessons. It wasn't always easy, yet no matter how busy she was, she always took the time with me. She was a truly superb teacher."

Dr. Rice started out at the University of Denver as a piano performance major, being highly proficient at the keyboard. (Years later, she would perform onstage at Constitution Hall with celebrated cellist Yo-Yo Ma.) But during her sophomore year, after traveling to the Aspen Music Festival School, she met prodigious twelve-year-olds and decided she needed to switch majors. She tried English, but it wasn't for her. She tried state and local governments, where a class project was to interview the city water manager of Denver. To this day, Dr. Rice describes him as "the most boring person I've ever met."

Fortunately, in the spring quarter of her junior year, at age eighteen, she wandered into a course in international politics taught by Dr. Josef Korbel, a Jewish, Czech-American diplomat and political scientist. Dr. Korbel had served as Czechoslovakia's ambassador to Yugoslavia and had chaired the UN's Commission for India and Pakistan. In a remarkable twist of fate, his daughter, Madeleine Albright, would go on to serve as the first female US secretary of state from 1997 to 2001 under President Bill Clinton, and Dr. Rice would serve as the second female secretary of state under President George W. Bush. Dr. Rice told us:

> Dr. Korbel shaped me in many ways, and he became one of the most central figures in my life, next to my parents. I found his class fascinating, and he kept pulling me forward. He called on me all the time in class, even when I didn't want to be called on. I wasn't shy, but I was still learning, and I was in his class mostly as an escape from music. He gave me a confidence to speak.
>
> After the University of Denver, I went to Notre Dame to complete a master's degree in political science. I then returned to Denver and didn't know what to do. I couldn't find a job. I was thinking about going to law school. I went to see Dr. Korbel, and he coaxed me into a PhD program, which I began. He was my advisor. I'll never forget how, in our first PhD colloquium after I gave my presentation, he called me aside and said, "You would make a terrific professor."
>
> I had such respect and admiration for him that I took the idea seriously. I hadn't been thinking about a career in academics, but he helped me start down that path.

During her PhD studies at the University of Denver, she interned at the State Department in 1977 during the Carter administration, then studied Russian at Moscow State University in the summer of 1979. She graduated with her PhD in 1981. She'd been a fellow at Stanford's Arms

Control and Disarmament Program. Stanford hired her as an assistant professor of political science, then as an associate professor.

In the mid-1980s, at a meeting of arms control experts at Stanford, she met Brent Scowcroft, who had come to give a talk. He had served as national security advisor under President Gerald Ford. Dr. Rice asked him a question that she later described as "fairly sharply put." She recalled:

I asked if he was going to be head of the Scowcroft Commission on Strategic Stability. I think I said, "Isn't that just a way for the president and Congress to abdicate their responsibilities?" So it was not all that polite, actually. You kind of want to get noticed when you're young, sometimes by being petulant. By the way, I always try to remember that tendency when some young person tries to take me on today. But he came up to me afterward, told me he'd been reading some of my work, and asked if I could come to the Aspen Strategy Group to speak about the Soviet Union and what was going on. From then on, we kept in constant contact.

When George H. W. Bush was elected president, Scowcroft returned to the White House in 1989 as national security advisor. Dr. Rice became his Soviet expert on the United States National Security Council, and both Scowcroft and H. W. Bush became mentors. She told us:

You need strong mentors who will advocate for you. The president [George H. W. Bush] really knew how to make somebody a part of a team. We finally met Gorbachev in Malta in 1989. There was this kind of a reception, and the weather was awful. We were on a Soviet cruise ship, and there were hammers and sickles on everything.

I was next to George H. W. Bush, and when Gorbachev approached, the president motioned to me and said, "I'd like you to meet my Soviet specialist. She's a professor at Stanford. Her name is Condoleezza Rice, and she tells me everything I know about the Soviet Union."

Gorbachev muttered in Russian to the people around him, "Well, I hope she knows something," not realizing that I could understand him.

The president stayed firm in his introduction. His words demonstrated to me—and to everybody in his hearing—that I might look young, I might be Black, and I might be female, but I was the person the president listened to. He wasn't speaking those lines merely so Gorbachev could hear them. It was for everybody in the room to hear—everybody who might have been questioning those things in me, including our entire national security team traveling with him.

That taught me a lot about mentoring right there. He instilled his authority in me. It was a powerful moment.

Later, George P. Shultz took Dr. Rice under his wing. He had served as Ronald Reagan's secretary of state from 1982 to 1989. "He was somebody on my speed dial," she said. "I always wanted to check my instincts with George. He would tell me exactly what he was thinking. I believe having a person like that in your mentor universe is vital."

A TWO-WAY STREET

Dr. Condoleezza Rice has had more mentors than we can mention in this book. As Shultz noted in the *LA Times*, "Everybody claims her as a protégé."[8]

She has also mentored many people in return, noting: "There's this notion that we sometimes have, 'I got there on my own.' Nobody gets there on their own. There's always somebody that's advocating for you, working for you."[9]

In our interview with Dr. Rice, it became clear she believes strongly in the mandate of investment. So, in this chapter, we'd like her to have the last word. Specifically, we asked about her hopes for America, whether better leaders indeed can be made, and whether transformative mentoring will be one important vehicle to help. She responded:

Mentorship is a two-way street. If you're a mentor, you have to invest in the person you're mentoring. You have to believe in them. And if you're a mentee, you have to earn mentorship.

Nobody is perfect. I make my fair share of mistakes. With the people I mentor, I know they're not going to get every situation right. But I also know they're going to be honest, have integrity, and they're not going to be outworked by anybody. If ever they feel in over their head, they're going to come to me and ask for help. They're not trying to impress me. They're going to be real.

Mentees need to be brought along. Sometimes, with the people I mentor, I have to rein them in a bit. I might say, "You know, you're not really ready to do that. You have great opinions, but your opinions are still uninformed. I know what you're capable of, and you'll be ready soon."

America is far from perfect. Yes, it has a rough history. But what's remarkable is that our country is capable of tremendous growth and change. Yes, Jefferson held slaves, and he didn't really mean it at first when he said, "We the people." But we are getting there as a country, and that phrase "We the people" has become more inclusive over time. In my own lifetime, I have witnessed the expansion of the meaning of "We the people" to encompass people like me.

Our leaders need to stop apologizing for us. They simply need to stop. Show me a country that has tried harder than the United States. Look at the other countries of the world—let them examine and admit to their problems with racism, or their human rights violations, or their lack of freedoms. Then they can lecture me about the problems I have in my own country.

America is not a perfect nation. But we have the essential ingredients for success. We have principles, and we understand the need to invest in the next generation of quality leaders. This can be done, and it needs to be done.

KEY TAKEAWAYS

- Effective mentoring always comes at a cost. It requires an investment mandate. The investment must be made by both the mentor and the mentee. If you are mentoring someone, it helps you to know about this cost from the start. Similarly, if you are being mentored, it will help you realize it will cost you something too.
- Both parties have responsibility. A mentor must provide time, wisdom, focus, and attention. A mentee must respond to the guidance and apply to the rigors of the course. A mentor must invest in the mentee, and in return, the mentee must invest in receiving guidance from the mentor. If only one party is committed, the relationship breaks down.
- The investment of mentoring produces not only quantitative results but *qualitative* results. A quantitative result is that a leader will become more effective at doing their job. A qualitative result is that a leader will become their best self who will positively influence others. For example, as one of Condoleezza Rice's stories showed, a leader will know how to answer a difficult question with wisdom and tact.

A Conversation with Mary Barra

As the chair and chief executive officer of General Motors, Mary Barra is the first woman to lead a major automaker. She became CEO of GM in January 2014 and chair in January 2016, put the pedal to the metal, and never looked back.

Under Mary's leadership, General Motors has not only remained an industry leader as America's largest automaker, but is also undergoing an unprecedented transformation as part of the pivot to an all-electric future.

Personally, we have strong reservations about a future where electric vehicles are mandated. Neither should EVs be heavily subsidized at the expense of individual customer preferences and the economic well-being of Americans. While we strongly support an energy future that embraces all forms of energy, including fossil fuels and alternatives, this transformation poses enormous opportunity and enormous risk.

There is no doubt in our minds that Mary runs a forward-thinking, innovative, and principled business. Under Mary's leadership, General Motors has not only remained an industry leader as America's largest automaker, but it's eyeing a future with the greatest possible opportunity.

Mary believes that technologically advanced electric vehicles are the future, and what is beneficial for people's well-being and the environment will also benefit shareholders. She envisions a world with zero crashes, zero emissions, and zero congestion. In this vision, lives are saved, the planet is healthier, and customers gain more of that precious commodity: time.

We sat down with Mary to ask her about some of her most significant mentors who have influenced her along the way. Interestingly, while she told us about several, she asked us not to name them. In the forty years she's worked at GM, she has had so many good mentors that she's afraid she'll forget a name and leave someone out.

❖   ❖   ❖

1. Walk us through the mentoring you received in your formative years. Who helped Mary Barra become Mary Barra?

There were many people who helped me along the way. In my younger years, I was inspired by my mother. She truly believed that opportunity is available to everyone in this country, and if you work hard, get yourself an education, and believe in yourself, then you can achieve anything. She instilled that dream into me, and I still believe in it today.

My mother was strict as a parent. She was demanding, but fair. Many of the lessons I learned from her have helped shape who I am as both an employee and a leader. For example, growing up, I liked math and science, and grades were important to me. I remember after a test I would worry that I didn't do well, and my mom would always ask me, "Did you do the best you could?" I would say yes, and she'd say, "Then that's all that matters." That's a mentoring lesson for today: hard work beats talent. Talent helps, absolutely, but there is no substitute for hard work.

Both of my parents came from humble backgrounds, which helped shape their work ethic. That in turn shaped mine. Neither of my parents had had the opportunity to go to college, but both wanted me to go, particularly my mother. In fact, she had a number of nieces and nephews, and she let every one of us know she wanted us to go to college. She didn't really care what we studied. But we were going to go to college, because that's how a person achieved more and made their life better. It was this focus on achievement that led me to become an engineer and that led my brother to become a physician. So, I would certainly say my parents, and in particular, my mother, were influential in my formative years.

A lot of my teachers also encouraged me along the way and were invested in my success. I had a science teacher who just kind of adopted us all. We went to her classroom between classes or when we had free time, just to hang out. Her own children were going to the University of Michigan, and she recognized that some of her students didn't really understand the college process, so she took a few of us to the campus just so we could see what college looked like. We sat in classes, toured the labs, and saw the dorms. It was all quite informative. That was definitely mentoring—showing people opportunities when they don't know those opportunities exist.

After I graduated from high school, I went to the General Motors Institute [now Kettering University], and I studied electrical engineering. I was eighteen and started as a co-op student, meaning I worked for three months at General Motors, then went to school for three months at GMI, and I did that for five years. It paid for college.

You can imagine the environment back in 1980, when a young woman walked onto the floor of the plant. But I never said, "I don't belong here." I just reminded myself that I was going to GMI, and this was my assignment. This was where I was supposed to be. I'm not saying I always loved the environment. Sometimes I was the only woman in the room. But, again, my mother had instilled in me the confidence to know I belonged. My job was to see opportunity, work hard, and better myself.

2. How important is it for women to have male mentors, and vice versa?
It's important to have both, because you'll get different perspectives. Whenever I have an important decision to make, I look for multiple perspectives. One of the things I ask for as CEO, especially from my

senior leaders, is to have a point of view. Don't agree or disagree because that seems like the right thing to do. Have your own point of view and embrace it.

After I graduated from university in 1985 and went to work full-time for GM, any number of people invested in me, gave me advice, and helped me along. I was working as a controls engineer at the plant that built the Pontiac Fiero.

My supervisor was in his fifties at the time, and he was completing his college degree at night, so he knew about hard work himself. The plant was a challenging environment in those days, but he really helped me. If things didn't go well for me, he got to where he could almost read my face and see if I was upset or if I felt completely overwhelmed. He had several daughters and would talk to me in a fatherly way, telling me not to worry about things, next time I was going to do better. Or he'd say, "I know that didn't go well, and you're really disappointed, but let's talk about it. How could you have changed the outcome?"

As a young college graduate, I always wanted people to like me. I was a people pleaser. But when you enter the working world, sometimes things don't go as you'd hoped. I was normally quiet, and one thing my supervisor encouraged me to do was speak up and find my voice. He'd say, "Don't just sit in the room and politely wait until everyone has said everything and then say, 'Yeah, I thought that too.' Don't hesitate to say something because of fear." That was definitely mentoring, and I took that to heart.

By contrast, his supervisor wasn't nearly as nice. One day he called me into his office for an annual evaluation, and it didn't go so well. Keep in mind, this was my supervisor's boss, and he hadn't worked with me closely. Everybody was rated on a scale of one through six, and I think I scored a three. I was devastated. In school, I had strived for all A's. So, when I received a three, I figured I might as well quit my job. I remember that as I walked back to my cubicle, it was all I could do to keep from crying. But when my supervisor heard what had happened, he just said,

"That wasn't right. I see your work. It's better than the rating he gave you." He didn't sugarcoat things and couldn't change things for me, but he reminded me this was a tough environment, and that there's always room for improvement.

As I continued to work in the plant, our personnel director was a woman. GM had a fellowship program where, if you were selected, and it was very selective, they'd send you to business school or to get your master's degree. I applied to Stanford Graduate School of Business and was wait-listed. Our personnel director called Stanford and vouched for me. This was 1988. You can imagine that if that kind of call happened today, it wouldn't move the needle much. But back then, her call helped. I needed to write two more essays, and then I was admitted. I wouldn't have gotten into Stanford had it not been for her. I received my MBA from Stanford in 1990.

3. What kind of mentoring did you receive after you earned your MBA?

At the start, I held a variety of engineering and administrative positions, and I managed the assembly plant in Detroit/Hamtramck. I worked as an executive assistant to the chairman and vice chairman. I worked in communications for a while. For each assignment, I can look back and think of at least one person who was a mentor to me. As your career progresses and matures, so, too, do your mentoring needs. For me, that mentoring eventually helped me start to connect to my own purpose. Soon I came to realize, in large part because of my mentors and coaches, that my purpose was to help others become their best self. After my MBA, I started to recognize that even though I was still in many ways a mentee, I needed to think about how I could start being a mentor to others as so many had been to me up until that point.

One of the things that I learned, and in turn try to pass on, is the importance of listening. In 2008, I became VP of Global Human Resources. Candidly, I didn't have a lot of HR experience at the time, but

I felt I could make a difference. Since I'm an engineer, I'm also a problem-solver. I immediately began identifying areas where I believed we could improve the company's performance. One was our vacation policy, particularly a program that allowed you to buy four extra vacation days. It felt like the program had outlived its usefulness, so I eliminated it without taking the time to listen and understand whether it had indeed outlived its usefulness. The next day there was such a backlash, and I learned a very important message.

I had failed to listen and understand. People were using those extra days when they needed the flexibility to manage work and their personal lives and, in particular, to be there for important personal moments—like caring for a parent, attending a child's game, or attending an important event with their partner. I course-corrected, and we reinstated the vacation policy—fast.

From that experience, I learned that the people around you can be mentors. Listening leads to awareness, and listening is extremely important. As a CEO, I hold regular and deliberate dialogue sessions, or, as we call them, "diagonal slices," to listen to employees' concerns and answer their questions. These diagonal slices are one of my favorite sessions as CEO, and are often the most insightful ones.

I was given the opportunity to lead Global Human Resources during GM's restructuring, but after two years, I was asked to run Global Product Development. This was a big stretch, because although I'd worked on the manufacturing/engineering side of the business, I'd never worked on the product before. Mentors often give you tasks you don't think you can do—at least at first. But looking back, this was a critical role, eventually positioning me to be in consideration for CEO.

When I became CEO, many members of our board mentored me and shared their learnings from other companies. Of the many lessons they taught me, one of the most important is the need to be empathetic. It is truly foundational to any form of leadership. They have encouraged me to see that to create a better company, you need to engage with people and win hearts and minds. You need to understand the feelings of others. You can't just tell people what to do. People need to see and feel the ownership of what they're doing.

So many people at so many levels have invested in me, and that's one reason I've stayed at GM for my entire career.

4. Who became an unexpected mentor for you?

It may not necessarily be "unexpected," but I can't talk about mentorship without acknowledging the role my husband, Tony, plays. I'd met him back when we both were studying at GMI. He was two years ahead of me, and we married as soon as I graduated.

Tony is fond of saying, "There's no crying in baseball." It became a metaphor for any of life's difficulties. Emotions are important, but crying won't get the job done—particularly in a leadership role.

He's been with me through my whole career. Especially as I moved into more senior roles, not only did he become my biggest supporter, but he also became my biggest critic—always constructively. If something wasn't going well, and I came home complaining or worried about a problem, he would give me the kind of feedback that can only come from someone who knows you well. He would say, "Well, did you think about this?" or "Have you considered things from this angle?"

That's a very different kind of learning, where a person has deep insight into your life. You trust that person because they care about you. The information isn't always appreciated at the moment, but it's always needed. We've got some of that going both ways in our marriage. We always want the best for each other, and we want each other to be our best selves.

Today, our kids are in their early twenties. I wouldn't call them mentors necessarily, but since I've become a public figure, they certainly have given me their viewpoint about decisions I've made. Our son is a car person, even though he's not in the industry, and he sends me critiques on our vehicles. He doesn't sugarcoat things, so his perspective has merit.

I mentioned I was a people pleaser when I was young, but by contrast, our daughter has an amazing ability not to worry about what others think. It's a strength. She's very comfortable with being herself and has her own opinions and perspectives. I look at her with a lot of pride, and there've been times when she's told me not to worry about things.

Can your family mentor you? Yes. They play a big role in your life, helping you see your blind spots and encouraging you to be a better person and a better leader.

5. Talk to us about how you mentor other people today. As CEO, do people ask you to mentor them, and if so, how do you manage that?
Throughout my career, I've mentored a lot of people, and it still happens today. It's part of my purpose to create an environment where everybody can thrive and be their best self. Mentoring is at its best when people can see you in action on a day-to-day basis. You can regularly encourage them, give them constructive feedback, and lead by example.

As a mentor, it's so important to listen. You want to understand what's important to the person you're mentoring, what they aspire to do, how can they find balance in life, and how they're going to be most fulfilled. When you mentor well, you don't project onto a person what you think they should do or be. You help them discover those paths and become their best selves. I never want to be too prescriptive with someone I'm mentoring. I say things like, "Here's what I'm thinking, but you can choose to discard this . . ." or "I could be wrong about this, but here's what I'm thinking . . ."

I do have one bit of prescriptive advice I give to all our employees: Do every job like you're going to do it for the rest of your life. Don't rent your job. *Own* your job. If you own your job, then you invest in it. You build networks, and you make processes more efficient. When you own your job, you're always working to make it better. Then you get noticed.

One of the best pieces of advice I ever received from a mentor is one I give to my mentees today: Do the right thing, even when it's hard. When you're CEO, you're worried about financials and earnings. You want to make the right decisions for the business, for your employees, and for your customers. Some of those decisions can be difficult to make. People often want to deliberate for three months about what they should do. Look, there is no choice. There is only one thing to do.

It's the *right* thing. You always have to do the right thing, even when it's hard.

4.

Confidence

Her parents emigrated from India in 1969 to the small town of Bamberg, South Carolina, three years before she was born. The town of some twenty-five hundred residents was about half Black and half White, and they were the only Indian family. Her father wore a turban. Her mother wore a sari. When she was born, her parents named her Nimrata Nikki Randhawa, and many years later, she would be accused of denying her Indian heritage and changing her name so it sounded more Americanized. But the accusations were part of a smear campaign.[1] The name she has used from birth is her legal middle name. It's a Punjabi term of endearment for the youngest in a family. Boys are called Nikku. Girls are called Nikki. It means "little one."[2]

When the Randhawa family first came to Bamberg, nobody would even rent them a house. Finally, a kindly doctor befriended them and located a place for them to stay. He invited them to his church and into his social circles and encouraged the townspeople to accept them. Slowly, the townspeople did. But it wasn't all easy.

When Nikki was still small, every girl in town competed in the Little Miss Bamberg pageant. She was excited. The little girl prepared and practiced her talent. But when she and her sister showed up on the day of the pageant, they were disqualified. Her mom asked why.

The pageant official shrugged. "Well, there's no place for them. We have to have a Black queen, and we have to have a White queen. But we don't know where to put your daughters. No matter what side we put them on, that side will be angry."

The official handed Nikki a beach ball as a consolation prize and tried to whisk her along. But her mom put her foot down. "At least let her do her talent," she insisted. "She's practiced really hard."

They agreed. So the little girl sang what she'd rehearsed.

This land is your land. This land is my land.

The irony wasn't missed by the crowd. Or perhaps her indomitable spirit won them over. When the last note was sung, the crowd rose to its feet, clapping, cheering. Nikki's first standing ovation.

Who is she today?

Nikki Haley.

In 2011, she defeated an attorney general, a lieutenant governor, a congressman, and a state senator in a five-way primary. She went on to become the first female governor of South Carolina and the first minority female governor in the country. When she took office at age thirty-eight, she became the youngest governor in the United States, as well as the first female Asian American governor.

She served as governor until 2017, when she was confirmed by the US Senate in a 96–4 vote for her next job: twenty-ninth US ambassador to the United Nations. In 2024, she became even more prominent when she made a run for the US presidency, receiving more than 20 percent of the votes in some primaries. After concluding her campaign, she joined the Hudson Institute and remains an important political force.

WALKING BEYOND THE WHISPER

How did Nikki get from there to here? From that little girl who wasn't allowed to compete, to the highly effective world leader? Beyond the hard work and determination, Nikki will tell you that one of the biggest factors contributing to her success is that she found her voice. She learned what it meant to stand up for herself and for the rights of others—and be truly confident.

This is the fourth pillar of transformative mentoring. The first three are trustworthiness, values, and commitment. The fourth is confidence. Keep in mind also the steel rod of this book—that the best kind of transformative mentoring fundamentally alters a person's capacity to be their best self, which produces a compounding effect on society. Confidence is necessary for this to occur.

Confidence, particularly how Nikki's story shows it, means not shying away from who you are or what you can do. Not only is confidence required for profound life change to happen, but it also is required to influence people for good.

More on this in a moment. But first consider how Nikki's parents were her biggest transformative mentors in her earlier years, and hard work was the family rule (remember the investment mandate). Her parents mentored by example and, little by little, instilled confidence in their children.

Her father, Dr. Ajit Singh Randhawa, who attended Punjab Agricultural University and the University of British Colombia, had accepted a new position at Voorhees College in South Carolina. Her mother, Raj Kaur Randhawa, had a law degree from the University of New Delhi and had been selected to become one of the first female judges in India, although it wasn't considered safe for women to be on the bench, so her family convinced her to decline. In America, she switched careers, studying for a master's degree in education to become a teacher.

Nikki's parents saw how families could build wealth in the United States, and then pass that along to their children to give them better opportunities. They were concerned they couldn't do that very well on two educators' salaries, so Nikki's mom started a clothing boutique on the side. Raj didn't know how to run a clothing company at first, but by hard work and determination, she figured it out. Each day, Nikki's mother taught sixth-grade social studies from 8 a.m. until 3 p.m., then ran her clothing company from 3 p.m. until 6 p.m. She started the company in her living room, and after it grew, she moved it to a shopping center, then to a five-thousand-square-foot store, and then to a ten-thousand-square-foot store. The work was all done in the name of providing better opportunities for the children.

Before she was four years old, Nikki learned to read. Kindergarten was a breeze for her, but her first-grade teacher didn't like Nikki's early reading prowess and acted unkindly toward the girl. Anxious, Nikki started chewing her hair in class. Bored, she started to get into trouble. Toward the end of first grade, her mother called a meeting with school officials and arranged to have her daughter tested. Nikki's test results soared. Her math was strong, and she was already reading at a third-grade level. School officials let her skip a grade immediately. She spent only a few weeks in second grade to finish out the school year, then the next fall she started in third grade.

After she skipped, Nikki was teased by her new classmates for being so young. But her new teacher, Mrs. West, could see she truly was smart. The teacher prompted Nikki to read words off the board and solve equations aloud to show the other students that she was good at math. "She didn't just tell the kids to stop making fun of me," Nikki told us recently. "She helped me show the class that I was just as capable as they were, and that won the kids' respect. She helped me prove to them that I deserved to be in the room. I will never forget her for that."

Nikki's parents wanted to instill confidence and build skills in their four children. Nikki's mom enrolled her in cooking and dance classes. Her older sister excelled in the extracurricular classes, but Nikki didn't. When she was ten, she took cooking lessons every Saturday for an entire summer before the teacher finally told her mother, "Let's face it. She can't cook." Her mother's solution was to enroll her in art classes, trying something different. Nikki described to us:

My mother wanted me to know what it felt like to be good at something. She wanted us to know that you can find your place if you work hard and prove yourself. She would say, "Whatever you do, be great at it. Make sure people remember you for it."

As a family, we didn't fit into the community—not at first. But my parents never let us complain about it. My mother's solution was always to work hard, and she drilled that into us. My mother would often say, "Don't complain. *Do something* about it. Figure it out, and get it done." She wanted us to be the best, and she wanted us to stand out at what we excelled at.

For instance, she didn't want me to play the saxophone or the clarinet in the school band. It was the French horn for me. That horn was bigger than I was, but she wanted me to be good at it. If I was going to be different, then I was going to stand out in a great way. She wanted me to challenge myself and learn to succeed.

You have to realize that my mom was not lovey-dovey at all. She was not emotional. If we started crying, she'd say, "Get a glass of water and go to your room." She didn't want us showing any emotion, because to her that was a weakness. But my dad was the opposite. He was gentler. If we had a test at school, he'd say, "Just do your best. That's all you can do." My mother taught me strength. My father taught me grace. That's what got us through.

Dad was more sympathetic to us being different in the community because he was the one who lived it the most by wearing a turban. People would point at him or whisper and say things behind his back, and he would hope we didn't hear any of it. He was stoic and strong and always held his head high. So I learned from both of them. I learned grit from my mother, but from my dad I learned how to walk beyond the whisper.

In many cases today, we need to encourage and even push mentees to do things they might not want to learn—at least not at first. We have to teach them to do things they are unfamiliar with. We have to challenge them to be great. That's how people develop confidence. I challenge everybody who works for me, and I do it in the name of trying to make them better.

The bookkeeper at the clothing company run by Nikki's mother was leaving for another job. Her mom needed to find somebody quickly. As the two women were in discussion, Nikki happened to walk by. Her mom grabbed Nikki's arm and said to the bookkeeper, "Train her! She can do it."

"She's only thirteen," the bookkeeper said.

"Doesn't matter," said Nikki's mom. "If you train her, she will learn."

At first, Nikki didn't realize that being a bookkeeper wasn't a typical job for a thirteen-year-old. She applied herself, learning how to keep accounts and managing sales records. She figured out how to do the payroll and write all the checks, both to employees and vendors. When she was only sixteen, she successfully traversed her first audit. Along the way, she discovered she was good at numbers. Her penchant might not have been art or cooking, but numbers made sense to her. Her self-confidence soared.

"My mother wouldn't give up until she found something that I could do well," Nikki told us. "For me, that was accounting. Absolutely, it helped me become who I am today."

Nikki completed high school at Orangeburg Preparatory School, then graduated with a degree in accounting from Clemson University, a leading public research institution in upstate South Carolina. A life-defining moment happened during her sophomore year. She and a group of friends were relaxing on the university lawn when some Indian students walked by, all talking with thick accents. One of Nikki's friends, not realizing her nationality, called out to the Indian students, making fun of them. Nikki described the incident to us:

> I didn't know the Indian students personally, but I knew what it felt like to be made fun of for being different, for looking like I didn't belong. So I got really angry at my friend and told him to knock it off. To his credit, he wasn't trying to hurt anybody. He just didn't know any better. Afterward, he told me that what I said to him changed the way he thought about brown people.
>
> I remember thinking, *This is what I have to do.* I saw it was my job to be proud of where I came from. I would no longer feel inferior because of being Indian. It was also my job to defend those who were being bullied or misunderstood or who didn't have a voice for themselves.
>
> That was my defining moment. That's when I realized it's my job to defend people when no one else will. I knew that never again was I going to shy away from who I was.

THE ESSENCE OF CONFIDENCE

A great deal of mentoring research has been conducted that pertains to specific sectors of life, including business, sports, entertainment, STEAM (science, technology, engineering, arts, mathematics), faith-based organizations, mission-driven nonprofits, and social movements. Research has clearly shown that a good transformative mentor can produce a significant, lifelong, positive impact on a mentee's life. The benefits for both extend beyond an increase in pay or a promotion at work. A mentor's influence is broadened and a mentee's self-confidence is bolstered.[3]

In our surveys conducted with Dr. Sonnenfeld, we found that a significant across-board impact of effective mentoring was "confidence building."

One of our research assistants, Stephanie Posner, was having Shabbat lunch with a group of students and Rabbi Mark Wildes, founder and director of the Manhattan Jewish Experience. Stephanie asked Rabbi Wildes how people can know when they have done their best. Immediately and without hesitation, he answered that mentors are key. In fact, he considered that there is an important dual function of mentoring: to hold people accountable for giving their best effort, and to help people realize when they have done enough. Mentors can be the centering force in a person's life. An effective mentor can instill true confidence by helping mentees realize when they have given their best, when they have done all they can, and when it is time to move forward.

When you are confident, it means you believe in yourself and your abilities and judgment. You know your strengths and skills, just like the rabbi pointed out, and you're also aware of your weaknesses and vulnerabilities. You are reflective about your actions, but you have learned not to second-guess yourself. You have learned to start each day by making an unspoken pledge to walk in wisdom and humility. At the end of each day, as you reflect over the actions you took, the conversations you had, and the decisions you made, you are trusting and satisfied that you did the best you could, but you are also learning and reflecting on the mistakes you made.

A confident person is ultimately a more efficient worker and a more effective leader, as well as being a more balanced person outside of work. If you are insecure, time is wasted worrying that you aren't good enough or that people don't like you. You find yourself having too many conversations with coworkers or friends (or yourself), rehashing old events. Conversely, when you have learned to be confident, you are more resilient. You are able to handle life's challenges without being crushed. You trust your ability to prepare well, decide well, work well, and mitigate well.[4]

Transformative mentors can help instill confidence in their mentees. In Nikki Haley's case, her parents helped infuse a sense of certainty into her. Her mother exposed Nikki to a variety of activities, hoping Nikki would discover what she's good at. Nikki didn't find a proclivity to cooking or art, but she did find it in numbers and accounting.

Notice also that Nikki's teacher Mrs. West didn't put the bulk of her work into silencing Nikki's antagonists. Rather, she helped Nikki display her intelligence to her detractors. In the process, Mrs. West empowered Nikki to realize she was smart, and that she did belong.

This confidence came to a head that day on the campus lawn when Nikki stood up for the Indian students. The mentoring she had received from her parents and teacher had paid off. She knew she had power and a voice, and she was going to use her voice for good. She knew she was capable of giving her best and that her best would help others.

WITH THE HELP OF A MENTOR

To be an effective transformative mentor, you must support your mentee in becoming confident. Mentees are looking to prove themselves, and yes, eventually they need to hold their own. The mentor's job is to bring mentees along, build skills into them, help them find their talents, steer them to learn and master new skills, introduce them to others, and facilitate them in giving their best. A mentor will drive home the message that "You belong here," and "You have good things to say," and "You are capable of giving much to the world."

When you're young, it's easy to feel like you're not ready to be in that room yet, whatever your "room" is—perhaps metaphorically, perhaps literally. You sense that people are scrutinizing your skills, judgment, and credibility—and often they are. One of the best things mentors can do for mentees is to ask for their opinions, and to ask in public. Sometimes it's for the sake of hearing the opinion. Other times it's to make a point. A mentee's opinions do matter.

I (Dina) had the opportunity of mentoring a young woman this way when I worked at the White House. A number of us were seated around a table, briefing the president about various matters. I was the only woman at the table, and when this young woman walked in, no one else stood to give her a seat, so I gave her mine. She was a junior policy and protocol person, and her role was to brief the president about the rest of his day. She needed to be directly in on the action.

Two years later, she sent me a note and thanked me. "You literally gave me a seat at the table," she wrote. "That changed the way I thought about myself. I had never sat with the president before, and I needed to that day. I always thought I was just a low-level staffer, but your action helped me see myself differently. It gave me confidence that what I was about to say truly mattered—and it did."

One story of a woman I mentored needs a bit of context first. In 2017, I was working as the deputy national security advisor to General H. R. McMaster, one of the greatest people I've ever worked with. I had the privilege of working on the foundations of President Trump's Middle East policy that eventually led to the Abraham Accords. These were a series of historic peace treaties facilitated by the U.S. administration that normalized diplomatic relations between four Arab states—the United Arab Emirates (UAE), Bahrain, Sudan, and Morocco—that joined Egypt and Jordan in making peace with Israel. No other president in more than fifty years had made the kind of progress President Trump made in transforming the Middle East and bringing real peace. Jared Kushner spearheaded this historic policy initiative. He was extremely respected by the leaders of all those countries. We worked closely as a team to plan the president's first trip overseas as president to Riyadh, Jerusalem, and Rome, the seats of the main "Abrahamic" countries—Saudia Arabia, Israel, and Italy, the home of the Catholic Church.

Our core team was comprised of Jared, attorney Jason Greenblatt, attorney Avi Berkowitz, and a key White House aide, Josh Raffel. Working in this role and managing many of the key relationships in the region was one of the greatest honors of my life. I remembered how my dad had served in President Anwar Sadat's military when he sought to make peace with

Egypt. Fifty years later, I worked on the foundations that helped put together another historic set of peace treaties between Israel and Gulf countries.

Others in the room included President Trump; General McMaster; Gary Cohn, who was negotiating all the economic partnership opportunities to be announced in Riyadh; White House Communications Director Hope Hicks; United States Intelligence Community official Cliff Sims; and Ivanka Trump.

Ivanka and I worked closely on that trip. She helped recruit me to the White House. She was extremely talented in bringing people together in a bipartisan fashion to promote and accomplish some of the signature legacies of the Trump administration. She led the way on some highly important initiatives, including the child tax credit and family leave efforts. She also led the massive expansion of apprenticeship programs in the United States that included significant new funding for vocational programs. These programs help ensure that millions of Americans will be educated and trained to receive well-paying jobs in critical industries as a result of her hard work. Apprenticeship is one of the ultimate examples of mentorship at its most meaningful.[5]

Another way mentors can build confidence in their mentees is by bringing them into real-world experiences or giving them real-world projects (even if the projects are beyond their current capabilities), and then letting them figure things out. The mentor doesn't hover over the mentee or manage the project directly. But the mentor is available if the mentee needs help. Training such as this can build genuine confidence in a mentee. The mentor understands that a mentee may make mistakes, or even fail. But that's okay. It's part of the learning experience. The mentor offers unconditional support and embraces failure as a part of learning. This helps build a mentee's confidence, even after failure.

Years ago, I (David) experienced this kind of mentoring from Lieutenant Colonel Carl Strock. He was my battalion commander with the 82nd Airborne Division (an elite parachute division) in Iraq, and he went on to become a three-star general. He was an exceptional officer and role model, and someone I admired and for whom I wanted to perform.

About a year after arriving at Fort Bragg fresh out of Ranger School and being assigned to my unit, I began a two-week intensive course to become a "jumpmaster," the person responsible for overseeing all of a plane's paratroopers in a parachute operation—everything from making sure the jumpers are properly rigged to personally identifying the drop zone and sending them out the door. Being a jumpmaster was a big deal for every aspiring hotshot young officer in the 82nd, and I was excited for the opportunity to be awarded the coveted jumpmaster wings. The two-week training period ends with several exams, including the prospective jumpmaster doing a timed inspection of a paratrooper in which the trainers deliberately build in errors into the timed exam that could risk the life of the jumper if not identified and remedied. If you miss even one of the errors, you fail the exam and the course.

As I finished inspecting the jumper, I failed to notice that a small piece of his reserve chute was sticking out of one side. During a jump, if his main chute had malfunctioned and he pulled his reserve, it might not have opened. That little piece of reserve canopy was all it took. It was less than an eighth of an inch of fabric, but it meant I'd failed jumpmaster training. While it seems relatively minor now, at the time I felt devastated and embarrassed by my failure. I had passed Ranger School with flying colors and was rated at the top of the heap in my battalion, but had very clearly and very publicly failed. Early the next morning, I walked out to our training area to do battalion physical training with my head hanging. It felt like all eyes were on me. Lieutenant Colonel Strock pulled me aside and said, "Listen, you're going to go back in three months and retake the course. Everything's going to be fine. You're a great officer. An outstanding leader. Everyone has setbacks. You can't let this get inside your head."

I can't tell you how much that meant to me. Thanks to his encouragement and faith, I was able to put the failure behind me. Everybody experiences failure in life, and I have many times since. We all fail, and when we do, it's easy to lose confidence. But mentors help you through, so you learn and grow from your mistakes. Your confidence is rebuilt. Sure enough, I retook the course, passed it, and became a jumpmaster. I also gained a healthy dose of empathy for later years when, as a CEO, I would help mentor others through their inevitable failures.

PUSHING THROUGH FEAR

How did Nikki Haley's confidence play out later, and how did mentors continue to help her along? Nikki's first job out of university was for the FCR Corporation, a waste management and recycling company. Then she returned home to work as bookkeeper and later CFO for her mother's company, which had grown into a million-dollar business.[6]

Her burgeoning confidence helped her succeed in both business situations. In her first job, she was an accounting supervisor to the company and six of their subsidiaries. Nikki was self-admittedly a newcomer but determined to prove her place as an equal. About two weeks after she started, she walked into a boardroom where the executive team was set to meet. Nikki sat at the table. The CEO was running late. As the CEO rushed into the room and sat, the CFO turned to Nikki and said, "Hey, why don't you go get Paul a cup of coffee?" Nikki described the moment to us:

> I remember not knowing what I was going to do, but also knowing that how I handled that moment was going to dictate how they treated me forever.
>
> So I said, "Absolutely." And I leaned over to the phone in the middle of the conference table, paged my assistant, and said, "Kim, will you please get Paul a cup of coffee?"
>
> I stayed confident and professional. That shifted the way they treated me. They never asked me to get another cup of coffee again.
>
> That's the essence of confidence. Knowing that you deserve to be in the room, and then acting like it.

In 1996, Nikki married Major Michael Haley, a business leader and military officer with the South Carolina Army National Guard. Nikki's first foray into politics was to serve on the board of directors of the Orangeburg County Chamber of Commerce, then the Lexington Chamber of Commerce. She became treasurer, then president, of the National Association of Women Business Owners, then served three terms in the South Carolina House of Representatives.

She won her first election to the House not by knowing much about politics, she said, "or even knowing if I was a Republican or Democrat at the start. But by being convinced that there were too many lawyers at the statehouse, and that they needed one really good accountant."

She had many detractors at first. She was told she was too young. She was reminded of her two small children and was told she should dip her toe in the political waters at the school board level. But one mentor, Deb Sofield, believed Nikki could do it. She was an author and motivational speaker who was highly involved in South Carolina politics. She took Nikki under her wing and taught her everything from what to say to what to wear. "I would call Deb," Nikki said, "and ask her what to do. She'd say, 'Buck up. Walk in there and show them what you're made of. Act like you deserve to be in the room.' It was tough love from her. I wasn't going to make it by being soft or scared."

The stakes were upped when Nikki decided to run for governor, and even more when she was appointed ambassador to the United Nations. She described one of her mentors during her time at the UN.

When I began the role, I wasn't given a lot of time to get up to speed on things. I did a lot of reading and studying. Henry Kissinger became a mentor. [Kissinger was secretary of state and national security advisor under presidents Richard Nixon and Gerald Ford.] He reached out to me and said, "I'd love to have lunch with you sometime, if I can ever be helpful."

I jumped at the chance. We began to meet every other month for lunch, and what Kissinger did for me was teach me how to see situations through my opponent's eyes. I had learned that as governor when dealing with the legislature, but it's very different when dealing with an international adversary, or even when you're dealing with an ally who you don't agree with.

He would say things like, "Okay, if you're going to be negotiating sanctions on North Korea with China, look at it through China's eyes. What is China thinking right now? What is China worried about?" He would tell me how countries think, and what their end goals were. If you can understand the psyche of a country's culture, then you can understand how to negotiate with them. He taught me how to push past fear and think empathetically.

Kissinger didn't have to do this for me. There was no reason for him to mentor me other than he wanted to pay it forward. He had the experience and the information, and he wanted to give me the information so I could use it.

Personally, one of the best things about the mentoring relationship was that he loved to see me on the world stage. He was so encouraging. After I gave a talk, he would call me and say, "That was brilliant. You were fantastic." He liked to see what he was teaching me go through me and end up in real-life situations.

Nikki Haley is a strong proponent of mentoring today. She declares that you don't need a massive support system of mentors, but you must have a few select supporters who believe in you. Those mentors must help instill confidence. She told us:

Mentors help get you up to speed. They support you unconditionally. And they know how to challenge you, which helps instill confidence. Ultimately, mentors help you push past fear. They don't simply give you advice. They help you move into new roles that make you uncomfortable at first. When you are put in difficult situations, you find out how strong you are on the other side. That's one of the biggest lessons I've learned in life—to push through fear. If you don't push through fear, you never know what could have been. You have to go to places that are uncomfortable, so you get used to what fear feels like. When you push through fear, you live life.

KEY TAKEAWAYS

- A transformative mentor must build confidence in a mentee. This means the mentee finds their voice, not shying away from who they are or what they can do.
- Mentees are looking to prove themselves. A transformative mentor will drive home the message that "You belong here," and "You have good things to say," and "You are capable of giving much to the world."
- An effective transformative mentor will encourage a mentee to undertake new and difficult challenges, even at the risk of failure. Sometimes the mentee won't want to do this at first. But overcoming challenges builds confidence. A mentee must learn to push past fear.

A Conversation with Sarah Huckabee Sanders

When Air Force One landed in Iraq, Sarah Huckabee Sanders was on board. It was Christmas 2018, and Sarah was the thirty-first White House press secretary, the third woman ever to hold that position. Hundreds of troops had gathered in a hangar at a remote military base west of Baghdad, expecting to see senior military personnel disembark from the plane. Instead, the Commander in Chief and First Lady of the United States stepped off the aircraft and walked into the hangar. The troops erupted in applause at the surprise visit.[1]

A comment from a young soldier, however, surprised Sarah the most. After greeting the president and First Lady, the soldier walked over to Sarah and said, "Thank you. I love the way you handle yourself. You have a tough job."

Sarah shook her head. "My job is to take questions. But you take bombs and bullets. *That's* a tough job."

The soldier tore a sleeve patch from his uniform, handed it to Sarah, and said, "We're in this together."

Sarah stared at the patch, the emblem of the 3rd Cavalry Regiment. The inscription on the patch read "Brave Rifles," the regiment's historic motto. Overwhelmed, Sarah couldn't muster any words. She did the only thing she could think to do. She hugged him.[2]

Sarah had been tested in a different way. She was the first White House press secretary to require Secret Service protection—something only the president, vice president, and their families usually receive.[3] A Hollywood actor had publicly encouraged people to kidnap Sarah's children,[4] and Sarah had been asked to leave a small restaurant in rural Virginia because of her job at the White House.[5] A heated national debate had resulted, with some people in favor of Sarah, others supporting the restaurant owner, and still others questioning the legality of refusing service.[6]

Sarah is no stranger to the battles and rewards of politics. Her father, Mike Huckabee, an ordained Southern Baptist minister, served as governor of Arkansas from 1996 to 2007. Sarah worked on her dad's gubernatorial campaigns and when he explored bids for the presidency in 2008 and 2016.

She hadn't anticipated being in a White House position—at least not so quickly. After receiving a degree in political science and mass communications from Ouachita Baptist University in 2004, Sarah worked as a field coordinator for her father, then was a regional liaison for congressional affairs at the US Department of Education under President George W. Bush. She also founded a political consulting service and helped advise the campaigns for several senators. When Donald Trump was elected president in 2016, Sarah became principal deputy White House press secretary, and then five months later, she became press secretary.

Sarah served our country during a controversial season in politics, yet she held her own, showing grit and determination—and she never lost her sense of humor—qualities we have observed and admire immensely. After concluding her job, she had friends and allies in both political parties. Recently, we spoke with Sarah, who now serves as the Republican governor in her home state of Arkansas. We asked her four questions about the people who influenced her the most.

❖ ❖ ❖

1. Your father, Mike Huckabee, is well known in political circles. How has he influenced you?

He's definitely the person who's had the biggest impact on my life. He's been there for every big thing that's ever happened to me. The traits and characteristics that defined him as a great leader are things I've tried to replicate or emulate as best I can.

For example, I experienced a difficult work environment for part of the time I was at the White House. But I managed to navigate it pretty well and come out without a lot of enemies. I think part of that is because of the biggest lessons I learned from my dad: First and foremost, always treat people the way you want to be treated, and always focus on the people first. All the other stuff will work itself out.

He was governor during Hurricane Katrina in 2005. A massive number of people fled New Orleans to escape the flooding. Literally within about twenty-four hours, Arkansas saw a 1 percent population increase, which is huge for a small state.

I remember watching my dad as he gathered his team and cabinet and said, "Look, we're about to be totally overwhelmed with people. Most have no homes. They've lost everything. Some don't know where their family members are or if they're safe. They're going to be desperate and cold and hungry and tired. Think of them as your own relatives. Take care of the people first. We'll worry about the paperwork later."

Because of his background as a pastor, he had strong contacts with church camps all over Arkansas. The camps have kitchens, cabins, heat, showers—all the facilities that people would need for temporary stays. The camps also had huge volunteer bases with the affiliated churches who could help. He reached out to the camps and was able to spread the hurricane victims out across the state, so people had places to sleep. No single community was overwhelmed.

That was such a formative time for me, watching him deal with a situation that could have become much more difficult. Instead of letting that happen, he focused on helping people. When you're in politics, it's easy to focus only on the policies. But when you prioritize people, that changes your approach. You must humanize policy. That's had a monumental impact on the way I approach everything I do today.

2. Who were your most formative mentors during your school years?
Two teachers had huge impacts on me. In ninth grade, my dad had just become governor, and we'd moved from the small town of Hope to Little Rock, the state capital. I started a new school and didn't know anybody. The civics teacher, Sam Stuart, encouraged me to participate in a thing called mock trial. The team is given a case, and students act as lawyers and witnesses. You compete against other schools.

I didn't want to be on the team initially, but I didn't know any other way to make new friends, and Mr. Stuart kept asking me to be on it. To get on the team you had to try out, and I decided to go for it. Eight students were selected, and I made the team. I started to make new friends and I found that I absolutely loved being in mock trial. Our ninth grade was a part of the junior high then, but we were competing against high schools. Nobody expected us to do well. We surprised everybody by going on to win the state championship. All the other teams were comprised of juniors and seniors. I mean, we were fourteen-year-olds with braces and bad haircuts going up against eighteen-year-olds.

When I had first moved to that school, it felt like my world had ended. But Mr. Stuart helped me get through that time. The experience of being in mock trial gave me a passion for debate and government, when previously I hadn't wanted anything to do with it. It helped set me on the path to where I am today.

In college, I had a professor named Bill Downs. He was a bit of a curmudgeon but a phenomenal instructor. He taught communications, and during my freshman year I accidentally got put in a junior-level class of his. I was cocky as a freshman, so when an adviser told me to consider switching classes, I said, "Nah, it's no big deal. I can handle it."

Our first big assignment was to write an extended research paper, maybe thirty pages. I waited until the last minute, then wrote it and turned it in, thinking how impressed Dr. Downs would be with my brilliance. Two days later, he asked me to stay after class. I thought, *Gosh, he really must have been impressed.* But then he showed me my paper. There were red markings everywhere. He said, "This is the biggest piece of garbage I've ever read, Sarah. You're better than this. This is not quality work. I know you wanted to stay in this class, but you're going to have to prove you're capable of being here. This will be the only time I ever give you a second chance, because in life you seldom get those—usually if you miss your chance the first time, it's gone. Let this be a lesson."

It was such a humbling moment. I realized that I didn't know nearly as much as I thought I did, and that I needed to pay attention to the people who were trying to teach me things. I worked extremely hard on my second paper for him. During the rest of my four years in college, I'm not sure if I ever worked on another paper as hard as I worked on that one. I absolutely killed myself. When I turned in the second paper, I got an A.

Those extra ten minutes he had taken with me were life-changing. He could have just given me an F or a D and moved on, but instead he chose to have the hard conversation.

I ended up taking every class I could from Dr. Downs. Over the next four years, I learned a lot from him, and I also became a better person. After I graduated, we stayed in touch. When I worked for the Bush administration, Dr. Downs often came to DC because he was part of a communications association. We'd meet for dinner, and he'd encourage me and tell me how proud he was of me.

Dr. Downs passed away in 2019 at age eighty-seven.[7] He was a remarkable person—not only a great teacher, but a great person who was willing to invest in others.

3. Tell us about your time in the White House. Who was most influential for you there?

I tried to approach my job as the opportunity of a lifetime that deserved the best I could give it. Everybody has days when you're not at your peak, and that happened with me as well. But my goal was to go in every day and give it everything I had, to be invaluable to the president, the country, and the people around me.

The people I got to know and develop relationships with, that's something I will value forever. They are some of the smartest, most talented people I have ever encountered. It was a case of peer mentoring, really; the entire team I worked with influenced me. Part of what helped us bond and form deep friendships is that we were under fire. The only way to survive was if we locked together. Not everybody was that united, of course, but it happened within our core team. To have people around me who were encouraging, and who I knew were fighting alongside me, that made a huge difference.

4. Talk to us about your interactions with President Trump. Do you feel like you were mentored by him?

He was definitely influential. Two moments stand out.

I wasn't planning to become press secretary. Ten years earlier, if you had asked me what my career goals were, they would have been more in step with becoming a political director. I was hired as a senior advisor in early February 2016, before he was elected, at the heart of the primary. My job was to help with strategy and outreach to women, Southerners, and evangelicals.

Within about two weeks of working as an advisor, the campaign manager asked me to do an interview on CNN, because they wanted more women on TV talking about the president. I'd been around the press my entire life, but I had never done any regular interviews, where I would get grilled. I guess I did okay during my first interview, because they asked me to do a another one. They liked that too. So every day for a week, I did another TV interview.

Donald Trump is good at spotting talent, and he highly admires competence. He was watching the TV appearances, and he called me. He was all business right away. There was no hello. He just said: "Don't do another thing. I don't know what they hired you to do, but you were meant to be on TV. That's all I want you to do. Every day, all day, as much as they can book you."

I said, "Mr. Trump, I don't know if I know how to do that."

"Yes, you do," he said. "You know exactly how to do that. You shouldn't be doing anything else—it's a waste of your time."

For the rest of the campaign, that's all I did. When Donald Trump won the election, Sean Spicer was hired as press secretary, and they asked me to come on as the deputy press secretary. I was hesitant at first, but I talked it over with my husband, and he said: "We'll never get a chance like this again. Let's see what happens." We just jumped into the deep end.

Certainly, there were some very difficult moments in the White House. One day, I was in a funk. We'd had a hard couple of weeks. People were attacking everything, even my appearance. The president and I were walking into an event, and he looked at me and saw that I wasn't myself. He stopped, almost got in my face, and said, "Sarah, you know why they pick on you?"

"No sir," I said. "I don't know what you're talking about."

"It's because you're good at your job. That's why they come after you. Don't ever forget: You're smart; you're talented; you're beautiful." Then, he slapped me on the shoulder and added in a way that only Donald Trump can do: "Don't let them get you down. Let's get back to work."

We walked into the meeting. It was a rare moment, but his encouragement boosted my confidence. I thought, "If he thinks I'm doing a good job, then I can do this." I blocked the criticism and got back to focusing on my job.

5. You are a mentor and role model for many people across the country. What's most important about being seen in this light?

I remember the first rally I went to after I had done my first briefing. Almost overnight I had become a household name in political circles, and I wasn't ready for that yet. A teenager came up to me, perhaps sixteen years old, and she was so excited. She asked for an autograph. I remember thinking, *Why does this girl want to meet me? No, you want to meet those other people over there.*

It was a light bulb moment for me. People were paying attention to what I was doing, so I needed to do a good job. If she saw me being a jerk to somebody, was she going to model that and be a jerk to somebody else?

That's the most important thing about mentoring. You realize you are a role model. So you better rise to that calling.

PART II
Transformative Mentoring in Practice

5.

Where Good Mentoring Begins

Wes Moore's path to success and significance all started with his mother, Joy, although there were many times along the way when she might have despaired.

Wes was born in Takoma Park, Maryland, in 1978. His father died when Wes was just three, so Joy moved her three children to the Bronx to live with their grandparents. By middle school, Wes was deep into academic and disciplinary problems, hanging out with kids who got into trouble for graffiti and other petty crimes. His mother took a drastic step; she pulled her son out of school and enrolled him in Valley Forge Military Academy, a strict boarding school in Pennsylvania.

That experience placed Wes on a completely new trajectory. In time, he would graduate from high school and then with a Phi Theta Kappa (honor society) degree from Valley Forge Military College, a Phi Beta Kappa degree in international relations from Johns Hopkins University, and a master's in international relations from Oxford University as a Rhodes Scholar. He served as a captain and paratrooper with the US

Army's famed 82nd Airborne Division, including a combat deployment to Afghanistan. He later served as a White House Fellow to Secretary of State Condoleezza Rice.

But none of that was in view when his mom was struggling to raise this unruly son. Nor was Wes's eventual career as an investment banker with Deutsche Bank in London and Citigroup in New York. She could not have foreseen his future turn to the nonprofit world, where he became the founder and CEO of BridgeEdU, an innovative social enterprise in Baltimore that reduced college dropout rates by helping disadvantaged students make the transition to college life. In 2017, he became CEO of the Robin Hood Foundation, one of the largest and most respected anti-poverty forces in the nation. He has helped the foundation continue to innovate and expand its strategies to lift New York City families out of poverty.

Today, Wes has written five books, including *The Other Wes Moore*, a *New York Times* bestseller that contrasted Wes's life with that of another man from Baltimore with the same name who fell into drugs and violent crime. Wes; his wife, Dawn; and their two children live in Baltimore, where he is the current governor of Maryland.

To be sure, his mother could not have envisioned this specific success for Wes, but she always believed in him and saw his potential for a bright future. How did Wes become such a proficient leader today, successful at such a wide range of endeavors?

As he stressed during our interview, an important key was that he was blessed with great transformative mentors, starting with his mother.

"MY SON WILL NEED YOUR ATTENTION"

Almost everybody we interviewed for this book cited either one or more family members as highly influential transformative mentors who helped changed the trajectory of their lives. Parents, in particular, can be a child's first guide, equipped with the passion and love to want the best for their children.[1] Research has shown that a positive parent–child relationship is one of the most important factors affecting a person's development.[2]

That means parents can be one important link in closing the leadership gap in America today. Why? Because parents, along with other family members, are uniquely positioned to do something that other influences often fail to do: instill a sense of values in the next generation that's so important to fostering maturity and balanced viewpoints. Journalist Matthew Continetti helps define the problem and solution:

> The question of how to avoid polarization and political violence ought to be at the center of public debate. We are caught in a leadership deficit doom loop. Our elected officials cater to the most agitated and unruly members of their coalition. Nor do they earn our confidence.
>
> The agents of change must be real people, building and participating in real institutions, concerned with the real wellsprings of human flourishing, such as family, community, and faith.[3]

The focus on family is particularly crucial. Parents build and participate in the very real institution of the family. Parents, in general, are strongly invested in seeing their child flourish.

But the pathway to effective parenting isn't always easy. Wes Moore described how he responded to his mother's decision to send him to military school, and how that single action put him on a far different and better path than he could initially imagine:

> I wasn't happy about my mother's decision—that's for sure. In my first four days of boarding school, I ran away five times. The sudden change from the Bronx to Pennsylvania during my eighth-grade year left me angry and bewildered. So did all the strict rules of a military school. I felt betrayed by my mother, which made me even

more defiant. Right from the start, school officials considered me a disciplinary challenge.

But when my mom had first visited Valley Forge before deciding to scrape together the resources to send me there, she'd noticed that one of the most senior cadets was an African American named Ty Hill, a cadet captain, one of the few African Americans to achieve that exceptional level of distinction on campus.

My mom basically informed the school that she wanted Captain Hill to meet me and look out for me. She was unabashed when it came to seeking help for her kids. When she met Ty, she said bluntly, "My son will need your attention."

Ty and I now joke that he didn't volunteer to be my mentor—he was "volun-told." But initially, when I found out what my mother had done, I was angry. I figured Ty was only paying attention to me because he had to. My lackluster response was, "Fine, whatever, I'll meet with this guy once a week." But I wasn't enthusiastic. Nevertheless, he quickly helped me to begin navigating the school. He took his responsibility seriously and went out of his way to keep checking on me. Slowly, my attitude began to change. I concluded that the guy was all right. Maybe I could learn some things from him. My focus grew, and my study habits improved.

Ty and I used to talk a lot about my home in the Bronx. He asked detailed questions about my neighborhood and the people I knew there. He listened. He helped me understand that despite the seemingly huge gap between the Bronx and Valley Forge, the two communities actually had much in common. Ultimately, people are people, and we all want to be treated with respect. When Ty broke down the ways that Valley Forge really wasn't that different from my home environment, it made me believe I could succeed at the school, just as he had.

We are still friends to this day. Ty gets a big kick whenever he sees me on television, or when he sees an article that mentions me. He remembers when some people thought I was a lost cause, but he saw potential in me as a future leader. He showed me how to think through problems, come up with solutions, and bring people together. That made all the difference.

A LIFETIME MENTOR

Who was the real mentor in this story—Wes's mother, or Ty Hill? Arguably both. Keep in mind that effective transformative mentoring results in a qualitative internal shift. A true mentor can fundamentally alter a person's capacity to be their best self, which can help influence other people and even change an entire society for good.

In Wes's case, the parent and mentor joined forces to become transformative agents in the life of the mentee. They worked to instill values and confidence. They invested in Wes, and they both made sure he sensed he belonged. It wasn't the first time Wes's mother had worked toward such an arrangement. Wes explained:

Before I went to the military academy, my mom worked multiple part-time jobs, which meant she never had consistent employee benefits. She finally got her first full-time job with benefits at the Annie E. Casey Foundation. She was the director of Grantee Relations, which made her the point person between the foundation and the community.

One of her grantees was this guy named Geoff Canada, who was then the president of the Rheedlen Centers for Children and Families, before its name changed to the Harlem Children's Zone. She got to know Geoff pretty well, and one day she called him with a question unrelated to their professional relationship. She said she had a fourteen-year-old son who was getting in trouble and struggling in his classes. She wondered if Geoff could spend some time with me. Just like in the situation that would soon follow at Valley

Forge, my mom was completely unafraid to ask anyone for anything that might help her kids.

Geoff was kind enough to say yes, so we started spending time together. His message was mostly that I should listen more to my mother and make better decisions. But we didn't have ongoing strong contact, because I soon moved away to attend Valley Forge. The amazing thing is that Geoff didn't forget about me. He stayed in touch as I got older. Years later, after I left the Army and returned to Baltimore, Geoff was helpful with my transition to civilian life.

When I started thinking about writing my first book, about my journey and the parallel life of another man, I went to Geoff for advice. He shared his own experiences as an author. He even gave me an endorsement for my book cover.

A few years later, Geoff was on the search committee when the Robin Hood Foundation was looking for a CEO. I had been involved in a lot of justice reform work, which made me a serious contender for the role. When we met about the job, Geoff gave me some highly useful advice, much of which I took—the rest I wish I had taken. He explained that running a foundation is a lot like running an educational institution. You're surrounded by really smart people, but you'll inevitably face resistance and a sense of entitlement. The big challenge is figuring out how to win your team's support for the changes you want to make. There will be pieces you can move around the board and pieces you can't.

After I became CEO, Geoff continued to support me with experienced advice. While I knew a decent amount about philanthropy from watching my mom do it, and from my work at BridgeEdU, I still had a lot to learn. Robin Hood was a much bigger organization, one of New York's premier nonprofit institutions. And New York City is full of powerful, strong-willed people in finance and politics and public service who would try to pull me in all directions. Geoff was so helpful, just by schooling me about that landscape.

In our discussions, we would compare being a CEO to being an air traffic controller—keeping the staff, community, and board members from crashing into each other. Robin Hood's board is full of successful people from diverse fields who care passionately about our core mission, but they don't always agree on how to achieve that mission. That made it tricky to lead an organization that already had its own cultural DNA. Geoff helped me see my role as respecting that culture and history while leading changes to help the foundation continue to thrive in a constantly evolving environment.

A big part of how parents mentor well is recognizing that nobody, regardless of how proficient the parent may be, has all the skills to do it themself. But as Wes said, "My mom was completely unafraid to ask anyone for anything that might help her kids."

If you're a parent, think about this: it's wise to ask for help from others. And the mentors you find for your children today can have a positive impact—not only for a season, but for decades to come.

WHEN PARENTS ARE "ALL IN"

In our own lives, we have both felt the power of a parent's unconditional support, affirmation, and championing.

When I (David) was young, my father became the president at a small college in rural Pennsylvania, Bloomsburg State College, at just thirty-four years of age. There were perhaps five thousand students there, and many came from lower-income, immigrant families where the parents worked at the coal mines, steel mills, and manufacturing plants throughout the state.

My parents, along with my younger brother, Doug, and I, lived in a campus house. It was about a mile from there to the far end of campus where the student dining facility was located. A couple times each week, we walked from the house to the dining hall for dinner. We didn't have to eat there as a family, but my dad liked to, and he always insisted we come along.

During each walk, I watched my dad greet everybody alike—professors, students, maintenance workers, guests. He made it a point to learn and remember everybody's name. It didn't matter who my dad talked to—from janitors to tenured professors, he treated everybody with the same level of curiosity, engagement, dignity, and interest. My mom was the same way.

If my dad ever saw trash on the ground, he'd stop to pick it up. Or if something wasn't taken care of with a building or landscaping, he'd call the staff member responsible and have the problem fixed. He wanted everything to be excellent. It was a lesson for me about high standards.

When we arrived at the dining hall, we would never cut to the front of the line, even though my dad could have. Our family stood in line and waited, and we talked with the students around us. Inside, we grabbed our meals and sat with other students, talking about their interests and concerns.

Doug and I always loved the campus meals because the dining hall had soft-serve ice cream. But there was more going on that had a significant impact on us. As president, my dad could have acted aloof or disinterested, but he chose to mix and mingle with people, listen to them, find common ground, and treat them as equals. Watching him, we learned to relate to people from all walks of life.

Mom shared this mindset. Each year, she and Dad invited every incoming freshman student to their house for dinner. My parents planned and prepared ten dinner receptions over the course of a year, and they invited about a hundred twenty students to each reception, twelve hundred students total. It took a lot of work, but Mom was always warm and welcoming. She and Dad both wanted to have their fingers on the pulse of what it felt like to be a student at Bloomsburg.

My father is an exacting man with high standards, and he would constantly push me to do better. If I got an A, he'd ask me why I didn't get an A+. If I left my bike outside and he came home late, he'd wake me up to tell me to put it away. The discipline wasn't wrong, although it took me a while to realize its benefits.

What I never doubted was that he was always there for me. My father wasn't a sports fan, yet he made a point to attend each of my football games. He always stood in the far corner of the top of the stands, wearing his trench coat and hat. During one chilly game my senior year, a torrential rain started to fall. We kept playing even though the stands emptied. I remember looking up from the field. My dad stood like a statue, unmoved. He was the only one left within the stands. He had come to watch his son, and nothing could deter him. That's how I feel about my children today. They have every ability to succeed, and I am there for them no matter what.[4]

I (Dina) know that my parents feel the same about me. Their support is constant, and their pride for their children is without bounds. Throughout my life, they have consistently seen more in me than I've seen in myself, and they have always believed that I would go far. Parental affirmation truly matters to a child. A parent becomes an agent of transformation when they say to a child, "We see more in you than you see in yourself, and we believe you will go far."

Like many parents, I take this same approach with my own daughters. Dave and I both have jobs outside the home, as is the case in most families today. According to the Bureau of Labor Statistics, among two-parent families with children, some 60 percent of families have both parents employed.[5] Any single parent or family with a similar arrangement experiences both the struggles and benefits of having parents work. You want to be there for your children, yet work is calling.

My daughter Ava played varsity volleyball, and, despite traveling out of town regularly for my job, I pledged not to miss any of her games. It's no small matter.

Often, important work or client meetings conflicted with Ava's games. The scheduling was often extremely tight, but I rescheduled my meetings or rushed to the games as soon as the meetings were over so I could arrive just in time for her opening whistle. When Ava was a sophomore, she made the varsity team but wasn't a starter yet. I frantically rushed to be at one of her games, but she wasn't put in for the first match. I sat and sat. For the second game, she was put in with just seven minutes remaining. But in those seven minutes, she scored four points! It was one of her best performances ever. I started crying. I took pictures of her and posted them on Instagram.

People say it's *quality* time that matters in parenting, not *quantity* time, and I know that working parents juggle this equation every day.[6] Personally, I think both matter. I didn't know when my daughter was going to play, so I wanted to be there right at the start. The quantity of time allowed me to see the quality of experience, the seven minutes when she shined.

Can parents find a work-life balance? I get asked this question a lot, especially from younger women at the start of their careers. My answer is there's probably no such thing as complete balance in parenting.[7] I haven't always been a perfect parent, and no one-size-fits-all approach exists. Being a parent is complicated these days. But I try to communicate to my children three things: first, that I love them unconditionally; second, that as a leader I'm trying to have an impact in the world; and third, that they can have an impact too—and their impact will look different from mine.

My friend Dr. Valerie Montgomery Rice told me how she and her siblings had grown up poor. Her mother was a single parent and worked long hours at a clothing factory. After her mom worked a shift, her mom's clothes would smell so bad from the chemicals that she'd need to take them off before coming inside. But the mother would go into the bedroom where her children slept and whisper in their ears, "You can be anything you want to be."

Her mother found the right moment to communicate value to her children. She wasn't sure whether her children even heard her. But they did.

Today, Valerie is president and CEO of Morehouse School of Medicine. She was the first Black woman in America to run a medical school.

DO YOU LOVE WHAT YOU DO?

Back to Wes's story. Two big takeaways stand out to us.

First, we honor Wes's mom, Joy. She is truly amazing, a role model for parents everywhere. Despite her personal and economic struggles as a single mother, she had an intuitive sense of the importance of setting up her children with the right transformative mentors—those who would reinforce her own high expectations. She fearlessly reached out to authority figures who could help her son and teach him things he refused to learn from her. She established a strong base of effective mentoring for him that has carried on to today.

Second, we love the deceptively simple observation that Wes learned from Geoff Canada, the other mentor that his mother found for him. People are people, and groups are groups, wherever you go. Knowing this has clearly helped Wes.

It's easy to be intimidated by any new environment or organization, whether it's your first day as part of a varsity high school team, an elite college, a military unit, a famous corporation, the State Department, or the West Wing. But if you treat everyone with respect and keep your eyes and ears open to behavioral standards, it's possible to adapt to just about any organization.

THE PRODUCTS OF OUR EXPECTATIONS

Wes told us a story about the other man with the same name as his. Perhaps it is no coincidence that Wes first linked the story back to his mother.

My mother made sure I found great mentors. She knew that there are certain lessons a kid might not absorb from his mother, but he will absorb them from someone he can look up to, like a cadet commander. Sometimes, if you need to get through to someone, the key is changing the messenger, not the message. She went out of her way to find mentors who believed the same things she believed, but who could reach a stubborn teenage boy.

I think often of something I learned from the other Wes Moore, the young man from Baltimore who got into drugs and crime, then was sentenced to life in prison for murder. When I interviewed him for my book, I asked if he believed that people are the products of their environments, a saying we hear often. By that theory, the main difference between the two of us was that I was yanked out of the Bronx and sent to a different environment, while he got stuck in the Baltimore region. But the other Wes replied, "Actually, I think we are all products of expectations. For better or worse, what people believe about us, or what we believe about ourselves, that's what we become."

The other Wes Moore and I both lived up to expectations. The difference is that I was blessed with a mother who had high expectations for me, even though she didn't have a lot of money or connections. Mom made sure I was exposed to mentors with equally high expectations for me. The other Wes grew up with different expectations that came from everything that surrounded him. Tragically, he lived accordingly.

None of us can truly succeed without people in our corner who believe in us—parents, teachers, leaders, and clergy. Someone else must envision what's possible for us and help us believe we can make the most of our gifts. Someone has to help us raise the bar of our own expectations. If I can help others do that, true transformation can happen in people's lives.

If you can convince your mentee that your belief in their potential is unlimited, even if all they can see right now are limits, that alone is a huge win. Perhaps setting positive expectations is the most important task of any mentor, more valuable than sharing any practical advice or strategies. Wes Moore's mother personifies this principle.

KEY TAKEAWAYS

- Among all family members, parents are uniquely equipped to be a child's first transformative mentor. Research has shown that a positive parent–child relationship is one of the most important factors affecting a person's development.

- No parent can successfully perform all the tasks of parenting alone. Wes Moore's mother was "completely unafraid to ask anyone for anything that might help her kids." As a parent, it's wise to ask other proficient leaders to become transformative mentors for your children.

- If you can convince your mentee that your belief in their potential is unlimited, even if all they can see right now are limits, that alone is a huge success. Setting positive expectations is one of the most important tasks of any transformative mentor, perhaps more valuable than sharing practical advice or strategies.

A Conversation with Alex Gorsky

As the former chairman and CEO of Johnson & Johnson, Alex Gorsky knows what it means to lead.

During his more than ten-year tenure as CEO and chairman of Johnson & Johnson, from 2011 to 2022, Alex led the company of some 145,000 employees in the research, design, manufacturing, and distribution of three distinct health care segments: pharmaceuticals, medical devices, and consumer products—everything from household staples such as Band-Aids, Listerine, and Tylenol, to cutting-edge artificial hips, cancer treatments, and surgical robots.[1]

Health care isn't an easy business, but with Alex at the helm, the company was given the number one ranking on *Barron's* 2016 list of the "World's Most Admired Companies," and the number one position in the pharmaceutical category of *Fortune*'s 2021 list of the "World's Most Respected Companies."[2]

Following high school, Alex was admitted to West Point, where he earned his bachelor of science degree. Six years of military service followed. He graduated from Army Ranger school, then went on to serve as a field artillery officer, and finished his service with the rank of captain. Alex continued his education at the Wharton School of the University of Pennsylvania, where he earned an executive MBA.

Alex began his career at Johnson & Johnson in 1988 and steadily rose through the ranks. From 2004 to 2008, he worked at Novartis Pharmaceuticals. Then he returned to Johnson & Johnson for the final decade of his career.

Mentoring has been an important piece of the company's success. Alex was the driving force behind two employee resource groups: the Women's Leadership Initiative and the Veteran's Leadership Council. He was named honorable mentor by the Healthcare Businesswomen's Association, and he sits on the board of the Travis Manion Foundation, a grassroots group that mentors veterans.

We asked Alex to tell us about the people who believed in him and changed the course of his life.

❖   ❖   ❖

1. You were born in Kansas in 1960, and grew up in Fremont, Michigan, in a close-knit family of six children. How would you describe your parents and your family of origin in helping you become who you are today?
My parents, Al and Loretta Gorsky, were highly inspiring. That's the best word to describe them. They were my first mentors, and they instilled in all six of us a sense that we could do anything we set our minds to, as long as we were willing to work hard. My grandparents had emigrated from Russia and Croatia and knew what hard work was all about. They passed this work ethic to my parents, and they passed it to us.

My father, a Korean war veteran, had a successful civilian management career at Gerber Baby Products and retired among the top executives. He was also in the Army Reserve. I thought it was normal that every father got up at 3:00 a.m. one Saturday each month, put on a uniform, and drove three hours to a reserve unit where he'd work all weekend. Sometimes I'd tag along with him, then do my homework at the reserve center while he was busy. He was a role model of hard work combined with service. He became a two-star general in the Army Reserve and is in the Hall of Fame at Fort Benning.

My parents provided for us the right blend of discipline, challenge, support, and unconditional love. They didn't give their love conditionally. It was 100 percent support all the time from them. My father could be harder on us at times, while my mother, who worked as a teacher's aide, was more supportive. They found that balance between them. In our household, you were never idle. On Saturday mornings, you were up at the same time as the rest of the week. On Sunday mornings, you were up and went to church. There was always an expectation that you would be active and involved. The church was the center of our life and community. In immigrant communities that was typical in those days.

My mother and father had a way of bringing other people into our family. If you were a friend or had a problem at home, my parents welcomed you in. You might spend four or five hours on the weekend just sitting around our kitchen table talking to my mother. It was a kind of mentorship for me—just observing the way they lived. People were always made to feel welcome.

We had a gathering of my old classmates from West Point at our house in Michigan a few years ago. They all came to me afterward and said things like, "You are so lucky to have a dad who at eighty-eight is engaged and tells stories." He was a mentor figure to me by doing that, sharing his knowledge, wisdom, experience, with me and others. He did that to the very end. He'd show up to our annual shareholder meetings at Johnson & Johnson, and he'd be smiling, nodding his head in agreement as I was up there delivering the message. Afterward he'd say, "You did a really good job, but there are a couple of areas where I could give you a few tips." His advice was always given in love. And it came from a place of experience and insight. To be able to receive that lifelong mentoring from him was just awesome.

2. Your hometown, or at least the subculture in which you grew up, became a kind of mentor to you. Tell us about that.

Our family started out in Kansas City, Kansas, where my grandparents had immigrated. On every other block, there was a different kind of church. You had all kinds of events, food, activities—a fairly traditional kind of urban ethnic community.

When I was twelve, we moved to Fremont, in western Michigan, when my father was promoted by Gerber from a sales manager to a marketing manager. The family dynamic changed. My two younger brothers had been born in quick succession right before we moved, just in time for my older siblings to move on. So I became the oldest in my family and was given a lot of responsibility, which played a role in my development.

Fremont had a different feel than Kansas City. It was a rural town of about thirty-five hundred people. Gerber was a very successful company there, especially in the 1960s and '70s. There were a handful of attorneys and doctors in the town, but other than that, folks were either farmers or they worked professionally for Gerber. That had an impact on the school system. You had three hundred executives in town with college educations. That elevated the tax base and culture of the city, and the school attracted phenomenal teachers.

3. Were there any teachers who became mentors to you?

Ann Werner, my high school English teacher, was the hardest teacher I've ever had. The first day of class, you went in and diagrammed sentences, and at the end of the semester, you researched, wrote, and handed in a twenty-page paper. She taught you how to do critical thinking, and if a paragraph didn't start with a theme and have three supporting points and a conclusion, then I'm sorry, you didn't pass go or collect two hundred dollars. And you had to footnote your points. The rigor, discipline, and critical thinking that she first taught, then reinforced, then inspired—that's something I carry with me to this day. I'll be in a meeting and say, "So, what are your points?" Or, "What does that add up to?" Each year at West

Point, in an average incoming class of thirteen hundred, three or four hundred would fail plebe English, but I aced it because of Ann Werner.

Two other teachers, Paul Blake and Barres Bultman, had a big influence on me. Paul Blake was my American literature teacher and also my football coach. Barres Bultman was my history teacher. Blake taught me Emerson, Thoreau, Hemingway, Ezra Pound. Even in tenth and eleventh grade, I was exposed to all the top authors. I'd read almost all of Faulkner by the time I was a senior.

These two teachers joined together our senior year to teach a capstone class called "American Trends." One would talk about what was happening in American literature, and the other would talk about what was happening in history. Then they would parallel how one would manifest itself in the other. For example, how the Depression manifested itself in the literature of Hemingway and the lost generation.

At the same time, Paul Blake was tough as nails on the football field. I was a quarterback. In one of the first games I ever started, I threw an interception. A kid ran for a touchdown, and I was booed off the field. Blake came over, put his big arm around me, and said, "Son, if you want to play this position, you better get tough skin."

No truer words were ever spoken for my later life as a CEO. Much later, these two teachers presented to me the Robert F. Kennedy Human Rights Award. Ethel Kennedy and Harry Belafonte were in the audience, and presenting the award were my two former high school teachers. If they were presenting an Academy Award, it couldn't have been as meaningful.

4. After West Point, you spent six years in the military, accepting a somewhat unusual posting in Greece at various nuclear warhead detachments. Then you came back to the United States and launched a high-powered business career. Who were the mentors from these seasons?
The uniqueness about the position in Greece was that you went to the Defense Language Institute first and studied Greek for a year. Then you went to your first assignment, considered a hardship tour, then you got to

pick your next assignment. I thought this was all too good an opportunity
to pass up. The language training proved invaluable later in the business
world. There are all these great Greek leaders, and if you show up and
start speaking Greek to them, you're immediately their friend.

As for specific mentors, my battalion commander Colonel Tim
Morgan took me under his wing. He was a long-distance runner, and at
the time I was a marathoner. We ran together all the time, and as we
ran, he mentored me. Through him, I got a chance to meet General
Harrison, the division commander, and got a great job in a select unit.
Harrison was steely-eyed and hard-core when it came to his job, but he
would go out and enjoy life too. It impressed me that an incredibly successful military leader could also step outside his environment and enjoy
other pursuits. Many soldiers I served with taught me the value of diversity, service, and teamwork.

The outstanding mentor of my business career has been my
brother-in-law, Roy Cosan. He's six years older than me and went to work
for Johnson & Johnson right out of college. He's a very thoughtful person,
and I have tremendous respect for him. When he first started dating my
sister, he'd come to my swim meets and football games and be interested
in what I was doing too. He was like a big brother. If I did things he didn't
like, he'd let me know.

When it came to business, Roy put a premium on developing people
and leadership, not just on making money. He encouraged me to get into
health care, because you can help people, it's high technology, and it's a
bit of a recession-proof industry. So I joined Johnson & Johnson as a sales
representative, then sales manager. But I didn't want to stay at that level,
and I realized I needed to go back to business school. That's when I
decided to go back to Wharton and get my MBA. Fortunately, the company supported me. The studies gave me the framework to understand
how business works.

Over the years, Roy and I both worked at Johnson & Johnson in different positions and levels. We ended up in the same Johnson & Johnson

division, where he was responsible for business development and I for marketing, and we shared a common wall between our offices. Our leadership styles are very different. Roy would admit that he never had the patience to do what I do, and I admire his ability to just be there in the moment. If you asked people in the organization, "Who's the most influential leader you've ever worked for?" many would say Roy Cosan.

5. How can transformative mentorship create highly proficient leaders who build trustworthiness that positively affects our country?

A critical feature of transformative mentoring is you must find somebody close enough to have an informed opinion, but far enough away not to have an agenda. Too often, mentors have no context, so they may be mentoring at a sixty-thousand-foot level, which you will need to turn into something relevant. On the other hand, you may get a mentor who has good intentions, but their advice is given only to retain you. It's about what's good for them. I have seen people fall into that trap.

You need informal mentors who you develop relationships with just because of your roles, management styles, and personal connections. Along the way, mentoring takes place, and it can be very beneficial. But if you rely only on informal mentors, then you run the risk of missing opportunities. So a formal mentoring program is a critical component in your overall development. Having both informal and formal mentoring, fostering it, encouraging it, even making it part of the way you evaluate leadership, is very important.

Leadership is by far one of the most important aspects of our society. Without it, you're never going to accomplish common goals, and without common goals, the divisiveness and fragmentation that results will lead to the stagnation of our economy and the disintegration of our society. Good leaders can bring people together and provide that unifying glue. They inspire us to do more than we ever could do on our own. That's why I think developing and inspiring and mentoring future leaders is so important.

Leadership can be challenging today. The minute you're a leader, you're in the spotlight and you're a target. In today's social media environment, the criticism that comes your way will be in surround sound and on steroids. Mentors and supportive leaders will help you navigate the rough waters.

As for the common goals of Americans—first, we need to be a force for good on a global scale. Countries are independent of us, of course, yet human rights and democracy are so important. There must be a common good for everyone, in every country.

Second, the idea of innovation has always been part of our common culture in the United States, and we need to continue to innovate. Americans are never satisfied with resting on our laurels, and we don't ever want to be put in a box. We want to find new solutions to challenges and go forward together.

Last, leaders must teach and model purpose-driven missions in every organization and business. Leadership is not about you. Leadership is about helping people. Mentors can help emerging leaders become part of a mission that's greater than themselves.

6.

The Indispensability of School

She was attending an exclusive luncheon for high-level business leaders in New York City when a fellow CEO asked what she did for a living. She named her company, and he fired a quick barrage of questions—Did she lead marketing? Was she in sales? What was her place at today's meeting?—even implying she didn't belong at the luncheon. She attempted to answer each question as straightforwardly as she could, but the effort seemed futile. Instead, when it was time, she simply took her seat onstage. The emcee introduced her, and she rose to her feet. The applause sounded.

She was the keynote speaker.[1]

Until 2023, Rosalind "Roz" Brewer was the CEO of Walgreens Boots Alliance (WBA), a global powerhouse of drugstores and health care brands. The company she led consists of Walgreens stores across the United States, Boots pharmacies in the United Kingdom, the New York–based pharmacy Duane Reade, the cosmetics brand known as the No7

Beauty Company, Benavides pharmacy in Mexico, and Ahumada pharmacy in Chile. All told, WBA has a presence in nine countries with some thirteen thousand stores across the United States, Europe, and Latin America. Roz Brewer's company was the largest ever run by a Black woman,[2] and it employs more than three hundred fifteen thousand people, including some thirty-five thousand pharmacists.

Perhaps her name and face aren't as instantly recognizable as those of some other leaders today, but besides the responsibilities and prestige of her role, her list of accomplishments and "firsts" is sky-high. She was one of only two Black women CEOs of Fortune 500 companies in America,[3] and the third Black woman in history to achieve the mark.[4] In 2019, she became the first Black person to serve on Amazon's board of directors. Earlier, she was the first Black COO and group president of Starbucks. Before that, she was the first Black CEO and president of Sam's Club, a division of Walmart. She has been called "a game changer," and in an exhibit about innovate leaders at the Smithsonian, her photo sat between Jeff Bezos, founder of Amazon, and Janet Yellen, former chair of the Federal Reserve.[5] Currently she serves as a member of the President's Export Council, advising the president of the United States on trade.

In each position, she has led to win. A self-described agile learner, the first thing she does at the start of any new job is read and study. Armed with information, she brings to bear her guidance, influence, and perspective. The result is boosted sales, modernized procedures, and diversity initiatives that help people and companies thrive.

Roz credits a familiar institution for helping her achieve such high success. Ask her about her most formative mentors, and she will steer the conversation to this institution. Yes, she'll talk about the ethic of hard work she learned from her parents and family, then she'll talk about some of the mentors she's had on the job. But soon the conversation will circle around again to this key formative place. She credits it as the foundation of everything good that followed.

School.

A SUPPORTIVE EDUCATIONAL CLIMATE

Roz's educational influences wove their way through her formative years. She was born in Detroit, Michigan, in 1962, the youngest of five children. She describes how her siblings all helped her learn. Both parents worked on the assembly line in the automotive industry, and they hadn't gone to college or even finished high school. Yet from a young age, all five of the Brewer children were instilled with the importance of helping one another and continuing on to higher education.

Roz enjoyed school and found some of her first heroes there. She described her grade school as one of the best public education facilities in Detroit. The principal became one of her first inspirations. She told us:

> He was a Black man named Ennis Stafford, and had this great stature about him. I loved to see him walk down the hallway. I thought he was just like a king.
>
> He knew every child's name in school. But then he'd stop, lean in, and talk with me personally. And I was like, *Wow, that's what I want to be.*
>
> To me, he was a giant of a man. He would make sure we were doing everything right, and he cared about everybody he talked to. That's what I really admired about him. He was a combination of role model and mentor early in my life.

Standardized testing was big at Roz's grade school, even in first grade, and she scored particularly well in math and science. If a student's math skills were sufficiently high, school administrators put that student on track to learn music. Roz was plucked out of class one day. Initially she thought she was in trouble, but she was taken to the music room. The teacher showed her a selection of instruments and told Roz to pick her favorite. After looking them over, she picked a violin. Her parents supplemented her violin lessons at school with private lessons at home, believing that music would help her get into college. She learned how to play violin, and piano too. "I am really proud of my public school education," Roz said.

Not everything went smoothly at school, but the support given to her—and the mentoring by her educators—was all part of the greater forward momentum that her parents began and desired to see continued in Roz's life. One day in third grade, Roz was observing how the teacher worked through a math problem on the chalkboard. The teacher seemed to be taking the long way around to reach the answer, but Roz's older siblings had already taught her shortcuts for the same kind of problem. Roz raised her hand but was ignored, so she walked up to her teacher and offered to help. The teacher brushed her off, but Roz was stubborn. She wanted to show the teacher how to work the equation more quickly. Again, the teacher told her to sit. Roz didn't take no for an answer. The next thing Roz knew, her parents were at school, picking her up from the principal's office.

"My parents were adamant about my education," Roz explained. "Acting out in school, even in that kind of way, was unacceptable. They were so strict about education, they didn't want us to miss a thing. So that was the beginning of us having conversations about what it takes to be excellent and what's expected of you. They constantly raised the bar. For all five of us to go to college on the backs of two parents who never could, that was really heroic on my parents' part."[6]

She attended Cass Technical High School in downtown Detroit, a vocational school where students needed to apply for entrance and where they chose concentrations, similar to college-level schools. Roz got in and majored in chemistry and biology. During Roz's senior year in high school, her guidance counselor at Cass, Dr. Geneva Carter, pulled her aside and asked where she planned to attend college. Roz was set to go to Lawrence Technological University, a small engineering school in Michigan, then planned to work in the automotive industry like her parents. Lawrence was a good school, but Dr. Carter invited her to have higher aspirations. "You should think about Spelman," she said.

Spelman College in Atlanta, Georgia, is an elite, female-only, histori-cally Black, private educational institution that typically attracts high-achieving students. Roz repeatedly told her guidance counselor no, but Dr. Carter, a Spelman grad herself, persisted and won her over. In an almost unprecedented velocity for the process of applying and being accepted to college, Roz applied in May of her senior year, was accepted in July, and left for Spelman in August—eight weeks total. Roz doesn't know for certain what happened behind the scenes to facilitate her quick acceptance, but she has a hunch that Dr. Carter called Spelman and advocated on her behalf. Roz told us:

In terms of my biggest influencers, it was my mom, my dad, and Spelman. The decision to attend there changed the course of my career, and really the course of my life.

Spelman works to put leaders into society. When you graduate, you will know yourself better. Along the way, your classmates and professors will tell you the truth about yourself, because everybody wants to lift each other up. We didn't want to leave anyone behind. When you came in your freshman year, you wanted to graduate with all those same girls. If someone had to go home early, we would do fundraisers, just to keep our colleagues in school.

A lot of who I am emerged from my experience at Spelman. I lived on campus all four years, and those late-night conversations in the dorm proved invaluable. The conversations were really rich. I felt supported, and I had tremendous role models. The faculty and staff are committed to seeing you do well. At Spelman, I came alive.

One of Roz's favorite professors, Dr. Cornelia Gillyard, often lectured on organic chemistry with her eyes closed, concentrating in reverence for the formulas and equations she presented. Roz said:

We would be chuckling at first, wondering what she was doing. But then her passion for the material became clear. She would really work to prepare us for exams; she was second to none.

She had been in the same sorority I was in, so we were sorority sisters. Dr. Gillyard took the time to know us all independently and really shepherd us through tough material. You could call her on a weekend and she'd take your call. She was fantastic.

Our sorority was focused on service, so they constantly embedded in your head what you would do for the community. That kind of influence really makes you think when you transfer into the corporate world. It's so important to be part of a purpose-driven environment.

The entire university climate proved supportive for Roz. During her sophomore year, the university's chaplain knocked on her door. Roz's family had phoned the school earlier, asking an administrator to relay some difficult news. Her father had been diagnosed with cancer, and the prognosis didn't look good.

I hadn't grown up in church, but I found solace in the spiritual setting of the school. Students held prayer vigils for my father. That helped me get through.

Six weeks before I graduated, my father passed away. His loss was devastating for our family, and on top of things, I was trying to graduate. I was a chemistry major, and all my final exams had to be postponed.

The college really rallied around me. They took my schedule and lifted it off my shoulders. They postponed everything. The day after the funeral, I flew back to college. They gave me a bit of tutoring to get me back up to speed, then I took my final exams. I finished my finals and graduated. That doesn't happen every day. I'm not certain that would have happened at other schools.

EFFECTIVE MENTORS IN SCHOOL

Why does mentoring need to become a strong influence during a person's school years? As David Gergen, White House advisor to four presidents, writes: "Amidst growing perils to our democracy, one of America's best hopes for the future is to pass the torch to a new generation of leaders— young people with fresh vision and a fierce dedication to progress."[7]

We agree. The point of transformative mentoring is to make a difference in people's lives, and by doing so, to positively affect our nation. We find ourselves in chaotic, polarized times today, and each of us thoughtfully must ask ourselves how we can make a difference. We discovered that transformative mentoring at the school level is an important factor. The process of creating and sustaining rich educational environments can be like the action of planting trees. An environment will be enriched immediately with a tree, and it also will be enriched *tomorrow* by that tree. In our journey of discovery to learn more about the power of transformative mentoring, we consistently heard from the people we interviewed that great mentors emerged from their school years and college experiences. Quality mentoring in schools helps people become their best selves, both now and for the future.

Dr. Veronica Fruiht and Dr. Laura Wray-Lake, building on previous academic work, showed that having a quality teacher for a mentor definitely affected a person's success and well-being in positive ways. Over a six-year span, students and parents were studied and surveyed in some fifty-five middle schools and eighty high schools across the country. Findings showed that effective teacher-mentors not only boosted test scores and academic skills in their students, but also reduced behavioral problems and helped students become more socially adjusted. Specifically, students who had a school-based mentor in their younger years of school had a better GPA in twelfth grade. They also completed more years of postsecondary education.[8]

At the college level, peer-to-peer mentoring is being increasingly encouraged and employed. Studies show that when college students have good mentors, first-year attrition rates are reduced, and values and ethics that reflect academic and personal integrity are increased.[9] Simply put, schools can be rich places for mentors, and mentoring at schools can work wonders.

Some administrators have begun to deliberately place mentors in their schools, particularly to help at-risk youths. Students in this category can face a raft of challenges, everything from homelessness to early parent-hood. But the embedded mentorship programs are working. Educator Jessica Valoris was positively mentored in high school, and because of it, she felt "noticed" for the first time and encouraged to have a voice. After she graduated from college, she worked for nearly five years in Washington, DC, for an organization called the Future Project, helping students get ahead through mentoring. Jessica helped students get to class on time, gain confidence through artistic expression, and in some cases become the first in their family to graduate. The students she worked with responded pos-itively, and some have gone on to become mentors themselves.[10]

Mentoring in schools is nothing new. Yet we hope to revive, redefine, and elevate its importance in newer and larger ways—particularly in a transformative sense. What might that look like? A case study from twentieth-century Americana points the way.

In the early 1930s, an unassuming newspaperman named Fred Birney convinced the Houston school board to let him volunteer weekly at San Jacinto High School. Few high schools back then taught journalism, but Fred saw the need to help students learn to report and write.

One student was the fifteen-year-old son of a dentist. Under Fred's tutelage, the boy became the school's sports reporter. He was skinny and shy and so softhearted he could hardly bait a fishhook, but under Fred's leadership, the boy began to thrive. Fred spotted his raw talent and recep-tiveness, entered him in newswriting competitions, and promoted him to different staff positions as he matured.

Slowly, surely, the teen learned how to write. His sentences grew stronger. His articles grew more powerful. The more the teacher believed in the student, the more the student believed in himself. One lesson after another burrowed its way deep into the boy's heart. Yet Fred saw the need to teach one more essential practice about the profession: trustworthiness.

"You've got to remember that everyone you write about is a human being," Fred told the boy more than once. "Not just a headline."[11]

In other words, Fred didn't merely show the boy how to report and write. He instilled the higher career mandates of ethics and character. He taught the boy that all leaders have a higher responsibility to society. It's not enough to simply learn the nuts and bolts of a profession. The boy also needed to learn how to be fair and unbiased. He needed to become a principled person.

Many years later, long after the boy had grown up, he explained the effect of being taught about trustworthiness from the adult volunteer at his school. He described how the mentor had, in fact, changed the course of his life.

We learned a great deal from Fred Birney. He was a very strong believer in accuracy and fairness in reporting.[12] [He] made clear that there was a sacred covenant between newspaper people and their readers. We journalists had to be right, and we had to be fair.[13] He was my first mentor, no doubt about it. Things could have been a lot different for me without Fred.[14]

The boy's name?

Walter Cronkite. He grew up to become "the most trusted man in America."[15]

If you're under thirty, you might be astonished to realize that this title was once given to a journalist. Evening after evening, America watched Walter Cronkite on TV and expected him to communicate the day's news accurately, fairly, and without an agenda. Walter Cronkite delivered. He did his job so credibly, so unbiasedly, that he earned the trust of an entire nation. Veteran journalist Andy Rooney said about him: "[Cronkite] was absolutely in favor of giving the American people what they needed to know, not what they wanted to hear."[16]

In today's world of clickbait headlines and deliberately slanted news sources, could something similar ever happen again? Can trust be rebuilt? Not in journalists alone, but in leaders everywhere?

This is what we hope.

The power of transformative mentors can help—from the schools on forward.

UNDERSTANDING COMES
THROUGH EDUCATION

Back to Roz Brewer. The mentoring she had received in early school right through college helped her hike the pathway to the top—as well as navigate one difficult supervisor and two public crises that happened later in her career. Perhaps unsurprisingly, both of these crises had to do with racism. One of the many significant ongoing challenges for America today is to bridge racial divides. What Roz's story shows is that mentors in educational settings can help create solid foundations of empathy and courage in people, so they work toward equity and inclusion.

The difficult supervisor was the easier challenge for Roz to handle. While Roz was still at Spelman, representatives from Kimberly-Clark recruited at her school. Roz was hired as a research technician and began working for them as a bench chemist, doing long-range research for the global paper-based product company. In her role, she was curious, asked a lot of questions, and studied a lot of data. That translated well to business, and she rose quickly in her job.

For the next twenty-two years, she worked for Kimberly-Clark in numerous leadership roles, including marketing manager, director of skincare products, vice president for nonwovens, and president for manufacturing and operations. Along the way, she continued her education at the Wharton School's Advanced Management Program at the University of Pennsylvania. She also graduated from Director's College at the University of Chicago School of Business / Stanford School of Law.

For a few years, she worked for a difficult man at Kimberly-Clark who she prefers not to name but describes as "the toughest leader in the company." The man was highly proficient at using four-letter words and tended to manage by tongue-lashing. Roz learned to stand up to him, and eventually they came to have a good working relationship. Roz told us:

> Certainly, I had some unusual mentors in my life. His model of management didn't work well for me—him being so brutal—but he was bright and very effective. For instance, if we were in meetings and reviewing the end of a quarter, he could be very tough, saying absolutely what needed to be said. He wanted corrective action. And then the employees became better from it. So I took notes from the toughest.
>
> I was shy and insecure at first and would never speak up in meetings. He would ask questions, and he knew that I knew the answer. So he'd call on me and forced me out of my comfort zones. He saw something in me that I didn't see. After a while, I got comfortable with it. He gave me a voice, and in hindsight I really appreciate that. He taught me to be fearless, and as a CEO today, I need to be that way.

But she still had to face those crises. Roz's first crisis occurred in 2015, when she worked as CEO of Sam's Club. The controversy stemmed from an interview with CNN where Roz offered some remarks about diversity and inclusion.

The interviewer asked her: "You are a rarity in the corner office in America, and it is something that so many people want to see change. Not only are you a female CEO; you're a minority CEO. Where do you fall on who has to make the change and how it is going to happen so that there are more women like you represented in the top echelons of corporate America?"[17]

Roz responded with an anecdote about meeting with a supplier earlier that day:

> My executive team is very diverse, and I make that a priority. I demand it of my team and within the structure. Every now and then, you have to nudge your partners, and you have to speak up and speak out. I try to use my platform for that. . . . I try to set an example. I try to mentor many women inside my company and outside the company because I think it's important.
>
> And I talk to my suppliers about it. Just today we met with a supplier, and the entire other side of the table was all Caucasian males. That was interesting. I decided not to talk about it directly with [the supplier's] folks in the room because there were actually no females, like, levels down. So I'm going to place a call to him.[18]

Her remarks seemed innocuous to many. Similar questions were often asked of me (David), when I was a CEO. My answer was always clear and from the heart. From my earliest days in the Army to my days as a CEO, I'm a firm believer in diversity. People from diverse backgrounds make us better and stronger as a team, because different experiences offer different perspectives and strengthen a team's overall effectiveness. However, we always need to note that diversity and inclusion must not take precedence over merit or the overall success of the organization.

Roz expected her suppliers to reflect diversity, just as her customer base is diverse. Roz told us that she considered her comments "pretty unremarkable, a very blank statement."

But her comments triggered a social media firestorm, and even generated death threats toward Roz and her family. She needed to call in a security team to stand guard around her house, which she found deeply troubling. Critics called her a racist, insisting that she discriminated against White people. People called for a widespread boycott of Sam's Club.

Walmart president and CEO Doug McMillon stood by Roz and issued a statement saying, "Roz was simply trying to reiterate that we believe diverse and inclusive teams make for a stronger business. That's all there is to it, and I support that important ideal."[19]

We asked Roz about the incident. Here are her words:

I probably could have shut down the initial question, but I'm not a person to shy away from difficult topics or speaking my mind. I want to show people what it means to lead as an anti-racist executive.

Keep in mind that this was a blanket question asked during the holiday season, when many leaders are asked about their company. There was another CEO, a well-respected White male, who was asked the same question a day later, and he responded the same way as I did. For his comments, we heard nothing at all. But I ended up on every terrible website you could think of.

The entire controversy reinforced why I had joined the company and aligned myself with who they are. Walmart stood for inclusion and diversity, and they stood behind me. That my comments had generated that amount of fury was a reminder to us all that when it comes to racial issues in America, things are intense. Ultimately, the incident raised consciousness around the issue.

The second controversy erupted in the spring of 2018, when Roz was COO of Starbucks. Two Black males arrived for a meeting with a colleague ten minutes early at a Starbucks store in an upscale business district in Philadelphia. They sat down. A barista asked them to either order something or leave. They refused. Their colleague had not yet arrived. The barista called the police, and the two men were arrested. The incident was filmed by customers, and the footage went viral—along with the ensuing outrage.

Roz had been with Starbucks for only a short period of time, just under six months. Her twenty-three-year-old son saw the incident in the news and texted her right away, saying she needed to do something. Roz agreed. She and the CEO, Kevin Johnson, responded at once, publicly and personally apologizing to the two men.[20] They also shut down all Starbucks stores in the United States (more than eight thousand) for a day of racial bias training.[21] Under Roz's leadership, Starbucks designed and implemented a mentorship program aimed at connecting employees who are Black, Indigenous, or people of color with senior leaders.[22]

We asked Roz specifically about mentoring across racial divides and the role that education can play. She said:

Incidentally, the man who mentored me back at Kimberly-Clark was a White male, and we created a bridge of understanding between us. I think it's easy for minorities to come into large work-places and feel undervalued, like a token. But when it comes to men-toring across racial divides, I think you're going to find more similarities than there are differences, in terms of value systems.

That's what happened with the mentor and me. We both learned from each other. Today, we call this cross-education. If you are a White middle-aged male, and you have opportunity to mentor a young Black woman, it would be a fallacy to assume that you will be doing all the teaching. What will happen, if you are open, is that you also will be educated about the life of a young Black woman. You will learn about her world, about her family dynamics, about the challenges she faces at work. A lot of work still needs to be done in the area of bridging racial divides, but I'm optimistic about these shifts in awareness. Respect, empathy, and listening are a package deal. You can teach me as much as I can teach you.

Perhaps you're a White leader and you're not sure if you could or should mentor a young Black person. I understand that apprehension, but as long as you don't come in trying to present yourself as the savior, then absolutely a mentoring relationship is acceptable. The key is relationship building. That comes through education.

EDUCATION TO BE "BEAUTIFUL"

Notice how Roz always brings the discussion back to education, something that she sees as both highly worthwhile and lifelong. Transformative mentoring and education go hand in hand, and in the overall scope of the process, education is not simply about teaching facts; it's about teaching discernment, appreciation, understanding, and how to function in the world. Mentors help educate people's inner lives.

Internationally renowned artist Makoto Fujimura lived with his family three blocks away from the Twin Towers in New York City at the time of the 9/11 attacks. He reveled in the paradoxical beauty exhibited afterward as America pulled together as one country from out of the ashes, and he noted how our nation is not simply "America the Beautiful" because of the view from the top of Pike's Peak; it is beautiful because of the sacrifice seen in the bravery of the first responders who sprang into action after the attacks.

"It's one thing to educate and raise our children to be good and 'successful,'" Makoto wrote, "but it's another to raise them to be beautiful—not superficially beautiful on the outside, but truly beautiful on the inside."[23]

Through deliberate and purposeful education, that spirit can reside in every citizen.

KEY TAKEAWAYS

- Schools are formative places, often establishing in young leaders the foundation of everything good that follows. Quality mentoring in schools can help people become their best selves, both now and for the future.
- Mentoring in schools is nothing new, yet we hope to revive, redefine, and elevate its importance in newer and more expansive ways—particularly in a transformative sense. The best kind of mentoring creates profound change in a person and instills a sense of principled grounding. Ultimately, the mentor teaches the mentee how to reach their full potential and lead a meaningful life.
- One of the largest ongoing challenges for America is to bridge racial divides. Mentors in educational settings can help create foundations of empathy and courage in people so they work toward equity and inclusion.

SPOTLIGHT ON MENTORING

A Conversation with Stephen A. Schwarzman

P rivate equity mogul, philanthropist, and advisor to presidents—
Stephen Schwarzman believes in tackling big goals.

"It's just as hard to achieve large objectives as small ones," he noted, when we talked with him about transformative mentoring. "The difference is that bigger goals have more significant consequences. Since people can undertake only one personally defining effort at a time, I encourage people to pursue a goal that's truly worthy of the focus it will require to ensure its success." In other words, both small and big goals require your full focus and take similar amounts of effort, so it makes sense to shoot for the stars.

Born in 1947, Stephen has led a life practicing what he preaches. When he was ten years old, he started working for his father's linen shop in Philadelphia, all the while dreaming of a larger life, filled with adventure, purpose, and values. He excelled in academics and athletics at Abington High School and earned a track scholarship to Yale University. After graduating from Yale with a bachelor's degree, he served in the US Army Reserve, then earned an MBA from Harvard Business School.

Stephen started his career in finance at the investment bank Donaldson, Lufkin & Jenrette, then worked for Lehman Brothers. He became a managing director at age thirty-one, then head of global mergers and acquisitions at age thirty-six.

In 1985, he and his mentor, Peter G. Peterson (1926–2018), started their own private equity and financial advisory firm—Blackstone—with $400,000 in seed money. Initially, they focused on mergers and acquisitions, then branched out into business acquisition, real estate, direct lending, and alternative assets. From the beginning, Stephen and Peter championed a culture of excellence and transparency. They saw that it was important to hire top talent and to establish systematic processes to analyze risk.

Blackstone went public in 2007, and today, as chairman and CEO of Blackstone, Stephen is the head of one of the world's leading investment firms with more than $1 trillion in assets under management (as of June 30, 2024).[1] Blackstone owns approximately two hundred companies, employing more than five hundred thousand people. The firm is the largest manager of alternative assets (cash, stocks, and bonds), and is the largest single owner of property in the world.

Stephen's wife, Christine Hearst Schwarzman, is a successful intellectual-property attorney and philanthropist who graduated from Hofstra University and received her law degree from New York University. She is the founder of *No Guarantees,* an artist-driven theatrical production company, and she has won three Tony Awards as a producer.[2] Together, Christine and Stephen are enthusiastic supporters of education, arts, and culture.

As philanthropists, Stephen and Christine provide tuition assistance to underprivileged children attending Catholic schools in the Archdiocese of New York. In 2007, Stephen donated $100 million to the New York Public Library. In 2018, he established the MIT Schwarzman College of Computing, an interdisciplinary hub that helps MIT study the rise of artificial intelligence, helping to assure that such technologies are used for the common good. His 2019 gift to the University of Oxford created their new Centre for the Humanities, which studies the ethical implications of artificial intelligence and other new computing technologies. The

Schwarzmans have donated large sums to the USA Track and Field Foundation and the Animal Medical Center of New York.

Stephen serves on multiple councils and boards including the Council on Foreign Relations and the International Business Council of the World Economic Forum. He is chairman emeritus of the board of directors of the John F. Kennedy Center for the Performing Arts.

It's no surprise that in 2007, Stephen was one of *TIME*'s "100 Most Influential People."[3] In 2016, he topped *Forbes* magazine's list of the most influential people in finance[4] and in 2018 was ranked in the Top 50 on *Forbes*'s list of the "World's Most Powerful People."[5]

He has been honored internationally for his contributions to global finances. The Republic of France awarded Stephen both the Légion d'Honneur and the Ordre des Arts et des Letters at the Commandeur level, one of only a few Americans ever to receive both awards, which recognize significant contributions to France. Mexico gave him the Order of the Aztec Eagle, that country's highest honor for foreigners, for his work on behalf of the United States to support the US-Mexico-Canada Agreement in 2018.

We asked Stephen five questions about the people who have influenced him most.

❖ ❖ ❖

1. In your early years, how did your parents mentor you or teach you about life and values?

My parents, Joseph and Arline Schwarzman, taught me honesty, common decency, achievement, generosity, and the value of hard work, right from an early age.

After World War II, Dad returned from the service, inherited a small curtain and linen business from my grandfather, and was happy running the business as it was, even though I pressed him to expand. Dad appreciated his smaller circle of customers and told me outright that he was happy in life. Our family had two cars and a modest house in Huntingdon Valley, Pennsylvania, and Dad was able to send my brothers and me to college. For him, that was enough. I appreciated the kindness and contentment I saw in Dad, although I had a hunger to live larger. I dreamed of a purposeful kind of wider adventure, and I wanted to excel at everything I did.

Dad was incredibly generous. I remember when I was a boy watching him extend credit to newly arrived immigrants when they came to his store. "Just buy what you need," he'd tell them, "and pay me when you can." Regularly he donated to Boys Town in Jerusalem (an orphanage for boys), just as my grandfather had done. And like many middle-class Jewish families, we saved ten cents a week to plant trees in Israel. Giving was a part of my family's life.

While my father provided stability, my mother was the source of inspiration, and she had a strong sense of adventure. For example, when my brothers and I were all still at home, Mom decided our family needed to learn how to sail. So she bought a small sailboat, figured out how to sail it, and began entering us in races. She herself was behind the helm. My twin brothers and I admired her competitiveness and drive.

She always supported our forays into adventure too. For instance, in junior high, I considered running for class president. Mom encouraged me to go for it and to give the election all I had. I won.

2. Describe a few teachers or coaches who mentored you or made a big impact during your formal years of education.

When I was a teenager at Abington High School in Pennsylvania, I ran track. A legend named Jack Armstrong was my coach. He was constantly cheerful and never shouted or got angry. But he was deadly serious when it came to our training. Year after year, he took raw talent and forged his students into champions.

Was he a hard coach? Absolutely. Coach Armstrong pushed everyone in training and barked at anyone caught loafing. He taught us how to discipline ourselves to the breaking point—and to do that every single day. I mean, every time I ran a 440, I threw up afterward. Every single time. That's how hard he pushed us. He hated to lose, and he taught us how to give a race everything we had.

Coach Armstrong designed training regimes that worked. He taught me the merits of persistence, running extra miles, putting in the hard work, and training in harsh conditions. Other teams didn't train during the winter. But we did. He'd make us run lap after lap in the freezing wind and ice. When spring arrived, we were ready. We never lost a meet.

When he retired, he had a career record of 186 wins and 4 losses. Can you imagine winning that many times over the course of a career? His record had nothing to do with the merits of the kids he was given. Some years they were athletically gifted, and other years not as much. But his athletes kept winning and winning, year after year. It was his genius to inspire people by his sheer confidence and strength of personality. He had a simple message, often repeated, and I'd say it applies to more areas of life than just athletics: "Run as well as you can."

When I cofounded Blackstone years later in 1985, my experience of entrepreneurship was anything but a smooth, upward curve. The launch was so grueling that I have never understood people wanting to be "serial entrepreneurs," starting company after company. Doing it once was hard enough. On the hardest days, Coach Armstrong's influence helped me keep going. In 2005, when I gifted my former high school a new stadium, it was only natural that I dedicated it to Coach Armstrong.

Another person who had a big impact on me during my years of formal education was a Yale professor, Dr. Alistair Wood. I'd chosen an unusual major—culture and behavior—because it sounded fascinating to me. It combined psychology, sociology, biology, and anthropology, and I grabbed this major because I figured it would help me understand people's objectives and motivations.

But when I got to Yale, I discovered that I was academically underprepared. A number of my classmates had come from the best prep schools in the country, and they seemed to know exactly what to do at university, which I was still trying to figure out. They also did well at writing papers and taking exams. I got a 68 on my first paper and a 66 on the second. At Yale, that was a D. Maybe a D+. But basically, I was failing. I knew I could do better.

Dr. Wood called me into his office to talk about my papers. He told me outright that he saw potential in me and that, if I wanted, he would teach me how to write and think. We began to work together, him tutoring me, and I'll never forget his patience and kindness. He understood that teaching is about more than dispensing knowledge. A teacher must remove the obstacles in a student's way. By the end of that year, I made the dean's list, at the top of my class.

3. Did anyone mentor you early in your career, or give you powerful advice at the start?

My career has been a lifelong journey, and along the way, many people have helped open doors and offered expertise. I recognize that, without mentoring, I would never have reached where I am today.

Near the end of my senior year of university in 1969, I wrote a letter to W. Averell Harriman, seeking his advice about what to do next. He had graduated from Yale in 1913 and gone on to a thriving career in business and politics. I respected him greatly. Today, I always encourage young people to write or call the people you admire. Go ahead and ask for advice or even a meeting. You never know who will be willing to talk with you.

During World War II, Mr. Harriman had served under President Franklin Roosevelt as the US ambassador to the Soviet Union, then as ambassador to the United Kingdom and US secretary of commerce under President Harry Truman. He was governor of New York from 1955 to 1958, then served under President John F. Kennedy as assistant secretary of state and President Lyndon Johnson as undersecretary of state for

Political Affairs. A group of six federal government officials, known for their diplomacy, were nicknamed "The Wise Men," and he was part of that group. By the time I wrote to him, he was almost eighty and serving as America's lead negotiator in the Paris Peace Talks, seeking to end the Vietnam War.

To my surprise, Mr. Harriman wrote me back, inviting me to meet with him for an hour at his home in New York City. I ran out and bought myself a new suit, then went to the meeting. When I knocked on the door, a houseman in a white jacket and black tie ushered me into a sitting room where I could wait. The person ahead of me in line to meet with Mr. Harriman was none other than Robert F. Wagner Jr., the former mayor of New York and former US ambassador to Spain. When Mr. Wagner was finished, Mr. Harriman invited me into his office.

I told him I was interested in politics and wondered if I should head into that field. In response, he asked what I considered to be a strange question: Are you or your family independently wealthy? I told him no. He noted that if I was truly interested in politics, I should first go out and make as much money as possible. That would free me to think independently in a future political career.

To my delight, he invited me to stay for lunch, and we ate on trays in his office and continued talking. Two more pieces of advice from that conversation stand out to me, even today. He told me I could do anything in life if I set my mind on it. And he said that at some point in life, we all have to figure out who we are. The sooner we do that, the better it goes. We can then pursue the opportunities that are right for us, not some false dream created by others.

I certainly didn't have it all figured out at the start. But I took Mr. Harriman's advice to heart. My perspective on philanthropy today has emerged, in part, from that meeting with Mr. Harriman so long ago. For instance, over my years in finance, I became a great believer that education is the passport to a better life. Education helps a person pursue the right opportunities. That's why I've targeted education so often in my giving. Fortunately, I've been able to help a lot of students receive an excellent education.

My wife, Christine, is Catholic, and for years now, we've been sponsoring underprivileged students to attend private, academically excellent Catholic schools in New York. At these schools, some 90 percent of the students are minorities and 70 percent live at or below the poverty line. Yet 98 percent of them go on to college. We don't simply pay the tuition bills; we make efforts to let them know someone is looking out for them. I have their report cards sent to my office. We review the cards to see how they're doing, then we correspond with the students. We commend their progress and encourage them to keep doing well. When they graduate, I meet them and try to talk with them the way Mr. Harriman did with me. It's part of changing people's destiny.

I founded a program for university students called Schwarzman Scholars. We collaborate with the world's top higher educational facilities to help create an international community that bridges differences. Part of the program is to help students establish lifelong relationships with each other, so they can keep affecting each other positively throughout life. It gives them a network. Regularly, I talk to our scholars on Zoom or in person to encourage and support them. Schwarzman Scholars is not just a giving program. It's an empowerment program. After our scholars graduate, we help them find jobs and establish their careers. We're trying to affect, in a modest way, the destinies of a large number of people in the next generation.

4. Describe a time when someone influenced you significantly in your adult-hood years.

Pete Peterson was my boss near the start of my career. During my second year at Lehman, he became chairman and CEO of the company. Lehman was struggling then, and Pete came to the firm as a widely respected leader who was experienced in business and government. He'd cut his teeth as an investment banker, then risen to chairman and CEO of Bell &

Howell where he worked until 1971. He served as the US secretary of commerce from 1972 to 1973 in the Nixon administration, then came to Lehman.

After he helped take Lehman off life support, Pete sent out a memo to all employees, asking for fresh ideas and input. I wrote him a strategic plan about money management and investment banking. About a week after I sent it, Pete called me to his office. We had a good talk together, and at the end of our meeting, he said: "You seem to be a capable young man. You and I should work together some day."

That's exactly what happened. Over time, he became my friend and my mentor, and I enjoyed working for him a great deal. After working for Lehman for almost ten years, he left the company in 1984. When he did, it started going downhill again, and I left soon after that. Pete became my business partner when we cofounded Blackstone together in 1985.

Pete was always there when I needed advice. He was a team player, believed in transparency, and had excellent ethics. I never worried about him. When you start a company, you need to make a lot of pitches and you hear a lot of people tell you no, which can be humbling, but Pete knew how to handle rejection and keep going. Deal by deal, we built the firm together. He retired in 2007 and became our Chairman Emeritus. Then he started his own foundation, the Peter G. Peterson Foundation, which promoted fiscal responsibility. In 2010, he signed "The Giving Pledge," led by Bill Gates and Warren Buffett, which meant he was one of forty billionaires who agreed to give at least half his wealth to charitable causes.

Pete died in 2018 of natural causes at the age of ninety-one. I miss him greatly.

5. Describe how you are mentoring people today.

At the first firm where I worked, I discovered that you can learn something positive even from a negative experience. I learned a lot about mentoring from a few poor experiences in my first six months working in finance. During that season, I had a tough go of it, mostly because of a few people with whom I worked. Not everybody was difficult, of course. But some definitely were. Here's how part of that played out: no one really bothered to train me. This resulted in me feeling useless a lot of the time, and I don't think I found a way to accomplish much of anything. There seemed to be an expectation that I should have figured out everything about my job before I'd started work.

Today at Blackstone, we work diligently to create a climate that's the opposite of that. I want our new hires to have a different experience than I did. We're fortunate at Blackstone that we get to choose from the very best young graduates. We hire only one-half of 1 percent of people who apply. That's more selective than most of the world's prestigious universities. If I had to apply for a job at my own firm today, in all seriousness, I doubt I'd be hired.

Yet as talented and smart as our new hires are, it doesn't mean that every person we hire knows how to do everything. So, once we hire a person, we help them to smoothly transition into the company. I talk to every class of new hires at Blackstone for about two hours, and in preparation for those talks I think about what it's like to be a young person. I always tell them: "You don't have to figure out everything about your new job for yourself. There's nothing new in finance. It can feel intimidating when you begin here, but feel free to ask questions that enable you to do things with the least amount of anxiety and with the most proficiency. Don't be nervous here. What may seem new to you won't be new to the institution. Just ask for help. We all start somewhere."

As some of our new employees advance and take on more senior positions, we continue to coach our staff, and some become my mentees. I check in with them, encouraging them along. I want people to be self-actualized. I want our people to achieve everything they can achieve.

That's one of the biggest keys to good mentoring right there: Empathy. Putting yourself in another person's shoes. Mentoring can happen effectively when you constantly think about what it's like to be that person.

7.

The Deeper Meaning of Work

As the chairman and CEO of Microsoft, Satya Nadella leads a global giant, but it might surprise you to learn what he values most.

With more than two hundred twenty-one thousand employees worldwide,[1] Seattle-based Microsoft creates laptops and desktops and web browsers and video game consoles and software and cloud systems and artificial intelligence and more. Each day, three out of four computer users around the planet use Microsoft Windows.[2] Microsoft is worth more than $3 trillion, making it one of the world's most valuable companies.[3]

Following Bill Gates and Steve Ballmer, Satya is only the third CEO to lead Microsoft, although under Satya's leadership, Microsoft arguably is a different company. At its inception back in 1975, the company's mission was "to put a computer on every desk and in every home."[4] But the initial mission has largely been achieved, at least in the developed world. Today, the evolved mission statement reads: "To empower every person and every organization on the planet to achieve more."[5]

The current mission statement reflects a change of the company's driving principles. With Satya as CEO, Microsoft is asking different questions about what matters most in life. "It's not just the surplus you've created for yourself," Satya told *Forbes* magazine soon after taking the reins. It's: "What's the state of the world around you?"[6]

Armed with this fresh perspective, Satya has helped shape the company by ushering in a new and more empathetic corporate culture. Those who knew Microsoft in bygone days sometimes criticized the company for being "inflexible and rigid."[7] But as Satya told *Mint* recently, "Anything is possible for a company when its culture is about listening, learning, and harnessing individual passions and talents to the company's mission. Creating that kind of culture is my chief job as CEO. The culture change I wanted was centered on delivering a growth mindset, to be customer-obsessed, diverse, and inclusive, and working as One Microsoft to get us there."[8]

We sat down with Satya and asked him how he developed this new mindset. How does he foster a work culture where new and emerging leaders thrive? Not only does he want to develop highly proficient leaders; he also wants to build a culture of creativity and values that extends beyond work. Satya pointed to the people who have mentored him in transformative ways, and he described how the mentoring specifically shaped his view of work and professional achievement.

WHO BELIEVED IN SATYA?

One of Satya's most important mentors is Doug Burgum, governor of North Dakota and former president of Great Plains Software, which was later sold to Microsoft. Doug's influence has affected the way Satya does business today. Satya told us:

> When Doug first came to Microsoft, I was in my early thirties, and I worked under him. He oriented me around what professional

achievement looks like: it must be made human. That completely changed my life.

He told me: "You're going to spend more time at Microsoft than you're going to spend with your own children."

It's almost three decades later now, and that's been true. Work takes up so much of our lives. So it's vitally important to create a culture where there's a deeper meaning to work.

What exactly is that deeper meaning? To answer, Satya took us back to his first mentors. They helped frame his outlook and mind en route to his readiness to receive the answer.

He was born in Hyderabad, Telangana, in 1967, and grew up in India. His mother was a Sanskrit lecturer, and his father was an economist and civil servant with the Indian Administrative Service. His parents instilled a solid sense of confidence in him. Satya told us:

In terms of their worldviews, my parents didn't agree on most things. One was a radical Marxist. The other was super conservative. Yet they gave me tons of room to develop my own point of view.

For a middle-class kid in India, you can feel such pressure to succeed academically. But oddly enough for them, because they were both very bright people, they removed that burden from me and gave me a lot of freedom academically. I had a real love for literature, and they allowed me to explore my passions, and wanted me to think for myself. I attended IT coaching camps in summer, but I also played cricket and read all the Russian authors I loved.

At first while growing up, I had provincial ambitions. I wanted to finish high school, graduate from a local college, play cricket for my state, and work for a bank. That was the extent of my dreams. It was my father who said, "You've got to do something more."

My dad bought me my first computer, a Sinclair ZX80. He didn't predict my future with it. He just sort of dropped it off in my room, and it collected dust for a while. Then I plugged it in and started using it, and it ended up changing my life.

In retrospect, what my dad and mom really wanted to instill in me were big ideas. They wanted to know what I was thinking about and talking about, and they would really listen to me. I think one of the greatest gifts parents can give to their children is to take them seriously.

That listening mandate is highly important in a work culture as well. When I first came to Microsoft, it was all about being the smartest guy in the room. But we've learned that in order to succeed, we have to truly listen to each other.

Satya described how mentors in the sports world also expanded his worldview. Cricket is the most popular sport in India, and Satya said he was "obsessed" with cricket throughout high school and college. Once, during a high school match, the captain of his team noticed that Satya was not having a good day on the field. He took over from Satya and "got a wicket" (scored a point), but then much to Satya's surprise, he handed the spot back to Satya, giving him another opportunity. Satya went on to score several points in the same game.

He was only about a year older than me, and I've often reflected as to why he did that. Much later in life, I went back and asked him. He told me that it was a leadership decision. He recognized that I was having a difficult day, so he made the hard call to take over for me for a while. But then he put me back in. And why was that?

Because he didn't want to break my confidence.

All sport teaches you a lot, particularly team sports, which can have a huge impact on how you think about leadership. He wanted to bring out the best in me. He understood that he needed his entire team, and he knew that not everybody will have a good day all the time. He was enlightened enough, even as a high school student, to know that he needed me for the whole season, not just for one match. So he didn't pass judgment on my first failure.

Am I romancing this moment in hindsight? Perhaps. But the bottom line is that his example taught me a lesson that I still use today. At Microsoft, I was completing my annual reviews recently, and this story came back to me. I needed to take over for one person and do the review myself, but at the same time I cared about this person going forward. I didn't want them to feel disempowered, or like I had lost confidence in them. So I needed to bring that person back in. What always matters is the person.

The school years proved formative for Satya. In 1988, he graduated from the Manipal Institute of Technology in Karnataka with a bachelor's degree in electrical engineering. Then he moved to the United States where he earned a master's degree in computer science from the University of Wisconsin–Milwaukee in 1990 and an MBA from the University of Chicago Booth School of Business in 1997. He picked out one incident to illustrate the impact of those school days:

I had a group of friends in college who had great ambitions to do things. They also cared about me as a friend and wanted the best for me.

When I was in college, I was set to apply for a job at Sun Microsystems, so I prepared a résumé. A friend asked if he could look at it. He corrected a few spelling mistakes, then sent it off to the hiring manager for me. I was hired at Sun in 1992 and worked there before going to Microsoft.

That simple gesture on behalf of my friend struck me as important. He wanted to make sure I got the best shot. He cared about my achievements and my future. He wanted the best for me.

That translates to a question I ask myself today: How much do I care about another person's achievement? How much do I want the best for them?

It's also a question to ask in the broader sense of community. Do we care for each other and help each other succeed?

Satya's family life has also contributed greatly to his personal development, teaching him lessons he has applied to the corporate world. In 1992, Satya married Anupama, an architect and lifelong family friend, whom he lovingly calls "Anu." Four years later she became pregnant with their son. Two daughters followed.

When their son was thirty-six weeks in the womb, Anu noticed he wasn't moving around as much as he had been. She and Satya rushed to the emergency room. That same day their son, Zain, was born by emergency cesarean. He had suffered in utero asphyxiation and weighed only three pounds. Diagnosed with cerebral palsy, Zain was also legally blind, had limited communication, and was a quadriplegic. Satya told us:

As I look back now, I see there were vast differences between the way Anu and I reacted to the birth of our son. I'd had all these grand plans for our firstborn, and I was devastated at first. I felt that life had been unfair. I wanted to know why this had happened to us.

My wife just picked up and became very pragmatic. She never asked, "Why us?" She started contacting professionals to find the best way forward for Zain, accessing programs for children with disabilities, driving him to and from therapy appointments, showing Zain endless love and commitment.

I needed to step up and watch my wife's reaction and learn from her. By watching her in those first few days, weeks, and beyond, things started to change for me. Both Anu and Zain have had a profound impact on how I think, lead, and relate to people. They have taught me to be kinder and more empathetic. This massively changes you as a leader, as a human being.

The biggest lesson I have learned is this: you must be present for the people who need you most.

Indeed, a leader's impact can be greatly affected by their family, through the difficult times as well as the good, and we appreciate this lesson from Sàtya about being present. Sadly, Zain Nadella passed away in 2022 at the age of twenty-six.

MENTORING INSIDE THE WORKPLACE

Life is about people, and work is a huge part of life. So work must therefore be about people. Our need in America is to create trustworthy leaders who will impact companies, communities, and families so our entire nation takes a leap forward. Transformative mentoring is one of the biggest keys. It fundamentally alters a person's capacity to be their best self, and that transformation can have a compounding positive effect on our nation. In addition to the mentoring that happens at home and schools, one of the best places for transformative mentoring to occur is on the job. Mentors at work can help instill this mandate that we must focus on people.

We believe in organic mentoring—that which takes place in informal, natural ways. Yet we also believe in formalized mentoring, which often happens through work. Statistics show that some 71 percent of Fortune 500 companies have some kind of mentoring program, and within those programs, mentees are promoted five times more often than people without mentors.[9]

Our proprietary survey, conducted by Dr. Sonnenfeld's team at Yale University, asked questions of people from a variety of companies of different sizes, as well as from graduate students. We noted that slightly over half of our respondents who had mentors said the relationship was initiated through a formal program at work, a statistic we find encouraging and hope will only rise.

Also note that in our survey, when we broke out the findings between MBAs, executives, and the general population, we saw how people valued things slightly differently depending on which group they were in. Across survey responses, MBAs valued and sought mentoring to increase their job skills at a slightly higher rate than they did with life skills, although they still valued both. Executives were more equally weighted between the two. While the general population valued personal support at a slightly higher level than professional support, they also valued both. In other words, everybody values both job skills and life skills, although at slightly different rates.

As Satya's story shows so far, the type of mentoring that creates the most impact can happen in both organic and formalized ways. Mentoring does not merely help people climb the corporate ladder or infuse job-related skills (or win a cricket match). Transformative mentoring is concerned with the development of the whole person. It teaches us how to be present for the people who need us most. The best leaders understand the necessity of kindness, of benefiting other people's lives, and of considering the world around them. Well-run corporate mentoring programs that adopt the transformative approach will not only onboard new employees to prepare them for future leadership positions, but also train them in both career and personal development.[10]

Anthony Tjan is founder, managing partner, and CEO of the venture capital firm Cue Ball, a company that describes itself as "purpose-driven and people-first."[11] As part of his overall work, Tjan devoted three years to interviewing and researching successful leaders, and he came to a straightforward conclusion: "They do everything they can to imprint their 'goodness' onto others in ways that make others feel like fuller versions of themselves. The best leaders go beyond competency, focusing on helping to shape other people's character, values, self-awareness, empathy, and capacity for respect."[12]

We like that a lot. In Tjan's schematic for success, corporate mentoring programs can become stale or bureaucratic if seen or implemented as another obligatory HR program. Instead, he urges mentors to focus on the authenticity of a relationship, building rapport and genuine dialogue with a mentee, rather than viewing mentoring as a box to check or a task to complete. He challenges mentors, when giving feedback to their mentees, to lean toward encouraging, optimistic, and upbeat thinking and communication rather than being cynical or pessimistic. This doesn't rule out necessary words of criticism or correction, but paves the way to give it a hearing. And he stresses the importance of selflessly considering a mentee's long-term effectiveness and impact. Even if a mentee is successful at your company, they might be more successful in the future at a different job, with a different employer, or in an entirely different industry. In that case, helping a mentee to find their long-term calling is one of the best things you can do for them.

"Most of us have experienced people, such as friends, religious leaders, and family members, who serve as our anchors and guides outside our workplaces," Tjan writes. "Why can't we bring this same high level of trust and support *inside* the workplace? In a lot of cases, we owe it to mentees to serve as something more than just career mentors."[13]

The type of mentoring that concerns itself with the whole person is increasingly common. One expert studied and contrasted traditional (and even archaic) approaches to mentoring at work with more relational types such as transformative mentoring. She found that, whereas in the past, a mentor would rarely if ever discuss her personal life or challenges with a mentee, today's mentors are far more comfortable talking about such topics. The attitude now is one where mentors can feel comfortable sharing their personal goals, challenges, and struggles with their mentee. The relationship becomes more reciprocal overall, and the connection experiences more depth, where matters of substance can be discussed. In the researcher's words, "We can talk about things that really matter: who we are and what we do."[14]

The strict hierarchy of mentor-mentee is flattened in these relationships. In the past, a mentor would dispense knowledge and remain more emotionally aloof while never shifting power to the mentee. In the models of transformative mentoring that we espouse, a mentor lessens the rigidity of the role and helps confer balance and responsibility to the mentee. Both the mentor and mentee learn from each other in ways that promote personal growth and healthy interdependence. Mentees still recognize that mentors have more work experience (and often life experience), yet mentors will recognize that a mentee may offer a fresh outlook from recent educational training or help offer insight into understanding a different people group or a younger generation.[15]

MENTORS BELIEVE IN YOU

I (Dina) have benefited greatly from having many excellent transformative mentors during my career at the White House, State Department, and Goldman Sachs, and I strongly believe it's important to have a trusted group of advisors you can go to for counsel that's related not only to work but also to all areas of life. Particularly for younger women. Let's face it, women have come a long way in the workplace, but the data on diversity and gender inclusion needs to be top of mind for every leadership team today. Empowering women is not only the right thing to do; it's also smart economics.

It's difficult for me to start naming mentors at places I've worked, because I'm sure I'll leave someone out. John F. W. Rogers, who recruited me to Goldman Sachs; Gary Cohn, the president and COO, who was also instrumental in recruiting me; and Lloyd Blankfein, the CEO at the time, are three who come to mind immediately. I had never worked in the private sector, but they were very focused on empowering women to make a societal impact, and they believed in me from the start. They were amazing mentors and constant supporters. Current CEO David Solomon supported our efforts to build One Million Black Women, and he remains a close friend and mentor.

Over the years, I've also had the privilege of being mentored by so many people mentioned in this book, including Ruth Simmons, Tory Burch, Condoleezza Rice, and Clay Johnson. I'm forever grateful to them.

Here's one way they helped. It's easy for me to take things personally, but my work mentors have taught me not to second-guess my decisions— and that's an important life lesson for anybody to learn. For instance, when you provide input in a meeting or give a presentation, you can come out of the meeting afterward and wonder if you said the right thing. You can absolutely obsess and replay things over and over in your mind. I now use a skill I call the "fifteen-minute rule." If ever I wonder about what I said, I give myself precisely fifteen minutes to reexamine things, then I never look back.

Mentors have taught me strength, and they've offered me some tough love. It was one of my bosses at Goldman who took me aside and said, "If you're going to be a decision-maker at the table—whatever table you're at—then you are going to receive pushback and criticism, by definition of being a decision-maker. So you need to determine whether you are going to be fully at the table. Gather the facts, use your best judgment, and make a decision. Some people will disagree with you. Know that you will need to explain and defend the choices you make as a leader."

That framed the quality of confidence for me. You won't always be error-free in your decision-making, and you won't always make the right decision. Life isn't meant to be perfect; it's meant to be meaningful. But to be a leader, you must be able to take pushback. Leadership and strength go hand in hand.

Here's an extended story of how a mentor changed my life. To pay for college at the University of Texas at Austin, I waitressed my first year, then almost randomly I had a chance to work in the Texas State Senate, first as an intern, and later as staff assistant and junior policy aide. My political beliefs were still being shaped back then, and I admit my service in the Senate, at first, was mostly to help pay for school.

After I graduated, I was accepted into two different law schools, and I was just about to enter law school when Senator Kay Bailey Hutchison called and said she believed in me and my potential. She asked me to defer law school for a year, come to Washington, DC, and intern for her.

I wasn't certain about making the move, but she encouraged me that a career path doesn't always follow a straight line. In hindsight, heading to Washington proved an invaluable life-changing decision for me. Sure, you can feel safe by taking a straight path in your career; you can even feel a sense of control. But if you don't take a little risk every now and again, you might miss a great opportunity that you couldn't foresee. Every decision doesn't always work out as you hope either, but that's okay, because you're going to learn a lot if it doesn't. If I had followed the pre-scribed path, I would have missed a pathway that's become incredibly meaningful to me.

Incidentally, my parents were not happy about my decision to defer law school and head to Washington, DC—particularly my dad, because he had wanted so much for me to have a stable career. He didn't think poli-tics was as stable as law. In fact, when I told them the news that I'd deferred law school, my dear father sort of shook his head and muttered, "I don't know why we ever left Egypt."

But here's where this story comes full circle. My internship with Senator Hutchison eventually led to another position with the House majority leadership and then to another role working for Governor George W. Bush, and another after he became president. It might sound strange to say that George Bush is one of my mentors, but he indeed became that.

When I first met him as governor, he was incredibly bipartisan in his approach, and I came to understand and value his policies. I worked on his campaign in 2000; then, after he became president, I was appointed assistant to the president for Presidential Personnel. When a president is elected, they're responsible for hiring literally thousands of leaders across different levels of government, and many will require Senate confirmation. It meant I needed to learn how to spot talented, dedicated, values-based individuals, and recruit those people for the president's vetting.

Along the way, I learned from President Bush at least two large lessons: first, you want team-oriented people who are all about the mission and the work; and second, good people make good policy. Who you place in those roles will implement policy for the sake of people's betterment. That was his focus, and that was how he led.

I worked for the president for eight years. About midway through that time, my parents visited the White House for the first time. You have to realize how big a deal this was for two people who had emigrated from Egypt. My parents didn't think they'd ever meet the president, and I didn't think they would either (he's a busy guy). But right when my parents landed on the grounds, the president happened to be nearby. He came straight over, said, "You must be Mr. and Mrs. Habib," and shook their hands. My parents were shocked. Then he added, "You know, you raised a great daughter. She's an important advisor to me. Congratulations."

It was a statement of belief. My boss *believed* in me.

That was the extent of their meeting. But I remember my father being very emotional afterward. The president's brief statement had won him over. I might not have taken the stable route for my career, but my parents' fears were assuaged. As the president walked away, my father turned to me and said with a tear in his eye, "There aren't many countries in the world like this. A man brings his little girl to his adopted country when she and her family don't speak a word of English. She grows up, and one day, he watches her serve the president."

President Bush has taught me so much. He and Mrs. Bush have mentored many people just by being such amazing examples of what a true partnership looks like as a couple. They've also been exceptional parents to their two children, now adults, Jenna Bush Hager and Barbara Bush.

Both daughters have made huge impacts in their careers. Barbara is the cofounder of a program called Global Health Corps, which has built a diverse community of health equity leaders around the world. Jenna was also instrumental in the creation of the Corps. In addition, she uses her platform as a leading journalist and bestselling author to provide inspiration and guidance to people everywhere. Through her Read With Jenna book club, she champions a diverse group of impactful authors, helping to further their reach while delighting and challenging readers everywhere. Amy and her husband, John Griffin, just celebrated twenty five years since founding iMentor, an organization that has transformed thousands of lives through mentoring.

I'm currently chairman of the Robin Hood Foundation, where I serve with John. It's the largest and most successful nonprofit focused on poverty alleviation in New York. I had served under John as vice chairman, when he was chairman. Among the many organizations that the Robin Hood Foundation support, several have mentorship as a critical mission.

Some of the greater leaders in the mentoring space are also friends. Their impact and profound investment in mentoring has made such a difference to so many women, both nationally and around the globe.

Amy Griffin, often known for her collegiate athletic prowess, is now the founder and managing partner of G9 Ventures. She's passionate for women's rights, and her fund invests in companies led by women. Amy has collated a passionate network of mentors who help women everywhere.

One of my dearest friends in the world, Dana Perino, has been incredibly successful. She's made it her mission in life to help and mentor others. We worked together at the White House and have been friends for more than twenty years. Her bestselling book *Everything Will Be Okay: Life Lessons for Young Women (from a Former Young Woman)* reached countless young women across the country, showing the profound yearning for guidance, advice, and mentoring.

One important business leader and friend is Reese Witherspoon. In addition to her excellence on screen as an Academy Award–, Primetime

Emmy Award–, and Golden Globe–winning actor, she pioneered and cofounded Hello Sunshine, the first major Hollywood media company dedicated to championing women's voices. I worked closely with Reese when I was at Goldman, and I know she's passionate about mentoring women. She started her company because she wanted to change the way women are seen in media. The mission of Hello Sunshine is to empower women by creating a platform to help them shape culture and the world around them. Reese ended up building one of the most successful enterprises in media. With the company firmly on track, and with its founding principles securely in place, we at Goldman were proud to advise her when she sold the company for a reported $900 million, the largest payout ever reported for a woman in Hollywood.[16] To this day, Reese continues to be an example for businesswomen everywhere.

Oprah Winfrey is a mentor the world over. I was recently with Oprah and heard her describe just a few of the many extraordinary accomplishments of her life. One of her greatest legacies is the school and leadership academy for girls that she founded in South Africa. Oprah is the girls' mentor, although she finds additional mentors for the students. One of the strong beliefs of the Academy is that education both levels the playing field and prompts people to rise. Each student at her school has experienced poverty and trauma but is taught to overcome through resilience, courage, and dauntless resolve.

Mellody Hobson, the co-CEO of Ariel Investments and the current Chair of Starbucks, is one of the strongest, most innovative leaders in diversity mentoring I know. Hers is a kind and powerful voice, and she's mentored countless others on corporate boards. Her specialty is teaching leaders how to effectively incorporate diversity into their leadership teams, and she's doing a world of good.[17]

FINDING GREAT MENTORS

I (David) also have benefited from having many excellent transformative mentors during my career. It's impossible to name them all, but I think of Bob Kimmitt, a West Point graduate and decorated Vietnam veteran.

Back in 1996, Bob worked as a lawyer in Washington, DC, had served at the highest levels of government, and had strong connections in Republican politics. I had graduated from West Point by then, served in Iraq, earned my PhD at Princeton, and written a doctoral thesis on military reform that I later published as a book, *The Downsized Warrior.* I was interested in public service, so I cold-called Bob, introduced myself, and asked for a twenty-minute meeting with him. He agreed, so I traveled to Washington, DC, just to see him. He invited me into his cavernous office. It was prime real estate, looking directly onto the White House. I told him about my career goals, and he said he'd be happy to help.

As a sidelight, Bob would tell you today that prospective mentees have much more control over connecting with a potential mentor than they might think. It's certainly fine for prospective mentees to become entre-preneurial in their pursuit of a mentor. If you're seeking a mentor, do your research, find who you want to learn from, and reach out, asking for advice. Almost everybody likes to be asked for advice, and it gives the prospective mentor a chance to pay it forward.

Sure enough, the next day, Bob wrote five letters of introduction for me to key people in Governor George W. Bush's campaign, all of which I followed up on. One positive response came from Rich Armitage. At the time, he was in charge of Governor Bush's defense policy. Governor Bush was set to give a speech at the Citadel, the Military College of South Carolina, to discuss defense reform. Rich ended up having me write part of the governor's speech, thanks to the work I'd done on my thesis, and I ended up staying in touch with both Rich and Bob. Funny enough, Bob and I soon accepted jobs working for different e-commerce companies. For several years we were competitors, in a sense. But we probably talked once a month during those years, and we became good friends.

After Governor Bush became president for his second term in 2004, Bob became deputy secretary of the Treasury. Bob helped me get my job as the Commerce Department's undersecretary of commerce for Industry and Security, and within two years, Bob helped orchestrate me becoming the undersecretary of the Treasury for International Affairs. During those years, Bob was not only my colleague but a life coach to me. He held a uniquely insightful, three-dimensional vision of opportunity, risk, and service to both family and country, and we have stayed in close touch ever since. There isn't a large decision I face today that I don't run by Bob first.

Bob reminded me recently that in life you will find both givers and takers. The takers are people who won't return your calls today but will as soon as they want something from you. The givers are in touch with you when they don't want anything except to maintain the relationship. He calls me a giver, and I hope I've always proved him right.

I also highly value one of Bob's life mottos, and it dovetails nicely with what Dina learned from Senator Hutchison. Bob told me, "Any time an opportunity comes your way that will not come around again, think long and hard before saying no." For instance, he was once considering a job offer that required a cross-country move. He and his wife disliked the idea of a move, but his wife said, "Well, it's not going to come around again. Let's go for it." Bob took the job. Years later, after Bob had been in government and was considering returning to the private sector, he was asked to serve as an ambassador to Germany. He knew the opportunity wouldn't come around twice. He accepted the appointment.

"I'M HERE FOR YOU"

What is the deeper meaning of work, according to Satya Nadella? He unearthed the secret of work's deeper meaning through the mentoring experiences he had along the way.

Satya discussed with us many more mentors, more than can be mentioned here. Both Bill Gates and Steve Ballmer proved to be important mentors and instrumental in Satya becoming CEO. Satya described how they taught him about high standards and helped position him for success. "They would talk to me like a peer," Satya said. "Once I became CEO, they didn't treat me like I was simply another member of their management team. It can be hard for some leaders to pass the torch; they can act like the next CEO works for them. But neither Bill nor Steve have been this way. They are there for advice when I need it, and they also let me lead and take the company forward."

Former Microsoft board chair John Thompson became a friend and mentor. He and Satya met regularly for three years after Satya became CEO. Satya said, "I needed to learn so much, and John had such patience for my situation. He made a huge difference. He could have approached me and said, 'Satya, we have a clock. We want to see whether you're going to make it or not.' But he didn't. He said, 'I know you can do this. I'm here for you.' He helped me grow into the role, become comfortable with the position, and ultimately become the leader I need to be."

Reed Hastings, co-CEO of Netflix, also became a friend and advisor to Satya. He invited Satya to executive meetings at Netflix so he could learn about the inner workings of another large company. Satya shadowed Reed for about a year, and Reed taught Satya valuable lessons about how large companies can pivot quickly. "He helped me see how you can connect your business to your worldview," Satya said.

In the end, the deeper meaning of work came back to the lessons that Satya first learned from Doug Burgum. Satya went on to explain to us:

Doug taught me that it's easy for work to become transactional. That's when you help somebody only because you want something from them. Or you only act positively only if there's something for you to gain. Doug explained that a work culture cannot be that way. Not at the core. We spend about half our life at work, and that's far too much time to be transactional.

Doug switched me on to work's deeper meaning: work is about people. That's what work needs to be at the core. The people you work with, the people you work for, the people you lead, the customers you have. I want the people I work with to be more successful after they have interacted with me.

Success is not measured in how much market capital I grow—not ultimately, anyway. Success is helping people have better lives. I ask myself that question regularly: What's my equation with the people I lead? The modeling, the coaching, the caring—it all goes into helping other people achieve more of that kind of success.

I mean, what is an institution, anyway? An institution is about its people and its culture. It's about the lived experiences, and you want those lived experiences to be really good.

We weren't surprised to hear that Microsoft has a mentoring program today based on similar values as Satya described. But has it been good for business?

Since he became CEO in 2014, Satya has led the company in several successful acquisitions, including LinkedIn, the code-storage service GitHub, Mojang (the maker of the popular game *Minecraft*), and the acquisition of Activision Blizzard. He has stewarded the company's jump into the portable PC market and cloud computing services. The *Los Angeles Times* lauded him for bringing Microsoft "back from the brink of irrelevance."[18] And since Satya took the helm, business has soared.[19]

KEY TAKEAWAYS

- Mentors at work don't need to talk only about work. Today's mentors take a holistic interest in their mentees. They talk about work and life, and the arrangement is often reciprocal, where mentees are encouraging and teaching their mentors too.

- Your career trajectory doesn't always need to follow a straight path, and transformative mentors can help point this out and help you navigate the transitions. Risk and reward go hand in hand. Sometimes your best opportunities will prompt you to follow a path you didn't foresee at first.

- As Satya explained, life is about people, and work is a big part of life. Anything is possible for a company when its culture is about listening, learning, and harnessing individual passions and talents to the company's mission. As Satya said, whether at work or at home or anywhere: "You must be present for the people who need you most."

A Conversation with General Joe Dunford

To say that retired four-star general Joseph "Fighting Joe" Dunford has had a distinguished career would be a giant understatement. From 2015 to 2019, he served as the nineteenth chairman of the Joint Chiefs of Staff, the top military leader in the country. Before that, he led all United States and NATO forces in Afghanistan, and prior to that he served as the thirty-sixth Commandant of the Marine Corps.

He's seen as quiet, intellectual, and unassuming, but Dunford has a character of steel. He earned his "Fighting Joe" reputation by leading the 5th Marine Regiment during the 2003 invasion of Iraq. Almost paradoxically, he claimed for much of his career that he wasn't competitive, and he attempted more than once to leave the Marines. Still, from the day Joseph Francis Dunford Jr. was born in 1955, he was clearly destined for leadership.

The trajectory of General Dunford's life extended from taking responsibility for his five younger brothers when they were children, to heading all the military forces of the United States. This pathway put him in a position to speak into the ears of both President Barack Obama and President Donald Trump.

Along the way, Dunford earned a bachelor's degree in political science from St. Michael's College in Colchester, Vermont, and two master's degrees—one in government from Georgetown University and one in international relations from the Fletcher School of Law and Diplomacy at Tufts University. He also graduated from the United States Army War College, Ranger School, Airborne School, and the Amphibious Warfare School.

His military career spanned nearly four decades, and his civilian awards include being featured on *Fortune* magazine's list "The World's 50 Greatest Leaders." Even in retirement, Joe Dunford keeps on giving—for instance, by serving on the board of the Travis Manion Foundation, one of the nation's leading organizations that serves veterans.

Though a fighting man, General Dunford's leadership style is nonconfrontational. His ability to get things done and keep people working together, even people of differing ideologies, is often credited to the example he sets for others to think strategically and empathetically.

We sat down with him to find out what, and especially who, shaped his life in terms of mentoring.

❖   ❖   ❖

1. Let's talk about your early years. Who came alongside you to set the course that followed?

My dad had served as an enlisted Marine in Korea, then for forty years he was a city cop in Boston and retired as a deputy superintendent. I also had uncles who served in World War II. So, for me, going into the military was kind of a rite of passage. But *staying* in the military, that was altogether different. I never intended to do that, and mentors changed my life there too. My father was a role model, a mentor, a great dad, and somebody I looked up to a lot. People used to say, "Hey, your dad is really an honest guy, always looking out for his people." That has a big impact in terms of the bar you set for yourself, in how you want people to see you.

Birth order and expectations in my family had something to do with it too. I was the oldest of six boys, eight and a half years from start to finish.

When I was ten years old, my parents didn't think twice about leaving me with the whole squad. A sense of responsibility and accountability came from my parents.

Then, the motto of our school, Boston College High School, was "be a man for others." You couldn't graduate without doing service projects. We helped younger students with reading and other subjects at a youth center, and we visited homes of the elderly to help out. Over time, service becomes part of you. The high school experience had a pretty big impact on me that manifested itself some years down the road. Here's one example: It was a Jesuit high school, and I attended from 1969 to 1973. Five of the priests there at the time were from Baghdad, and one was my guidance counselor. These were guys who had been kicked out of the country by Saddam Hussein in 1969, and they came straight to my high school. Later, I led the troops who secured Baghdad University in 2003.

2. Some of your mentors inspired you to join the military, and others helped keep you from resigning. How did they do that?

Back in high school, I'd had a spinal fusion and was told that I would never play sports again, never be able to do anything, really. I was a die-hard Red Sox fan, and I adopted the motto that no sporting event was ever sold out; it's just a question of how much you want to pay for a ticket. Sports motivated me, and I certainly wasn't going to sit around for the rest of my life. Despite my spinal fusion, I kept trying to get into the Marine Corps. Just six months after the fall of Saigon, December 1975, I made it in. I signed a two-year reserve contract with the Marine Corps.

Still, I only intended to do those two years. I had a very idealistic, almost romantic vision of the Marine Corps, but I experienced some disillusionment when I joined. I saw racial problems, drug problems, not enough money for training. After just eighteen months, I became a company commander, and I was woefully unprepared. I went from leading 40 Marines to leading about 175. I was twenty-three years old and completely over my head. I would not have stayed in the United States Marine Corps except for a few key people.

First, Sergeant Major Sam Fernandez, who had been a platoon sergeant in Vietnam, helped me through. His door was always open to young lieutenants needing advice.

Second, the battalion operations officer, Joe Bierly, took an interest in me. Not only did he have an open-door policy, but he provided guidance in almost everything I did in the company. I'd look at him and say, "Hmm, if guys like that stay in, there's got to be more to it than what I'm seeing." When my time as a company commander was over, I worked directly for Joe Bierly. Over the course of a year and a half, maybe twenty Saturdays, we went out in a jeep to plan training, just he and I and the driver. This was a three-hour period of instruction for me on whatever was the issue of the day.

Another key mentor was General Joseph Hoar. After I'd been in the Marine Corps for two and a half years, I went to my second rifle company, still only marginally prepared. I was in this one situation, and it was chaos. They didn't even have a good, serialized inventory of rifles. At that point, I resigned my commission and went up to see Colonel Hoar. I was very uncomfortable going to see him because he'd done so much for me. He gave me the talk, the Psychology 101 about trying to stay, but I wasn't budging. Next, I told my team. A guy named Gunnery Sergeant Ignacio from Guam blurts out, "Well, that's great, Lieutenant. What about the rest of us?" That night I didn't sleep. The next day I pulled my letter of resignation. Ignacio was the catalyst. It wasn't that I decided to stay in. It was I couldn't bring myself to get out.

I accepted orders to go to Okinawa, but I still wasn't comfortable with staying for the long term. I was responsible for all the classified material for the Marine Expeditionary Force headquarters. It was an office job. Basically, I was in a windowless vault doing page counts on nuclear code books and other classified documents. I did this for forty-eight hours, and I thought I was going to go crazy by the end of the year. I told Colonel

Hoar, and I'm sure he made some calls, because I soon got a phone call from General Stephen Olmstead. He says, "Hey, how would you like to be my aide?" What are the odds of that happening? Again, this was meeting the right guy at the right time. As I worked with him, he took a deep interest in me, as if I was one of his sons. He spent time talking to me about his experiences, and about what it was like to raise a family in the Marine Corps. We traveled all over the Pacific together. I was in his personal space; I was in his professional space. And I wanted to be like him. He was one of those guys—you kind of go, "Wow, I'd like to have the kind of impact that guy has."

So it was a combination of these very influential people early in my career. I did everything to actively look at other opportunities. It wasn't so much that I decided to make the military a career, but I was surrounded by people who made it really hard for me to leave.

3. You've named one man, besides your father, as having more influence on you than any other: General Carl Mundy. Can you tell us about him?
It was during a time when staying in the Marine Corps was getting tough. My wife, Ellyn, and I had three kids in preschool, and we'd always talked about me staying in only until the kids got into high school. In 1992, I was assigned to Headquarters Marine Corps. Shortly after checking in, I was standing in front of General Carl Mundy, Commandant of the Marine Corps. He said, "I want you to write a speech for me." I didn't even know how to type. I'd never written a speech in my life, but I put something together. A while later, he said, "Hey, you're going to be my speechwriter." About a year into it, he called me to his office and made me his senior aide.

From then until I became Commandant in the Marine Corps, this is the leader I called for advice. I spent three years working for him, and I could tell you a million stories about his integrity. He taught me so many things that go from being a father, to being a man, to being a leader. Working with him was one of the most profound experiences I had in the military. I was so fortunate. He interacted with my kids and my wife, and he called me his third son. He had the same integrity in private that he had in public. Even when he was under extraordinary stress, the way he treated people was amazing. I never saw him lose his temper.

The profound thing about leaders such as General Mundy is that the relationship isn't transactional. It's not just about getting you to the next assignment. It's transformational. They take time talking about things that you ought to think about and know. More importantly, they make themselves accessible. If you have a question, you're never without someone you can call. They're trustworthy, and they care about you as a person. It's not just someone trying to keep you retained.

A couple of incidents with General Mundy show his integrity—and became such a model for me. I remember one day a mistake was made—not by him. Someone in the organization released a message that said something like, "You're not eligible to enlist in the Marine Corps if you're married." That hit like a ton of bricks in the public space. It looked like General Mundy was going to be fired, and I was devastated. But instead of pointing fingers, he held a press conference, corrected the mistake, and took responsibility for it. He said to me, "Joe, if I didn't take responsibility for that, then no one would ever do anything without my permission again. I'm the Commandant. I'm responsible. That's the way it is."

The other incident concerned a one-star general who went on a news program and said things that were just terrible regarding race. The producers of the program showed the clip to General Mundy and basically said, "Okay, if you go on instead of him, we won't show the clip." Everyone was telling him not to do it, that they'd screw him. But he stood up, went on the show, and clarified things. That's the kind of guy he was.

On the human side, there's an anecdote that shows how far he'd go as a mentor. Once, while our family was ice-skating, our little boy had an accident and his arm was broken badly. It was reset in the hospital, and they kept him in overnight because he was so little and had gone through so much. The next day, General Mundy and his wife showed up at our house with a bag of toys and visited our son. A four-star general! I could tell you a thousand stories of similar kindnesses.

In sum, he was a leader who accepted responsibility, who communicated, and who took a personal interest in you. Whenever we were out walking, the conversations that I'd have with him were like gold.

4. You were chairman of the Joint Chiefs of Staff under both President Obama and President Trump. What is your secret for bridging divides and getting along with people who have different opinions?
In those settings, it was about maintaining a professional relationship but not a distant relationship. It was all about business. I was "General Dunford" or "Chairman."

I had read the history about General George Marshall. President Franklin Roosevelt was a gregarious joke teller in the Oval Office, but Marshall would never laugh when a joke was told. One time, the president called him "George," and after the meeting he said, "Mr. President, I'd appreciate if you'd call me 'General.'" When I was a junior guy, I thought, *Wow, what a stiff,* but as a senior guy, I realized there was a method to the madness.

I wasn't seen as part of either the Obama or Trump administration. As chairman, you have a responsibility to the president to adjust to his personality and to provide information in a way that he wants. They couldn't have been two more different types of leaders. But I had to adjust to the environment. I had to keep in mind what my job was. We had to deliver nonpartisan military advice no matter whether the president used it or not. As chairman, we have a statutory responsibility to provide advice, although no one in statute has a requirement to listen to our advice—I learned that from General Marty Dempsey [eighteenth chairman of Joint Chiefs].

5. You've had experience with mentorship, both formal and informal, throughout your career. Currently, you are a senior fellow at the Belfer Center for Science and International Affairs at Harvard University, where you mentor national security and intelligence professionals—so obviously mentoring is important to you. In the wake of all those who have believed in you over the years, now you are believing in others. Looking ahead, how might transformative mentorship fit into the overall cultural landscape of the United States?

The future operative environment will place new demands on leaders at all levels. To best prepare our future leaders for success, we must continuously assess and refine our leader development. I've always believed that a mentorship program is one of the primary ways we can develop and retain our leaders, whether in military or civilian life. One of the elements of mentorship, obviously, is to be a teacher and also a role model. You've got to remember that your influence is based on trust.

My first battalion commander told me three rules to success. I've long since forgotten the last two of them, but I'll never forget the first: *Surround yourself with good people.* That's the key to our nation's success today. We have to build better leaders. That's where transformative mentoring can help.

8.

Mentoring Across Genders

One of the larger issues that repeatedly surfaced in our discussions while researching this book was that of mentoring across gender lines. Can men effectively mentor women? Can women effectively mentor men? For some team members, the answer seemed obvious: of course, yes. Mentoring across gender lines can and needs to happen. But for others, the concept was more nuanced and not as straightforward, particularly in a post-#MeToo era.

If a middle-aged male business leader, for instance, reached out to a younger female intern and offered to mentor her, would that be considered appropriate today, or would that be seen as an unwanted advance? If the genders were reversed in that situation—a middle-aged female business leader reached out to mentor a younger male intern—would anything be different?

Some business leaders we spoke to and surveyed felt that this was a nonissue. Yet others indeed felt a reticence surrounding this practice. Too many public abuses had surfaced, they stated, so they were wary of mentoring across gender lines, and they had become so cautious that they didn't want to entertain the possibility of accusations.

Yet the cessation of mentoring across gender lines certainly isn't the answer—as we'll discuss later in the chapter—because it creates disparate opportunities, usually favoring men. Mentoring needs to happen, and transformative mentoring across gender lines is part of the solution to building better leaders. We've already shown how we are living in one of the most divisive times in our history. True, transformative mentorship is the key to creating trustworthy leaders, people of character, who build the bridges we need to become our best selves and reach our full potential.

And for us, this is more than just an academic question. With six daughters between us, we often wonder what barriers they may face—and opportunities they may discover—when it comes to developing the same transformative mentoring experiences that we have both enjoyed. Will they be able to form strong trusting relationships with bosses and coworkers, male and female alike? Will societal standards and our recent societal experience with the #MeToo movement get in the way?

As a start for wrestling with these questions, we want to present an example of someone we believe is doing mentoring well—Tory Burch, a close friend of ours, and a strong female leader who regularly mentors people of any gender within her company. We'll let her example offer a model of what seamless, effective, cross-gender mentoring can look like. Then we'll pull together some conclusions toward the end of the chapter.

A STRONG ROLE MODEL

She didn't go to business school; she didn't go to design school. Yet Tory Burch stands today on top of a multibillion-dollar[1] global fashion empire that she built from the ground up. She credits her success to an instinctive sense of personal style, a powerful vision to fill a niche market, and lots of hard work—plus valuable guidance from mentors in finance, talent management, manufacturing, and operations.

Tory founded her eponymous company in 2004 around the kitchen table of her New York City apartment. Tory Burch LLC began with a simple idea—to provide "beautiful clothes that don't cost a fortune."[2] The company concept is to offer stylish yet reasonably priced women's apparel, shoes, handbags, jewelry, and accessories. Tory has opened more than 345 stores throughout the United States and internationally, with flagship stores in Los Angeles, New York, London, Rome, Paris, Singapore, Shanghai, and Tokyo.

Her company is an activist brand, purpose-driven to the core. Tory helped build her company's culture with ideals she calls "Buddy Values," named after her father, Buddy, who "always treated everyone with kindness and respect."[3] The values are as follows: "We show up with honesty and kindness. We work with passion and humility. We act with integrity and compassion. We lead with excellence and humor."

Tory is on a mission, and her activism extends beyond the corporate culture that she champions. Social responsibility was always part of her business plan. Tory recently described to us how her experiences as a female entrepreneur have shaped and deepened her company. She continually desires to lead a business where everybody can flourish, both professionally and personally.

One of Tory's specific driving passions is to encourage women to know that it's okay to be ambitious. To clarify: she's not against *men* being ambitious. She has three brothers, three sons, and three stepsons, whom she loves dearly and wants to see succeed. Rather, she wants to help close the professional gender gap around this concept of ambition. Years ago, a reporter asked if she was "ambitious," and the question made her bristle. When a friend later asked her why, Tory realized she'd bought into the stereotype that women shouldn't be ambitious, or at least not show it. "From that moment on," Tory said, "I owned my ambition."

Tory pointed us toward a study done at Columbia University where researchers described a fictional venture capitalist to a group of business students. Both groups were told about this person's competencies, aspirations, and successes. But one group was informed that the entrepreneur was named Heidi, while the other group was told that the leader was named Howard. The results as reported by the study were these:

> Students felt Heidi was significantly less likable and worthy of being hired than Howard and perceived her as more "selfish." The more assertive a student found the female venture capitalist to be, the more they rejected her.
>
> The essence is that research has demonstrated a negative correlation for women between power and success. For men, the relationship is positive, i.e., successful men are perceived as more powerful and are revered.
>
> The assertive, authoritative, and dominant behaviors that people link with leadership tend not to be viewed as attractive in women.[4]

To combat such stereotypes, Tory established the Tory Burch Foundation in 2009, specifically to advance women's empowerment and support women entrepreneurs by providing access to mentorship, education, networking, and low-interest small business loans. I (Dina) had the privilege of serving on the board of the Tory Burch Foundation. To date, it's become the largest American foundation dedicated to investing in female entrepreneurship. The program's biggest emphasis is mentoring.[5] In 2017, Tory and the Foundation created the #EmbraceAmbition initiative to further address the double standards that surround ambition for women. Every two years, the #EmbraceAmbition initiative holds a summit in New York, which brings together activists, scientists, politicians, and thought leaders to discuss women's empowerment and the most pressing issues facing women and marginalized people today.

Tory's initiatives fascinate and inspire us. We've discussed how, as we have journeyed toward discovery around the topic of mentorship, the subject that came up repeatedly in our interviews and research was cross-gendering mentoring, specifically for the purpose of closing the gender gap. We all want women and men to have equal opportunities in businesses, organizations, and leadership positions, yet unfortunately this is currently not the case.

At present, women obtain some 57 percent of all undergraduate degrees and 59 percent of all master's degrees and hold almost 52 percent of all management and professional level jobs.[6] Yet a woman makes only eighty-two cents for every dollar a man makes.[7] Only a quarter of women in the legal profession are partners, just 16 percent of medical school deans are female, merely a third of tenured professors are women,[8] and just forty-one of the Fortune 500 companies are led by women.[9] In our own survey, we found that, due to mentoring, men received a significantly greater amount of new professional opportunities compared to women.[10]

When it comes to women mentoring men, and men mentoring women, the goal in the United States needs to be that both women and men receive equal opportunities and equal rewards for the same tasks done. How might this insight and equality best be grasped and accomplished?

Tory addressed this question by describing to us three main areas: first, how she had strong female and male role models in her own life; second, how she made career and homelife choices that recognized both her role as a mother and her role as a business leader; and last, how both men and women have mentored her, and how as a female CEO she mentors both women and men today.

STRENGTH FROM WOMEN AND MEN

Tory took us back to the people who first gave her roots and wings—her parents, Buddy and Reva Robinson. (Buddy passed away in 2007.) They were both positive-thinking, highly creative people, adventurers at heart. Almost every summer, they boarded a steamer ship and spent six weeks traveling. Tory described how their unique lifestyles and wanderlust proved a consistent inspiration for her and helped teach her courage. When she was a child, her parents would send her outdoors on non-school days. She'd play all day, climbing trees, helping her mother with the family's vegetable garden, or exploring the pastures and countryside with her brothers, Robert, James, and Leonard.

In her youth, Tory's mother, Reva, was an aspiring actress who had dated Steve McQueen.[11] Reva later found her niche as a floral designer, and Tory and her brothers helped in her business. Buddy was an investor who had inherited a stock exchange seat and a paper cup company, which he later sold. On the side, he operated a gentleman's farm in rural Valley Forge, Pennsylvania, where the family bred and cared for German shepherds. Tory told us:

My parents taught me how to care for people, to think beyond myself. Our house was a creative place and always open and welcoming to strangers, sort of a mix between the Swiss Family Robinson and Andy Warhol. Both my parents would help anybody they met. We had a constant mix of people coming and going, people who were down on their luck; maybe somebody just needed a place to stay for a while. At times, we'd have eight to ten people living with us, for up to six months sometimes, and often we didn't know them very well. I went to Quaker schools, and the entire community emphasized love, peace, and beauty. My mom, to this day, takes care of people who need help. She's an incredible example of strength mixed with femininity.

My father was astute and kind, and he helped me be strong. He had a welcoming personality and an unbelievable sense of style. He made all his own clothes, and people often said he should have been a designer. Others would try to replicate his style. If he had been raised a bit differently, he could have become an incredible entrepreneur.

Overall, my parents raised my brothers and me the same way. Their attitude was that if we worked hard and helped people, we could achieve anything. I never knew that by being a girl I might be treated differently. It never occurred to me to think otherwise until I got into the workforce and saw a very different perspective.

When Tory was six years old, her uncle was killed in a plane crash. It was her mother's brother, and the two siblings had been extremely close. In her grief, Reva sent Tory to summer camp in Maine for two months with her cousin, whose father had been killed. Tory said:

They wanted to get us out of the house and away from all the sadness. You can imagine it was pretty traumatic, even to be away from home for that long when so young. I didn't have a perspective to understand everything that was going on at home. My mother's brother was the closest person in her life, and my mother was experiencing such enormous grief and she wanted to prevent me from going through that.

But the cup was always half full for my mother, no matter how bad things got. If we were going through something hard, she'd say, "You wake up, and it's a new day." That helped me be strong. Every evening at summer camp, I talked to her on the phone. There was nothing said that was negative. It was always positive. We would talk about learning how to ride horses, or about playing tennis.

When visiting day came, I was ready to go home, but that wasn't an option. I wasn't allowed to feel sorry for myself. So I learned to persevere. I still have letters that she wrote to me that summer, where she was making sure I could stand on my own two feet. That taught me to be independent.

Overall, I could be quite shy when I was young, and my mother helped me overcome this. She thought I could achieve anything if I put my mind to it, and she had higher aspirations for me than I had for myself. She taught me how to believe in myself, have strength, and dream big without limits. If things didn't go right, she would say, "You are Tory Robinson," as if strength and confidence were built right into my identity.

THE POWER OF FEMALE MENTORS

Tory graduated from the University of Pennsylvania in 1988 with a major in art history, then moved to New York City where she worked in public relations for the Serbian designer Zoran, then wrote marketing copy for *Harper's Bazaar* magazine, then worked in publicity and advertising positions for Vera Wang, Ralph Lauren, and Loewe. These experiences all paved the way for her later powerful career.

In 1996, she married the investor Christopher Burch, and they had three sons together, as well as his three children from another marriage. They were married for ten years, and Tory continues to use his last name today. Through the ups and downs of personal relationships, Tory gained wisdom. In 2018, she married Pierre-Yves Roussel, the former chair and CEO of the LVMH fashion group. He became the CEO of Tory Burch LLC in 2019, a title Tory had held for fourteen years. With Pierre-Yves as CEO, Tory now devotes the majority of her time to design and creative work as chief creative officer and executive chair.

When her children were young, Tory described herself as a "full-time mom." As they grew, she began to explore various ideas for businesses to start. She worked on a book and contemplated going back to school. She was offered a high-level position with a prominent fashion company, but she turned it down because she had twin toddlers at home and had just discovered she was pregnant with her third child. During 9/11, Tory watched the news nonstop. A commercial kept playing with a tagline:

"Follow your dreams." In the midst of that dark season, she found inspiration. Three years later, after a lot of research, she launched her fashion company. Tory said:

Why did I turn down the job offer when I was pregnant? Women have to make those tough decisions. Often, we can't do everything at once. I had three babies under the age of four, and I wanted to have a career, too, but it wasn't the right time for me.

The years at home gave me time to think and dream, in addition to caring for my children. My family and mentors and I talked through a lot of ideas for different businesses to start. At one point I decided to stop talking about it, because it felt like I was having a different idea every minute. They weren't all fashion businesses either. What they all had in common was that they solved problems.

Then I saw a white space in the market. There was a certain mystique to doing a collection that was beautifully designed and well-made but wasn't at a luxury price point. I can't tell you how many people I cold-called for advice. I was definitely an information gatherer, and everyone had an opinion. I came up with this concept that everyone told me not to do: a direct-to-consumer model with an e-commerce retail feature. And right from the start, I wanted to start a company with a mission and a foundation.

Anna Wintour is one of Tory's earliest mentors in business. They met through a friend. Anna is the legendary editor of *Vogue* magazine and the inspiration for the hard-driving character Miranda Priestly in *The Devil Wears Prada*.[12] Anna helped Tory launch her first fashion show, gave her tips for approaching investors, and ultimately became a lifelong mentor. Tory told us:

Anna taught me how to be focused, and to be prompt. One of the very first memories I have of Anna, after we had known each other for a while, is this: There was a small dinner in Paris, which she had invited me to. On the way there, I got stuck behind a garbage truck—a terrible traffic jam.

I showed up at the restaurant late, after the first course. Anna is always early—and when you have a meeting, she'll tell you to be there ten minutes ahead of time. It was not an exciting moment for my twenty-seven-year-old self. I don't think I've been late ever since.

We got to know each other slowly. It definitely wasn't immediate. Something I truly respect about her is her honest and fair perspective. She has the ability to be incredibly straightforward, which can be hard to hear at times. But she will give you extremely valuable advice. Real mentors will do that for you. It's tough love.

She also taught me the importance of being who I am. It's so easy in this industry to look to the right or the left and see what everyone else is doing. But if you don't have a point of view that's your own and unique, then it's not interesting. You have to be who you are. It has to come from your heart and your instinct, or else it's not authentic.

She also taught me the art of saying no. The concept that you're not able to please everybody is something that's very freeing, once I understood it. If you can learn to say no in a way that's straightforward and honest, that's a very important skill.

THE BENEFIT OF MALE MENTORS

One of Tory's main male mentors has been Eric Schmidt, a Silicon Valley icon and the former CEO and executive chair of Google. Tory said:

The best leaders empower others. Both Anna and Eric do that. They are unconventional thinkers and both have creative minds. Eric is at the forefront of technology and has more experience around data and analytics, and he helps us think on a bigger scale. Just like Anna, he will tell me things in a very straightforward way.

Eric is interested in creativity and innovation, and he's a bit of an unlikely board member for a fashion company. But I've learned it's incredibly valuable to have people outside of the industry on our team. They see things from a different perspective, and that's transformative for us. I remember Eric kept using this phrase: "Cash is king." This was during a time when we could have used more cash. For me, it was an abrupt realization that we better figure it out.

At the same time, his expression made me think, *Okay, if cash is king, then culture is queen.* In other words, we are a business, so we better run our business well monetarily. Yet as a business we also have a tremendous responsibility with our values and how we interact with other people. That can be a great thing about mentors—you listen to them and get advice, but they also help you think differently.

Another male mentor for Tory is her brother Robert Isen, nine years her senior, who works for Tory Burch LLC. As chief legal officer and president of corporate development, he's in charge of in-house legal, new business development, and the company's real estate. Tory said:

Our whole family is close, and Robert's always been there for me. Robert is brilliant, and Robert has no ego, and Robert builds people up. He personifies our company culture. I could never have built the company without Robert—not in a million years. I've learned to surround myself with the most brilliant people I possibly can and then never worry that they outshine me in any way. I never want to take personal ownership of our company's success. I love it when other people shine.

As an entrepreneur, I take risks. But Robert is the measured voice of reason that's constantly in my head, pulling me back. That's characterized our relationship our whole life. He's protective. I don't think we've ever had a serious disagreement. It's been a real gift for me to have had him sell his company fourteen years ago and join me. Robert is a measured thought partner, and he's helped me build the company from the ground up.

SAYING YES TO OPPORTUNITY

When Tory Burch mentors people today, she almost always does so intentionally. But the spectrum of people she mentors is much broader than one person at a time. She's designed and implemented mentoring programs, not only for people who work in her company but for anybody interested in growth and entrepreneurship. She told us:

I have often mentored by creating introductions. When we first designed our mentoring events, one large goal was to invite some twenty established leaders and roughly one hundred emerging entrepreneurs and hold an open session. We'd have ten tables set up for one-on-one meetings. You would think that five minutes wasn't much, but even that short amount of time proved valuable, because it helped with networking. The emerging entrepreneurs would network with the established leaders, and also with each other, peer-to-peer. The introductions were the start of greater things.

What's also amazing is that almost every established leader who we asked to participate at those events has said yes. They are all highly busy people. But the events have proved fulfilling to them. The established mentors have described to me how they get as much out of the events as the mentees do. Saying yes to being a mentor gives people a sense of purpose, and it gives leaders the opportunity to feel good about helping others.

That's certainly woven into our DNA at our company. We've lived it and proved it over time. Doing good is good for business.

TODAY'S MANDATE OF
CROSS-GENDER MENTORING

Let's draw some conclusions. When it comes to cross-gender interactions in America today, it might seem straightforward that men can and should mentor women and women can and should mentor men—as Tory's story shows.

Yet even today, it's not so simple. After the #MeToo movement drew long overdue attention to the mistreatment of women in the workforce, it became more difficult for men to mentor women. One survey found that 16 percent of men in leadership positions expressed discomfort with the idea of mentoring junior women—triple what it was before[13]—and one executive reported that he would "think twice" about taking a younger woman under his wing.[14] It's easy to understand the concern and the desire to avoid risk of misperception or false allegation. But this overreaction is destined to harm women more than help them, and it's not the only barrier to cross-gender mentoring.

A few years ago, a prominent male leader made national headlines for publicly holding himself to "the Billy Graham rule"[15]—that he never travels, eats, or attends events alone with a woman other than his wife.[16] The well-intentioned rule, created by Dr. Graham and his leadership team back in the late 1940s when he was a young preacher who spent a lot of time away from his spouse,[17] is meant to uphold marital fidelity and personal integrity—both in optics and practice.

In the modern era, people have denounced the rule for being sexist, albeit unintentionally. Although the rule is meant to help leaders live with high standards, it can also enable gender discrimination.[18] Here's how: In the normal operations of any business or organization, any number of circumstances might crop up where an employee would need to meet alone with a boss of the opposite gender. During those meetings, career insight can be offered, insider information can be shared, and transformative mentoring may take place.

As *The Atlantic* notes: "If [a male leader] would share a glass of scotch at the end of the day with a male subordinate in a way that he would not with a female subordinate, that creates an unfair advantage for the men working under [him]. Leaders in both the private and public sectors have to be very careful about creating such unequal opportunities for mentorship and professional development."[19]

How can cross-gender mentoring interactions be safely conducted today?

To be clear, the Billy Graham rule never prohibited interaction between men and women, nor called men to wall off their lives from women they weren't married to, or vice versa.[20] And in an age of sexual scandals and power mongering, media outlets have noted that the rule, or portions of it, or at the very least the honorable spirit and intention behind it, is to be praised for its prudence.[21]

When it comes to modern transformative mentoring, and the vast opportunities for true change it presents, we call for a balanced approach, filled with integrity—similar to how Tory Burch has modeled it for us. In order for all people to have equal career opportunities, mentoring across gender lines should be encouraged. We understand and appreciate the cautions, yet mentoring is not tantamount to a romantic attachment, nor should transformative mentoring be viewed, understood, or practiced that way.

What keeps a mentoring relationship just that? Both mentors and mentees need to be smart, respectful, and cautious. Both a mentor and a mentee must stay professional and focused within the sharing and receiving of personal information, even as the information that is exchanged will sometimes be vulnerable. The responsibility is on them both. Sharing hopes, dreams, and challenges with a mentor or mentee might make the relationship more personal, yet the interchange does not need to be romantic.[22]

As Katelyn Beaty wrote in the *New York Times*:

To be sure, there's wisdom in married people avoiding settings that naturally cultivate attraction. Even men far outside the Christian world, and plenty of well-known liberals, including Ta-Nehisi Coates, keep some version of the [Billy Graham] rule. Alcohol and isolation put otherwise honorable people in precarious situations, and one needn't be religious to acknowledge moral vulnerability.

But reasonable people know the difference between a business meeting over breakfast and drinks at a hotel bar at night.

The answer is not to ask women to leave the room. It's to hold all in the room accountable, and kick out those who long ago lost their right to be there.[23]

An additional piece of the solution is that leaders need to establish clear and candid communication at the start of a mentoring relationship. It's good to define the arrangement for what it is and isn't, then lead from a place of integrity and honor. The mentor can take the lead. Using whatever words and communication style is natural to the mentor, he or she can establish the guardrails of the relationship at the start. If the mentor feels the relationship drifting off course, he or she can clarify what the relationship is all about.

For instance, the mentor may need to say something such as, "Just to be clear, what we're hoping to create between us is an effective mentoring relationship. We are two people working together in the hopes of you reaching your full potential." The mentor can talk about his or her responsibilities, and what the limits of those responsibilities are. They can discuss together how many times they meet, how long the meetings are, and where they meet.

A mentee has responsibility too. He or she may need to periodically remind himself or herself what the relationship is and is not. For example, it may be helpful to tell yourself something as overt as, "This person is my mentor. I value and respect this person's opinions and experience, yet there are lines we must not cross. We will not and should not become romantically involved."

Equally, it's helpful to understand that different genders don't always value the same leadership traits the same way. In our Yale survey, men were more likely to cite "power" and "prominence" as qualities that drew them to their mentor, while women cited "authenticity" and "good listener" at higher rates. This knowledge will undoubtedly affect how mentors approach prospective mentees, and vice versa.

CULTIVATING QUALITIES

I (David) was mentored by Ann McLaughlin Korologos, a prominent leader in Republican politics. She served in prominent roles in the Department of the Interior and the Treasury, and was eventually named secretary of labor under President Reagan, one of the very few female cabinet members at the time. She served as a board member of many blue-chip US companies and nonprofits ranging from Microsoft to Kellogg to Michael Kors, as well as not-for-profits such as the Aspen Institute and the Dana Foundation, a brain health research organization. Before her death in 2024, she owned and ran a beautiful art gallery outside of her home in Basalt, Colorado.

A very smart leader, Ann had a pragmatic concept of both mentoring and being mentored. She would simply watch people and see who showed promise, either as someone to learn from or (later in her career) as someone who could learn from her. When finding a mentor, her advice was to look ahead in time to where you want to be, then find someone who's already there.

I first approached Ann two decades ago when I was a member of the Henry Crown program, a fellowship for the Aspen Institute, because while I was in the private sector, I was interested in public service. So I called and asked if we could talk. She did a lot of listening at first, asking straightforward questions: What did I want to attain in a career? What did I want to learn? How did I want to grow? I think she could tell fairly quickly that I was serious in my aspirations. Her brother and father had both been in the military, so she liked that I'd graduated from West Point.

Ann talked about how leadership itself is hard to learn, particularly when you're leading large organizations, but leadership qualities can be cultivated in anybody. She often said that integrity, strength, and kindness are necessary traits for public service. We also discussed issues specific to governance. We kept in touch, and later when I worked for the Treasury, she became a good friend. A question she asked me more than once—and I know she asks this of herself too—was: "What are you not doing that you should be doing?"

One story in particular sticks with me. She told me about a young male mentee she had for an assistant. Basically, he just sat on a sofa in her office and heard every conversation she had. He was doing administrative tasks for her, too, but their mentoring relationship was mostly about him observing her day in and day out—and it helped in his growth. He went on to the London School of Economics, and today he's succeeding in big ways. Observing a good leader in action is a significant cornerstone of transformative mentoring. Find the person who's the best at what they do, and then just be around them. Keep your eyes open and see what you can glean.

Despite the challenges, having a strong mix of men and women leaders, and having them interact together within the bounds of transformative mentoring, is not only the right thing to do; it's also good business. Research has shown that companies that have strong gender equality in the workplace are 15 percent more likely to outperform those with little gender equality.[24]

We need men to mentor women, and women to mentor men, and for cross-gender mentoring to be done with safeguards, respect, intention, and care. This can happen. And it can happen well.

KEY TAKEAWAYS

- When it comes to career opportunities and equitable pay, women experience unique challenges. Cross-gender mentoring can help create understanding, right wrongs, and minimize gender gaps.
- The Billy Graham rule, or some variation of it, has no doubt guarded the integrity of many people throughout the years. By noting the intention behind it, we can respect the concept while also encouraging and even mandating valuable cross-gender mentoring opportunities in workplaces and organizations, handled with prudence and respect. Communicating the boundaries of the arrangement up front is wise.
- Having a mentor or mentee of a different gender than you can increase the depth of your life and offer new perspectives. It's the right thing to do, and it's also good for business.

A Conversation with Carlos Gutierrez

H e's been in the epicenter of revolution, at the top of global business, and in the heart of world politics.

Carlos Miguel Gutierrez was born in 1953 in Havana, Cuba. At age six, he and his family fled the country, leaving everything behind, to become refugees in the United States. Soon, Carlos would become a US citizen. His career began inauspiciously as a truck driver in the Mexican branch of the Kellogg Company. He rose through management ranks to become chairman and CEO in the United States, the only Hispanic CEO of a Fortune 500 company, and, at age forty-six, the youngest CEO in Kellogg's history.

In 2004, President George W. Bush appointed Carlos to become the thirty-fifth secretary of commerce. Carlos worked to promote American businesses, advocating free-trade agreements and comprehensive immigration solutions, and overseeing an agency with some thirty-eight thousand workers and a $6.5 million budget.

Although he studied at the Monterrey Institute of Technology in Querétaro, Mexico, he never finished a college degree. But today Carlos serves on the boards of several educational institutions and was named a scholar at the University of Miami. Now out of politics, he cofounded and chairs Empath, a skills intelligence software that enables large, complex organizations to identify and grow employee skills.

Despite all this achievement, Carlos identifies his family as his main source of self-esteem. He's married to Edilia and they have one son, Carlos Jr.; two daughters, Erika and Karina; and four grandchildren.

We asked Carlos to tell us about the people who believed in him along the way.

❖   ❖   ❖

1. Tell us about your earliest years. Who influenced you the most when you were young?

This may be exceeding creativity, but I put an event as a mentor in my life. Of course, I'm referring to the Cuban Revolution in 1959. My father was in the pineapple business, as a very successful businessman. He was forty, an up-and-coming entrepreneur, doing well, and could see a great future. But he was considered an enemy of the state by the Castro regime, and my father lost everything. Our property was expropriated. We fled to the United States, settling in Miami. I learned my first words of English from the bellhop at the hotel where we initially stayed. We arrived with few material possessions, but we had many dreams.

One day, a few years later, my father very calmly told us that we were never going to go back to Cuba. "Let's not kid ourselves," he said. "Let's not look back." He had that way of discarding things that were no longer relevant, and doing it in a very classy way.

All of that huge change made a big impact on me. I think immigrants feel a bigger sense of responsibility to succeed because of all that their parents sacrificed. One of my big motivators was the fear of failure. That's what got me up early—I just could not fail.

Maybe that's part of the whole Cuban experience. I learned that anything you have, you can lose, so you can never get too comfortable. I had that experience when I was almost seven, that decisive event, that turning point in my life. There isn't a day goes by in my life that I haven't thought of it.

2. Your father clearly had a huge impact on you. Tell us about how he mentored you, and about other family members who might have filled those roles too.

Despite several attempts, my father never was able to re-create the level of success he had achieved in Cuba, and he passed away a poor individual. But for me he was always Superman: his wisdom, his values, his self-confidence, his ability to deal with adversity with a sense of grace. On top of all that, he believed in me. Once, when I was having a hard time in the sales job in Mexico City, he told me not to worry because I would become CEO someday. I was driving a delivery truck route around to local stores, and I thought he was crazy, but he did have that belief.

I ran away from home when I was fifteen, and in that whole situation my father never belittled me. He never touched me, by the way, although he had a terrible temper. Sometimes I wished he would hit me, because disappointing him was more hurtful. One time I turned the car over and he said, "Okay, come on, we've got to go to the insurance company, and go talk to the parents of that girl who was with you, who may be hurt." It was just, "Let's get on with it." That's how he was.

He wanted me to go to university and become an agronomist. So, when I dropped out of college and went to work for Kellogg, he never agreed with it. He just said that I had better make the best of it, and he gave me advice about how to be successful without a degree, how to read things to get the skills I would need, and how to deal with people. He didn't like it, but his attitude was, "Let's move forward." I never felt dismissed; I always understood that he thought I had potential.

Even though he tried one business after another and saw them go down the drain, he didn't complain. He just went ahead and tried the next thing. That kind of resilience and strength impacted me. And he was also kind of a James Bond figure, just a very cool individual.

My older brother was also a mentor to me. We are very different, but he was always a big believer in me. I picked up the conservative side and my brother's life has been one amazing adventure, and we've been life-long best friends. He has this bold optimism. And I knew I could call him at any time.

When I talk about who has believed in me, I have to add my wife. We've moved homes about twenty-five times, so you've got to believe in someone to put up with that. We have undertaken this whole journey together. When I was going through rough parts—a thirty-year career is not always rosy—she was always there for me. She has a great deal of strength. When I was out traveling and doing my thing, she was raising three kids.

3. You've named people as mentors whom you didn't know personally and had little or no contact with. Tell us about that.

Bill Lamothe was CEO of Kellogg from 1980 to 1992, when I was still working for the company in Mexico. He came down for a reception, and as we were talking informally, he asked me some questions, which amazed me. He wanted to know what I thought about something in the company. I said, "Well, it's pretty good but doesn't necessarily fit with the culture"— something like that. And he said, "You know, we can learn from people like you in Mexico."

That shocked me. After that, I just started to follow him and pay attention to what he was doing. I'd only see him about once a year, and I didn't report to him. But I knew exactly what he wanted. I think every CEO in the world would want that—a salesperson working in Mexico City who would know exactly what he wanted and what his strategy was.

Bill Lamothe's vision was so clear, so simple, so honest, that I felt like I was working for him, even though he was about seven steps above me. I watched the way he managed people. I don't think I ever heard him scream, but when he stood up to say something, people just froze. Throughout my career, I would always ask myself, *What would Bill think about this?* We had no direct contact and he didn't give me advice. But he just led by example. I realized later that he had been behind a lot of my promotions; he had believed in me.

Another mentor whom I didn't know directly was Roberto Goizueta, the CEO of Coca-Cola from 1980 to 1997. I was running Kellogg, Mexico, at the time, and a copy of *Fortune* magazine hit my desk with him on the cover. I just stared. Here was this Cuban American, promoted to be chairman and CEO of Coca-Cola. He was a chemist, had a heavy Cuban accent, and had also fled Cuba—not the profile you think of for Coca-Cola.

He had learned how to do business on his grandfather's knee, and I found the same thing with my father. I'd hear the words of wisdom "There's no substitute for results," or "Tell me what you brag about and I'll tell you what you lack"—this gave me business direction. Goizueta would use humor to deflect pressure, and he'd show his team that you can be vulnerable and human but still withstand the pressure. He did business by a combination of skills, gut, and value. That's very much part of the Cuban culture—the principles and the honor of business.

So, having seen a Cuban American reach the top of Coca-Cola, the first thing that came to mind was: *Why can't a Cuban American dream about reaching the top of Kellogg?*

I had thought my father was just being nice when he'd said I'd be CEO, but it hit me for the first time that maybe there was a possibility.

4. You've mentored others along the way and invested in them. How would you describe your mentoring style?

I have mentored like it was done for me. For example, there was someone in the Mexico organization that I could see had leadership skills and good values. I didn't talk to him every day, but I just kept my eye on him. He eventually became the president of Kellogg for Latin America. When I went back to the plant ten or fifteen years later, there were people on the lowest rung on the ladder who remembered me and would come up and talk to me. One person had a tear in the eye. I just couldn't believe I had that kind of impact. I had mentored by example, sometimes without even knowing the person.

Another that I worked with moved to the top because he deserved to. He was also someone that I treated like Bill Lamothe treated me, in the sense that I didn't have to be there with him every day. He knew what I wanted, and I always paid attention to what he was doing. It wasn't a direct mentorship; it was just knowing who I thought had great potential and making sure they were being looked after. Being too obvious of a mentor to someone sometimes hurts them. If you get too close, you can actually hurt them.

A person can be a mentor just by being a role model. Like the CEO of Coke—I learned from everything he did, even though he didn't express it to me. But I consider him a mentor, if you think of a mentor as someone who made you what you are. Don't be afraid to tell a person he or she is a role model, read about them, and see yourself as if you were them in ten or twenty years. Some of the people who make the most difference in your life do so indirectly.

I like to think I mentored my three kids. Even though I wasn't there every day, I was making sure I knew what they were doing. They knew what I wanted. And they observed me. They saw that I believed in them, just as people believed in me.

You mentor your family by doing things that are in the interests of the well-being of your family. Foremost would be showing courage, determination, will, sacrifice. That's what sticks out when I think about my father. That's what he did. That's what I hope I've done for my kids.

President Bush believed in me. I don't know where he found me. I was never in politics. I was in Battle Creek, Michigan. But that move changed my life forever. After having been in government as commerce secretary for four years, I will never be the same. I took a 95 percent pay cut, but I would do it again. I respect President Bush greatly, and in my post I was able to watch him: his courage in going through that period of time when we were in Iraq, the tremendous stress he was under, and how he managed pressure under grace. His leadership was just off the charts.

5. From your perspective as an immigrant, how is it possible for a country to mentor a person? How has the United States impacted you?
I've found that immigrants and refugees are probably the most loyal, grateful people that we will find in America. I remember that gratitude in the people we were with when we came to Miami when I was seven. I just felt so grateful and so lucky to come to America. We all did.

Five years later, in a Brooklyn courthouse when we became US citizens, a judge said, "Never let anyone tell you that you're not as American as they are. In fact, you are probably more American, because you chose to be American." I kept that in mind. Americanism is an idea, not where you came from.

I came from a communist country, and I think that made the American people more welcoming. I worry today that it wouldn't be the same experience. We could have a new generation of loyal, wonderful, grateful people if we just kept that in mind and treated them well. We're glad they're here. They choose to become Americans.

My parents instilled in me a belief that, in the United States, one could achieve almost anything through hard work, determination, and the hunger and humility to learn. They taught me the noble American values of personal liberty and personal responsibility, and the importance of both to our free-enterprise system.

9.

Unlikely Mentors

As a chef, he is a luminary. As a television personality, he is a maelstrom. As a culinary icon, he has become a spokesperson for the fine-dining industry—surprising, because he helped knock it off its high horse.[1] A newly conjured word reflects his clout, an adjective that he didn't create and never uses, but one that bloggers and food critics employ to characterize certain restaurants, ramen, and ways of doing business.

Changian.[2]

What exactly is Changian? The *Washington Post* explains:

He could be called the defining chef of the decade. If you've ever eaten pork buns, or fried Brussels sprouts with fish sauce—maybe you didn't know they had fish sauce?—that is David Chang. If you've had ramen in a smaller city, circa 2014, that's David Chang. If you've heard Notorious B.I.G. or LCD Soundsystem in a restaurant. If you've sat before an open kitchen, in a place with a minimalist, plywood aesthetic. If your neighborhood has a restaurant started by a young chef with an attitude, and an eclectic menu of whatever the hell he feels like cooking, all of those things are David Chang.[3]

Regardless how "Changian" he has become, David Chang is a consummate business leader today. He heads a collection of influential, profitable, and people-serving enterprises, including eateries and TV shows.

His business group began in 2004 with a single restaurant: New York City's Momofuku Noodle Bar. *Momofuku* means "lucky peach" in Japanese, and it was a nod to Momofuku Ando, the Taiwanese Japanese inventor of instant ramen. Nine years later, *Bon Appétit* magazine boldly termed the Momofuku Noodle Bar as "the most important restaurant in America."[4] David never looked back. Over the years, his restaurant group grew to include four eateries in New York, three in Las Vegas, two in Toronto, and one in Los Angeles.[5] His restaurant Momofuku Ko was awarded two Michelin stars in 2009 and has kept them every year since.[6]

The TV shows began in a roundabout way. From 2010 to 2017, David made guest appearances on various shows, proving his ability to draw viewers. Finally, in 2018, he created, produced, and starred in the popular, limited-run Netflix documentary series *Ugly Delicious*, about food that perhaps didn't look like the primped-up cuisine that's often showcased on social media, but that tasted really good. The next year, he returned with a new series titled *Breakfast, Lunch, and Dinner*, in which he engaged notable personalities in conversation while eating around the world. In 2021, he produced and hosted another hit documentary series called *The Next Thing You Eat*. He's also produced a magazine, has his own podcast, and has written two bestselling books.

He is not without controversy. Critics have called David Chang many things, including "edgy,"[7] "the bad boy of the culinary industry,"[8] and "a noodle-slinging punk." The last moniker came from Pete Wells, the esteemed restaurant critic for the *New York Times*, who affably quipped that David had come a long way from his origins, and added: "[David's] opinions are sometimes contradictory, but they are always strongly expressed. He is probably the modern equivalent of Norman Mailer or Muhammad Ali in the 1960s and '70s—somebody whose success in one part of the culture allows him to sound off on the rest of the culture and where it is heading."[9]

We know David Chang as a friend and can attest that in addition to his undisputed talent, he is also reflective, a dedicated husband and father, and surprisingly humble despite all his success. He handles his celebrity status with casualness. His restaurants are not only unpretentious; they are *anti*-pretentious. He has talked candidly and vulnerably in the press about the good and the bad in his career—the triumphs and the difficulties—not only with his notoriety but also about his struggles to overcome clinical depression and bipolar I disorder.[10] He publicly owns his mistakes. An entire chapter of his soulful memoir, *Eat a Peach*, was printed with the strikethroughs and editing marks deliberately left in the text. The effect was to show his flaws as well as his desire to correct the person he once was. It's David picking up a bright red pen like a schoolteacher and circling his mistakes. In spite of all his accomplishments, he openly wishes that some events could have been different.[11]

We asked David about his multifaceted achievements and mentorship: Who made the biggest impact on his life? Who helped shape him to become who he is today? Of all the people we interviewed for this book, David's answers surprised us the most, because his story includes a string of "unlikely" mentors. Some people he thought would never become his mentors actually became strong supporters in the end. And some mentors let him down—one deeply. He laments the loss of the relationship, yet he has learned from and turned his grief into greater personal growth. That's an example from which we can all learn.

WHO BELIEVED IN DAVID CHANG?

David's father, Joe Chang, immigrated to America from North Korea in 1963 with fifty dollars in his pocket. He started out by working as a dishwasher in a restaurant.[12] Joe married, had four children, and eventually owned and ran two restaurants and a golf-supply business. David, the youngest child, was born in 1977. Despite the family connection with food, Joe and his wife, Sherri, who had emigrated from South Korea, discouraged their children from ever making a career of restaurants. Joe wanted David to become a professional golfer, and for decades the two of them didn't see eye to eye.

After his dad died in 2020 from complications from cancer, David wrote on his Twitter page, "Like many immigrant kids . . . I have a very complicated relationship with [my father]. But I loved him and often try to imagine what I would be like if I survived the Korean War and lived in America in the 1960s not speaking the language or knowing anyone. Puts things into perspective."[13]

David told us:

When I was growing up, I can't say my father and I ever talked much. He never really understood what it was like to be a kid in America. My dad had this weird way of motivating me. There was no "I love you." Never an "I believe in you." He just told me that nothing I did was ever good enough.

He wanted so badly for me to become a professional golfer. I thrived as a junior golfer, but I didn't have the heart to play golf professionally. I would meet kids on tour, and they were allowed to have other interests, but I was only allowed to have golf. I was always looking at the leaderboard, wondering who I needed to beat, haunted by who was going to beat me. That shaped who I became. I grew up viewing life competitively, and that's how I first saw cooking. There are only so many people in the world who are going to become executive chefs.

My older brothers always told me, "Don't worry. When you turn eighteen, Dad will become cool." They had always worked for him, but I wanted to become an entrepreneur. When that happened is when I learned how much my father loved me. Absolutely, my father became an unlikely mentor to me, a mentor I didn't want to have at

first. As much as I don't want to admit it, much of my business philosophy today is related to how he operated. Even the things I do
differently are intentional—because I want to be different than him.

You have to realize how difficult it is to make it in the restaurant
industry. When people tell me they want to open a restaurant, I
always tell them it's a bad idea. So many restaurants fail. There's an
old anecdote that goes like this: If you want to start a restaurant,
bring all your investors into a room, cook them the food you're going
to serve, then collect all their checks and light them on fire. Tell
them, "That's what I'm going to do with your money. Burn it all."

My dad knew about that anecdote. Even then, he invested in me
when he saw how committed I was. After I signed my first lease for
a restaurant, I was there all the time. Day and night. My dad saw
that and said, "Okay, because you're so ridiculously committed,
you're going to make it." He put his own business on the line to
secure my second loan. I don't know exactly how he did it, but my
monthly payments went from $23,000 to $5,000, all thanks to my
dad. Today, I understand how much he put out there to make that
happen. That's mentorship. My dad gave me the freedom to make
a choice without making it for me. He saw how committed I was.
Then he supported my decision.

"ONE OF MY BEST MENTORS"

David's parents were active in the Korean Presbyterian Church. After
high school, he attended Trinity College, a historic faith-based university
in Hartford, Connecticut. Although he was a religious studies major, he
was not devout in his own practices and says he "only got in because he
was Asian," and that he "smoked pot almost every day."[14]

But he found unlikely mentors at Trinity College—people and ideas
that shaped his worldview. He took every class he could from Dr. Ellison
Banks Findly, professor of Religion and Asian Studies at Trinity, and he

describes how she contributed to his ongoing love of philosophy and ethics. Whenever David examined religion in connection with Dr. Banks
Findly's teaching—both Christianity and Eastern religions—he continually wanted to know "why." *Why did people believe what they did?* Ultimately,
a sense of ethics became deeply rooted in him.

"Ethics is about trying to do the right thing," David told us. "Those
ideas—truth, honesty, friendship, building a team where people are
happy—those are things that never fail me. I tend to moor myself in those
constants."

A curious, philosophical mentor also emerged from university, although
it wasn't a specific person. David explained:

> The early Christian theologians had this philosophy called "via
> negativa." [Literally meaning "by way of negation."][15] It's the study
> of subtraction, of what isn't there. Basically, they figured that they
> could understand who God was and what God was like if they
> pointed to all the things he wasn't. Like, if God is not *these things*,
> then the opposite of that is what God is.
>
> I took that idea from Trinity College and applied it to cooking.
> I'd studied plenty of other chefs, but I knew I would never be as good
> at, say, French cooking as some of the others. So I went the other
> direction—deliberately, almost pathologically. Like, I love pork
> stock, but I had an instructor who hated it. So I chose to engage with
> it. If nobody was doing pork stock, then that's what I was going to
> do. If nobody was trying to become an expert in noodles, then I
> wanted to learn everything about noodles. I went and worked in a
> casino in Atlantic City, because it was the only place on the Eastern
> Seaboard that had a noodle bar.
>
> Much of my career happened because I took the contrary
> approach. I did the things that nobody else was doing. I did every-
> thing I wasn't supposed to do, just seeing what could be done.

After Trinity, David taught English in Japan for two months, then moved to New York City, enrolling at the French Culinary Institute, now known as the International Culinary Center. He worked in various elite kitchens in Manhattan, sometimes preparing food, other times answering phones. Then he moved back to Japan to study noodles, finding work in a soba shop. For a while he worked at the famed Park Hyatt Hotel in Tokyo. In 2003, he returned to New York where he worked at Café Boulud, on the Upper East Side, putting in long hours, and wrestling in the high-stakes subculture of competitive cooking, admitting that he essentially "struggled every day."[16] During that season, David helped his mother navigate a bout with cancer, which she would end up fighting for decades.

When the season was concluded, David realized his dream and opened his first restaurant. He was only twenty-six. Again he struggled, working constantly and spending three years in self-described "survival mode." Several times, his restaurant nearly closed. David told us:

When I came back from Japan, I realized there was no way I could make a facsimile of what I'd learned in Japan. I would have to do something different. So we just created our own thing, mostly by screwing up. I mean, there was lots of hard work that went into it too. I hired Japanese translators to translate all the best Japanese cookbooks and culinary textbooks. There was a lot of trial and error. In fact, I'd say one of my best mentors has been failure. The more mistakes I made, the more data I got that I could use. The data allowed me to make a decision. Failure has been a huge mentor.

Finally, he started finding his way, seeing gradual success while constantly trying new options. Chef Daniel Boulud helped by sending long-time customers from his restaurant over to David's. Sometimes David created bold, adventurous fare. He filtered out the dishes that didn't work while raising his game, eventually "wowing throngs with bowls of ramen and slabs of pork belly on fluffy steamed buns."[17] The first restaurant, Momofuku, worked. And worked well.

That was just the start. Today, customers can munch on thinly shaved American ham wrapped in Korean-inspired flatbreads at Momofuku Ssäm Bar. They can dine on exquisite truffle ramen with seared scallop, Istria black truffle, and chives at Momofuku Noodle Bar in Toronto. They can eat a sumptuous dish entitled Whole Plate Short Rib with Beef Rice at Majordomo in Los Angeles. Or, if they have the required three hours, they can experience an intricate and opulent ten-course meal at Momofuku Ko in New York.

MENTORS AND TORMENTORS

Have you ever experienced an unlikely mentor in your life? Or been an unlikely mentor to someone else? Unlikely mentors can come in many shapes or forms. Perhaps, like David Chang discovered with his father, you will be mentored by a person you didn't get along with at first, someone you never thought could encourage, support, or teach you things.

Or perhaps your mentor is unlikely because it's not a person at all, the same way David described how he was mentored by the concepts of via negativa, failure, and determined trial and error. Philosophies, concepts, and experiences are unlikely mentors, but they can definitely and radically affect your life.

Or perhaps you will find mentors in different industries than yours. They are unlikely because you wouldn't necessarily think to go to them for life transformation. But as you get to know them, you find that they teach you valuable lessons. For instance, David described to us how he has found a number of mentors in the business field. They aren't chefs or restaurateurs, but he goes to them for advice, and they sit on his board today.

Keep in mind that the best transformative mentoring fundamentally alters a person's capacity to be their best self, and that can have a compounding effect in our society. Some mentors can become "unlikely" in a negative sense: when their effectiveness becomes questionable. Perhaps they have mentored you for a while, but their influence isn't as helpful as you'd hoped. Or you might have been paired with a mentor because of a program, but you soon find out it's not a match. Or maybe the relationship started out fine, but over time you discover that you have outgrown each other. What then?

Moving on from a mentoring relationship can be a necessary part of life, according to Dr. Joelle Jay, an executive coach with the Leadership Research Institute. She describes how some mentors can move you away from your goals or even work against you. In that case, the mentors actually become "tormentors."

For example, she counsels mentees to watch for and guard against mentors who take credit for work you have done. If a mentor uses you as a dumping station for extra work when it's not within your regular responsibilities, that's not copacetic. If a mentor constantly tries to steer you in a direction you don't want to go or doesn't want to release you for a greater role even when you're ready for it, those are warning signs. She recommends articulating expectations clearly to a mentor, setting boundaries, and, if sidelined or frustrated, taking a step back so you can reframe your goals and discern what you want to achieve.[18]

Similarly, another mentoring expert recommends avoiding or ending relationships with at least three types of mentors: 1) egomaniacs who don't listen or who talk only about themselves; 2) whirlwind leaders who are too busy to accommodate you, who regularly need to reschedule with you; and 3) meritless leaders who have risen to their position in spite of their ineptitude, who consistently don't offer wise or helpful advice.[19]

It's okay to break up. If a mentoring relationship isn't working, or even if it's been good but has run its course, then there's no point in prolonging it, notes leadership specialist Carolyn O'Hara. When a breakup is due,

O'Hara recommends either having a quick, professional conversation where gratitude is expressed and the relationship is terminated, or simply letting the relationship naturally fade away. Most mentors won't act upset if the relationship is terminated, but if they do, then it's best to stay polite, listen to their perspective without becoming argumentative, and move on.

"Emphasize your appreciation above all else," O'Hara writes. "Don't focus on the relationship's shortcomings—emphasize the positive. Describe what you've learned from them and how those skills will help your career going forward. But don't stay in the relationship out of obligation—you'll only waste your time and theirs. And don't burn bridges—you never know when you might encounter them again."[20]

Even the best of mentors can make mistakes. Mentors become "unlikely" when they do things that affect you negatively. Or they might completely fail you or simply prove unable to fulfill the investment mandate. They might fail their organization, themselves, or even the law. If that happens, it's easy to feel disappointed, crushed, and betrayed. You might have shared deep or vulnerable stories with your mentor, only to have this person break that trust. Most likely, you looked to this person for wise guidance, only to have their mistakes or illicit actions leaving you feeling let down.

If mentors do disappoint, leadership coach Toni Feldstein notes that feelings of sadness or bewilderment are normal, but she also recommends checking your own attitudes and actions. Did you actually think your mentor was perfect? Did you place them on an impossible pedestal? Her advice: separate the person from what they taught you. Take the good and filter out the bad. Preserve the relationship if possible and continue forward.

She writes:

One of the reasons why it's so painful to recover from the fall of our mentors is that we innocently, and many times unconsciously, fuse message and messenger into one unit. Yet the power of the message is inherent to the message itself, not the person imparting it. This

distinction can make the difference between throwing out everything the teacher has taught us or being able to retain insights and
discernments amidst our disappointment.[21]

HELLO, IT'S SUNDAY MORNING

When it comes to an unlikely mentor, or at least an unplanned mentor,
who's had a large impact on me, (David), that would be Hank Paulson.
He was the CEO of Goldman Sachs until 2006, when he became the
seventy-fourth secretary of the Treasury under President George W.
Bush. Hank insisted on handpicking his team—choosing talent from
across the government as well as Wall Street to build a strong, solid, and
capable Treasury Department.

I became one of his three undersecretaries, responsible for the international portfolio. While I was there, Hank led the nation through the 2008
financial crisis. With the economy tumbling, and under immense pressure, and after many fits and starts, Hank worked with Congress to autho-
rize more than $700 billion in government aid to save the world's
collapsing banks.[22] Hank's success in those endeavors saw him named a
runner-up for *TIME*'s Person of the Year in 2008.[23] He now runs the
Paulson Institute think tank, and we still keep in touch.

Hank was an unlikely mentor in that he never formally mentored me.
One of our team members interviewed Hank for this book, and in fact to
this day he flatly denies ever filling a mentorship role. Hank described
how we first got to know each other. It was during the throes of the crisis,
and he said, "David, this is the economic equivalent of war. We need to
get things done quickly. We're not landing at Omaha Beach, and no one's
going to shoot you. But we're going to do some difficult things that will be
unpopular. So we need to have courage to do them." Then he set me and
others straight to work.

I was watching him, learning from him, being mentored more by
his example than anything else. Hank can navigate a crisis like nobody

I've ever seen. He is a force of nature, blunt, and extremely focused on his agenda. During the worst of the crisis, he called me like clockwork at 8:00 a.m. every Sunday morning. Week after week after week. I picked up the phone, and there was never any greeting. He just started talking, describing what needed to get done. He was all business. When he was done talking, he didn't say goodbye. He just hung up. The meeting was over.

I did not always agree with the actions Hank took to stem the panic and stabilize the financial system. In fact, the bank bailouts became a huge polarizing issue for the country and the Republican party. But there was never a doubt to me that, throughout the crisis, Hank acted with integrity and courage. Additionally, he was always a source of friendship and support to me.

By the end of 2008, it became clear that we were through the worst of the crisis. Toward the end of our time at the Treasury, we were flying back to Washington from an international trip a few days before the end of the administration. I asked Hank what I should do next in my career, and he said, in his typical direct style, "You should be CEO of a major company. That's what you should do. Tell you what, I'm going to call the five best CEOs I know, tell them how great you are, and I'm going to have you fly out and meet with them after we leave office."

He did exactly that, calling each of the CEOs over the next few days to tell them about me. In turn, I followed up with the CEOs. They were some of the most esteemed leaders in business at the time, and the conversations I had with them helped me visualize possible paths to pursue. That's how Hank was. He didn't coach you as such, but he could cast a broad vision for your life. He made seismic shifts that would open doors, and I could trust him.

That's a part of mentoring, for sure. Funny, it's been more than a dozen years since he was my boss. Every six to twelve months, he still phones me up, sometimes on Sunday mornings. There's never a greeting. I just pick up the phone, and Hank begins talking. He's always going to be the man in charge. He talks to me like I still work for him, telling me what I need to do and what's going to be best for the economy. When he's finished, he hangs up.

I love the guy, and these continue to be some of my favorite calls.

"EVEN IN HIS FAILURE, I LEARNED FROM HIM"

Back to David Chang. He told us about one more mentor, and parts of this story are difficult to hear. Yet this person was—and is—an important part of David's life and development. In the latter half of the aughts, David Chang met the global icon who would become perhaps his largest unlikely mentor. A gifted chef, author, storyteller, and arguably a genius.[24]

Anthony Bourdain.

David fondly refers to him as "Tony." He hosted a variety of travel and cooking shows over the years, including the award-winning documentary series *Anthony Bourdain: No Reservations* (2005–2012) and *Anthony Bourdain: Parts Unknown* (2013–2018). They met through their mutual literary agent, and both described their first meeting as "a blur."[25] Anthony took an instant liking to David, and the two were soon spending a lot of time together. In David's words:

> I never thought I would become friends with this guy. I was looking for more of a traditional "big brother" chef to mentor me, and he was the last person that I thought would end up doing that. He had his own challenges, yet he ended up becoming a lot more than a mentor to me. He gave me life advice, and helped me to navigate the media world. He was someone I could always go to. Everybody wanted advice from Tony. He became a mentor in ways that still sort of shock me.
>
> The fact that I have the career I have outside of the kitchen is because of Tony. I had done some TV, but basically my first time was for an app that didn't work as it should. That led to me hosting

the first season of *The Mind of a Chef* on PBS, which Tony narrated and executive produced. I didn't realize that he was teaching me the ropes.

He became my sounding board. Whenever I made a big decision, I would ask Tony. He would give me the truth, the brutal truth, even when I didn't want to hear it, and sometimes he could even predict my mistakes. He would say, "You're going to go through this, and you're going to make these mistakes, and then you're going to reflect." When I made them exactly as he said, never once did he say, "I told you so."

Like, I needed to end my magazine, *Lucky Peach*. I was really torn up about it. But he took me aside and said, "Just pursue happiness. Who cares if you lose the magazine? Don't lose sight that this is relatively nothing."

He was telling me not to get lost in the weeds. To just let it go. He was right: it's so easy to get caught up in negotiations, to fight your way into the middle of a conflict or transition where you want to win and win at all costs. I wasn't expecting him to say, "Just let it go."

In June 2018, Anthony was in France working on an upcoming episode of a TV show. After Tony didn't come down for breakfast one morning, a close friend searched for him and found Tony unresponsive in his hotel room.[26] He had hanged himself. He was sixty-one. His death shocked people all over the world. Anthony's mother, Gladys Bourdain, told the *New York Times*: "He is absolutely the last person in the world I would have ever dreamed would do something like this."[27]

David told us:

I was always in awe of how well he could navigate the world like he did. Clearly, he didn't do everything well. In the last few years of his life, he was at a different place. He was reverting. I think everything finally caught up with him.

You tend to judge your mentor as an ideal, a movie version of a mentor. But there is no perfection in any mentor. He was a complicated, imperfect person. Sometimes he could be a horrible teacher. Yet people must be allowed to falter. We need a deeper well of humanity to understand all the implications of that truth.

What would I say to people who have had a mentor who let them down? First, I'd point at myself. I am the mentor who has failed people. I've failed a lot. Second, I'd say we are not robots. Mentors will disappoint you. It's a fact of life.

When I think about Tony, he failed everybody, in a sense. But if you're at a point where you can be critical of your former mentor, maybe you can learn from your mentor's mistakes. Maybe you can take what you learn and give back.

It took Tony's passing for me to realize that all I did was work. He was on the road 250 days a year. Pre-pandemic, I was on the road up to 150 days per year, nearing the same hectic pace. So I'm examining the things that will become mistakes if I continue that direction. These days, I'm trying to be very deliberate with the media I'm doing, and I'm trying to be very present with my family. The lure of travel is so strong, but media can consume you. I need to put obstacles in my way so I don't go down that road. I've pulled back now. Thanks to Tony, I want to make sure I have some balance.

Even in his failure, I learned from him.

KEY TAKEAWAYS

- Unlikely mentors come in many forms—someone you didn't get along with at first who ends up teaching you things, a mentor in a different industry than yours, or even an idea that ends up transforming your life. Learn to be open to unlikely mentors.

- You don't have to stick with a mentor (or mentee) forever. If the relationship has run its course or shifted off track, or if you sense toxicity, the arrangement can be politely and professionally terminated.

- Mentors are not flawless, and we do them a disservice whenever we demand perfection from them. If a mentor lets you down, it helps to separate the person from what they taught you. Take the good, filter out the bad, adjust the relationship if possible, and keep going forward.

PART III
Transformative Mentoring for True Change

10.

Mentors as Uniters

E ven when Christine Lagarde makes a small move, it can influence the world's monetary systems. When she talks, people listen, and markets can rise and fall simply in response to what she says.[1] It is no exaggeration to say she is one of the most powerful women in the world.[2]

Think of her as the European counterpart to the American Federal Reserve Board Chair. Since 2019, Christine has served as president of the European Central Bank (ECB), the main banking authority of the "eurozone"—the nineteen European Union countries that currently use the euro.

A lawyer by profession, Christine is the first woman to hold the position at the ECB—and it's only one of a string of firsts for her. Prior to her current role, from 2011 to 2019, she was the first female managing director of the International Monetary Fund (IMF), an organization of 190 countries that fosters global monetary cooperation, promotes employment and sustainable economic growth, reduces global poverty, and safeguards the steadiness of the global monetary system. Before that, from 2007 to 2011, she served as the finance and economy minister of

France and, as such, was the first woman to lead the economics of any G-7 country.[3] She was France's minister of foreign trade for two years before that, with a brief stint as minister of agriculture and fisheries. And prior to that, she was the first woman to chair the international law firm Baker & McKenzie.[4]

Christine's current role as head of the ECB is to help keep the euro-zone's banking system safe, stable, and predictable.[5] It's no small job. Her actions directly affect some 341 million people in the eurozone.[6] By most measures, the United States is considered the world's largest economy, with a gross domestic product of about $22.9 trillion. China is usually ranked second, with a GDP of $16.7 trillion.[7] The eurozone is usually third, with a GDP of about $13 trillion.[8] None of the world's other econ-omies come close to these top three,[9] with Japan coming in fourth at slightly under $5 trillion.[10]

Make no mistake, Christine's actions can directly affect countries out-side the eurozone, including the United States—a fact she is very aware of. "If things go wrong in one part of the world, it is going to affect the rest of the world as well," Christine told *CBS News*, shortly after starting her role at the ECB. "We buy American products in huge quantities. The United States buys European products in huge quantities. Massive num-bers of European firms have set up shops in the United States. Vice versa. We penetrate each other's markets."[11]

Throughout her distinguished career, Christine has repeatedly proved her competency. As finance and economy minister of France, she earned universal respect for steering her country through the Great Recession of 2008–2009.[12] That was when I (David) first met her, when I was in the US Treasury. When she was head of the IMF, she cautioned world leaders against international trade disputes, then helped bring parties together and de-escalated tensions.[13] In her current role with the ECB, she has helped eurozone economies navigate the massive shock of the COVID-19 pandemic, as country after country went into lockdown mode, which slowed and sometimes halted economic activity.[14]

For her overall efforts, she has been called "the rock star of international finance."[15] But we know her best as a friend. We interviewed Christine to discuss her approach to her job and her role as a world leader. One of the things that impresses us most about Christine is her ability to reach across divides and bring people of differing opinions together. "The mandate to cooperate," uttered in various paraphrases,[16] is one of her consistent rallying cries. When it comes to finding solutions for the challenges of modern trade systems, she constantly encourages international collaborations. She champions flexible, rather than rigid, negotiation strategies. And she advocates domestic policies that help ensure equity for all people.

As a leader, she is a uniter—and in today's divisive world, we find that extremely refreshing. For that reason, we have included her as the only non-American profiled in this book. She is not afraid to speak her mind, yet she leads with a cool head and a steady hand.

WHO BELIEVED IN
CHRISTINE LAGARDE?

She was born Christine Madeleine Odette Lallouette in Paris, France, in 1956. Her father, Robert, was an English professor, while her mother, Nicole, was a Latin, Greek, and French literature instructor. Both parents were politically engaged and socially active, and they often went out to meetings in the evenings. Even at age four, Christine was given the responsibility of babysitting her younger brothers. "That certainly played a role in my upbringing and in the person I turned out to be," Christine told us. "You learn to take responsibility for yourself and for others around you. We had to stand on our feet and be strong."

Christine grew up active and involved. She was a Girl Scout, a lifeguard, a children's swimming instructor, and a champion synchronized swimmer. A high school teacher encouraged her to apply for an American field service scholarship, which would offer her the chance to study abroad and widen her worldview. Christine's father died when she was sixteen, and she came to the United States shortly afterward on the scholarship and attended the Holton-Arms preparatory school in Bethesda, Maryland. For her year at Holton-Arms, she lived with a host family, Bill and Marion Atkins. They were both very supportive of her, and Bill became a father figure to Christine. To this day, she still corresponds with them.

During her time in America, Christine perfected her English, and for the final two months of her year abroad, she interned at the US Capitol for Representative William Cohen (R-Maine), who later became the secretary of defense under President Bill Clinton. Christine considers Cohen one of her first formal mentors, and she reflected on that season:

> I had just turned eighteen. What is the likelihood of a young French woman being hired by the youngest member of the House Judiciary Committee who is investigating President Nixon for possible impeachment?
>
> I was tasked with answering the mail of Bill Cohen's constituents from the northern part of Maine—those who spoke French. My internship was such a short time, yet even then he instilled in me confidence and a sense of responsibility.
>
> At the end of my internship, he gave a little party, and I still have the pen that he gave me when I left. I mean, it's very silly. But it's the kind of thing that builds your confidence and instills in you the attitude of "I can do it." The confidence is so badly needed when you are young—particularly for women, I think.

Christine returned to France and graduated from law school at University Paris-X (now Paris Nanterre University), then obtained a master's degree from the Political Science Institute in Aix-en-Provence. After being admitted as a lawyer to the Paris Bar, Christine joined the international law firm Baker McKenzie as an associate, specializing in labor, anti-trust, and mergers and acquisitions. She worked in the Paris branch of the Chicago-based firm and made partner in 1987 by age thirty-one. By 1995, she was a member of the firm's executive committee. In 1999, she advanced to become the chair of the global executive committee of Baker & McKenzie (now Baker McKenzie). And in 2004, she became chair of the global strategic committee.

Christine told us about an early mentor at Baker McKenzie—one who taught her how to be a uniter within any organization, in a way that may seem unlikely. She learned that unity can be achieved not when a leader kowtows to people around her or accepts shoddy practices, but when she raises the standard of excellence and unites people with the vision and vigor of her leadership. Christine recalled:

When I started at the firm at age twenty-four, Monique Nion was the only female partner at Baker McKenzie in those days. She was managing partner of the Paris office, very demanding, but also very caring—and she was mindful of how tough it was to be a young associate in a big law firm.

She would come and check with me to see whether the assignments I had been given were not impossible. Sometimes they could be so difficult, it would put off a young associate completely. She gave me the little nudge, the little encouragement to move forward, keep working, keep researching, and feel comfortable and strong. That was her kindness.

She could be a really tough cookie, too, and she had learned to succeed in a highly demanding environment. Early on, Monique said to me, "If you want to succeed, you're going to have to know how to dress, address, and redress." Those were the three words she specifically used. She didn't explain to me right away what that meant. She let me just sort of figure it out.

Monique was always impeccably dressed. She went to the hairdresser once a week. Her nails were perfect, and she had this style and elegance about her. That's what she meant by "dress." The appearance and power that you express through the way you dress matter to your professional life.

By "address," she was referring to the fact that you have to learn to speak well in public if you're going to be a lawyer, because you're going to be advocating or pleading. Monique was quite specific about breathing. She would say, "Whatever you do, don't forget to breathe and pause, because that's the time it takes people to turn a page."

The last one, "redress," means to remedy, or set right what is wrong. I have needed to practice, in my professional life and in any organization that I've come to lead, something called the theory of "the little knife." I did not invent that phrase, but it references the fact that in any organization, there's always a couple of bastards— those who abuse the situation, do not contribute, talk behind your back, are unfair, dishonest, or harassers.

You have to identify those people early on, then take the little knife and get them out. You don't have to do it with too many, only one or two. Everybody else will fall in line and know that not only do you mean business, but you promote ethics and respect, and you're not going to tolerate nonsense. You're not going to be blind to the mediocre.

Jean-Pierre Raffarin, prime minister of France from 2002 to 2005, first identified Christine in the private sector as a highly capable person and recommended that she join the French cabinet. But before she could work with him, he resigned due to a failed referendum. The next prime minister, Dominique de Villepin, called Christine and asked her to be trade secretary. She agreed and quickly became known for her "no-nonsense, straight-talking approach."[17] Yet the world of politics was new to her, and she recognized a need for counsel. Christine describes de Villepin as a visionary, but she says he was not terribly interested in coaching or guiding the incoming staff. Instead, and discreetly, she received mentoring and political advice from Nicolas Sarkozy, then the president of France. She told us:

> [Sarkozy] helped me not to make too many mistakes in the beginning. For instance, in the National Assembly in France, if there's a question from a member of Parliament on your topic, you have to stand and answer the question on the spur of the moment, without briefing, unless the question comes from your political party.
>
> He's the one who gave me the tip "Forget about the noise." Forget about the shouting. Forget about the insults. Just look straight in the direction [of the camera] and speak to the public. Everybody watches those debates, and they don't hear the noise. They only see you speaking to them and addressing the topic.

The advice worked. Christine worked hard and paid attention to details. Four years after she started in government, the London-based *Financial Times*, one of the world's most credible news organizations,[18] voted Christine the best finance minister in all of Europe.[19]

WHEN LEADERS BECOME UNITERS

In her role today, Christine consistently works to unite world leaders so that they are better able to help people. We've traced a number of mentors in her life who infused her with this spirit of unification.

Think about it. Her parents gave her responsibility to keep her younger brothers safe, an early lesson on leadership and keeping people together. Her schoolteacher encouraged her to spend time in another country, broadening Christine's understanding of different cultures. An early employer bolstered Christine's confidence by placing her in the unique role of reaching out to French-speaking Americans, helping them navigate both their heritage and the opportunities that lay before them. An

experienced colleague at Baker McKenzie taught Christine to unite people around excellence, rather than mediocrity. And the president of
France instructed Christine on the fine art of diplomacy—cutting through
noise and criticism to speak to people directly, a powerful tool in bringing
diverse groups together.

That's our question for exploration as well. Can mentors help unite
America today, particularly in an age of divisiveness?

A recent think piece in the *New York Times* analyzes the current climate
of polarization, specifically as it relates to social consciousness and corporate activism. The article's author, David Gelles, imagines a future scenario in 2041 where today's partisan rifts have widened even further,
playing out in strict, hyper-partisan consumer brands. In this imagined
extrapolation, for example, Starbucks coffee might become the sole choice
of liberals, whereas Black Rifle Coffee Company might be the sole choice
of conservatives. He notes that Facebook or Rumble might become the
go-to social media site of Republicans, whereas Snapchat might be the
exclusive territory of Democrats. Even clothes could signify strict political
allegiances. Levi's jeans might become the new uniform of liberals,
whereas conservatives might wear only Wranglers.

The scenario is not unfounded, according to Gelles, and the big question raised by the article is essentially this: Should such divisions be promoted? Should today's corporate leaders continue to entangle themselves
in politics and culture wars to the extent that brands and allegiances
become hyperpolarized? Is that inevitable, even desirable? Certainly peti-
tions, protests, and boycotts can put pressure on companies to take sides
on an issue. But is it better for businesses to stay out of politics? Or do
conscientious leaders have a responsibility to jump into the fray and speak
out, and in doing so risk offending their employees, customers, and
shareholders?

Gelles framed the tension: "Determining when to speak out and when
to stay silent is one of the most fraught calculations for leaders these days.
Keep quiet on a given issue, and impassioned employees and customers

might accuse the company of callousness. Engage in a public debate about a partisan topic, and members of the opposing party may accuse the brand of playing politics."[20]

Certainly there are many sides to every issue. Some contend that when CEOs are drawn into political frays, that action only lessens shareholder value and works against the dynamics of our capitalist system. We respect that opinion and note that it has merit. Certainly, caution must be taken.

Our friend and collaborator for this book, Dr. Jeffrey Sonnenfeld, was interviewed for Gelles's article and leaned more toward an activist stance, noting that the climate of polarization "is permanently part of the social context of business. It's the job of CEOs to elevate issues and explain how it matters to them."

We know Dr. Sonnenfeld as a unifier and not a divider, so we asked him to explain his position more. He said, "I do not think that CEO engagement in social issues must lead to divergence among constituents and hyper-partisan brands. CEOs can address issues such as voting access, secure ballot counts, public health, diplomatic engagement abroad, and immigration in uplifting and educational tones—not in partisan and divisive ways. CEOs hate needless wedge issues, so it behooves them to work to transcend them."

Mentors indeed can be uniters—in strong, conscientious, ethical, world-changing ways. To be a uniter, you do not need to give up your opinions—and neither do you need to get involved in every battle. Rather, your challenge lies in knowing when it's wisest to become vocal about a cause, and then in expressing your opinions well.

While I (David) respect Dr. Sonnenfeld's opinions, and I agree that CEOs can be uniters rather than dividers, I approach the subject from the perspective of having been a CEO, so I differ from his position. That's okay. Thoughtful people can have different perspectives. My view is that a CEO's responsibility is first and foremost to his or her shareholders and customers, while also being strong and caring for his or her employees. That's not to say I advocate soulless business or corporate leadership driven solely by profit and loss statements. Corporate leaders must be responsible, and when it comes to a company investing in its surrounding communities, I contend that it's often in a company's best interest to do so.

But here is the challenge. Suppose a CEO speaks out publicly about a cause that's become a politically polarized issue. (The issue could lean in any political direction; that's not the point.) If the shareholder holds a different stance on the cause, that puts the shareholder in a difficult position. The shareholder is either forced to go against his or her conscience or is apt to stop investing in the company. Similarly, CEOs must reflect the needs of the customer. Is it fair, for example, for Coca-Cola to boycott a Georgia voter law and deny millions of customers their favorite brand?[21]

CEOs must wrestle with this tension. We must make needed changes in our companies to take moral stances, understand changing cultural climates, and assure that pertinent causes are addressed. Yet we cannot lose sight of our commitment to our shareholders, customers, and employees. Our shareholders are entrusting us with their hard-earned money— often in their 401(k)s and pension plans and retirement and savings—and our employees are entrusting us with their well-being. We must respect the trust they place in us.

My bottom line is this: To be a uniter, we can and must take stances grounded in principle, and sometimes we can be vocal about our stances. Yet we need to develop strict guardrails, too, being careful not to moralize to our clients, insisting they invest a certain way. Our commitments to social agendas cannot reject the basic principles of merit and competency, and we should not favor hot trends over substance, or allow our business decisions to be pushed around by the loudest voices in the room. We must always stay professional, and in the exhortation of Dr. Sonnenfeld, we must address issues in "uplifting and educational tones."

Ultimately, we have worked to underscore the spirit of true unification throughout this book, believing that transformative mentors can help unite the country and help us go forward together, rather than divide people and force them into polarized camps. Ours does not need to become an age of rudeness or hate. Nor, within this era of widespread division, do we need to become the *Uniformity* States, in which we all think, look, and act alike.

It is in every American citizen's best interest, however, that we remain the *United* States and strengthen our resolve to understand, respect, and get along with each other. As one trenchant political observer put it: If our society feels dysfunctional and divided, it is "not because we have forgotten how to agree with each other but because we have forgotten how to disagree constructively."[22] To correct course, we must commit to engaging in civil discourse, to getting outside of our own bubbles, and to fostering a better awareness and openness to the ideas of others.[23] This can be taught when mentors seek to develop the whole mentee, rather than simply offer career advice.

Rick Woolworth worked as a Wall Street executive for more than thirty-five years before cofounding Telemachus, an organization dedicated to mentoring emerging leaders. Regarding mentoring approaches, he has found that "[the] more holistic approach is dramatically more effective in helping people fulfill their true potential, [although] mentoring the whole person takes more effort, time, and thought."[24]

He recommends that mentors and mentees learn to discuss not only work-related situations but also behavior, values, relationships, parenting, finances, and even spiritual life. When he first meets with a prospective mentee, he begins with a simple statement: "Tell me your story. Start at the beginning and take your time—twenty to thirty minutes." He may ask a few questions as the mentee begins to speak, but mostly he listens. Right from the start, the straightforward exercise establishes the direction of the mentoring relationship—it's not simply about careers; it's about the development of the whole person. In turn, he will tell the mentee his story, including sections of his life that have been difficult.

Today we all too often find that we must be on our guard. Some people consistently make it their ambition to stir up hatred between people, creating false dichotomies, mistrust, and rage. But it is certainly possible to disagree with other people without being disagreeable. Social justice does not come down to the brand of jeans you wear. Real change starts by your willingness to listen well. You must think about issues intelligently and deeply. Then you can develop actionable opinions and express them well—in ways that do not belittle people, stir up rage, or further divisiveness. Transformative mentors can teach self-regulation, active listening, and empathy. We can model strong, effective, and respectful actions and attitudes.

We can teach America to be united again.

THE SECRET OF CONFIDENCE

As our conversation with Christine Lagarde drew to a conclusion, we asked her three important questions surrounding unity and mentoring.

First, we asked her to provide a bit of direct mentoring for you, the reader, to absorb as you wish. We are so impressed with Christine as a leader, her remarkable combination of strength, skills, determination, and grace, that we want you to be an immediate recipient. She has achieved remarkable success, and although she has not had the perfect ascent, she has learned from her mistakes and grown. So just imagine for a few moments that Christine is in a mentoring relationship with you. Here's what she said she'd do:

> The way I mentor anybody is to start by listening. I don't think mentoring is about lecturing to someone. I am always cautious about giving advice. You need to own your own decision-making process.
>
> So, I would want to listen to what you aspire to. I would ask about what you want to do in life, what the next step you see for yourself would be, and perhaps by listening I would help you figure out whether you are on the right path. By listening, I hope I could help you make up your own mind.

What would I tell the young people of the world? I would say: Don't be afraid of taking a risk. Particularly when entering your professional life. I have seen far too many young people be too risk averse.

You can find opportunities to thrive. You can lead the way and change things. It is good to be conscientious. But at some point, you just have to jump. You have to forget about your due diligence. Find the level of self-esteem and courage to overcome insecurity and take some risks. If you fall on your face, that's okay. You get back on your feet and start again.

Second, we asked Christine to provide a perspective on America's future. We welcomed the unique perspective of an outsider who also knows the United States well. She said:

Americans can unite around inspiration. You might not think you provide it, but this inspiration is felt by lots of people around the world. The inspiration that you generate outside of your country is far greater than you suspect.

Not every other country is inspired by the United States, of course. There are some countries where America is despised and not respected and even hated. Yet for the majority of the world's populations, and even for some individuals who live in the countries who despise America, the United States is the dream that still inspires people.

America is so much more than the borders of a country. It is an idea, a picture of freedom. Your country cannot be encapsulated even by the one word "democracy." America is the idea that anyone can achieve their potential. Anyone can have freedom. For many people around the world, the United States still represents that dream.

Finally, we asked Christine about the secret of her confidence. She comes across as very poised and self-assured. She routinely interacts in high-pressure situations with the most influential leaders of the modern world, and they listen to what she says. We wondered if her secret lay in pushing herself to take risks and overcome them, or if it was something different. Christine's answer surprised us greatly. This key to confidence is one of the most important things to remember when it comes to being a leader who is also a uniter. She said:

> Love. That is the secret of confidence. There is nothing greater than love. Love gives you strength, and your confidence is generated by that love. You must care for people. That is the secret.
>
> You will have occasions where you must fall back on that foundation. You might think: *Why should I stand up and give a speech? Who am I? Why do I have to pretend I know something about this subject, when all the people in this room probably know more than I do?*
>
> The answer to fall back on is that love, that warmth, and then you find that your confidence is generated by your love. You care for the people you are speaking to. You care for the people you are leading. Love gives you the power to lead.

KEY TAKEAWAYS

- Transformative mentors can help unite America today, but keep in mind that unity does not mean uniformity. True unity comes from pluralism and respect for differences and varying opinions. In a unified country, people are free to disagree.
- When addressing potentially polarizing issues, it's important not to create a wedge between people. Aim to transcend division by addressing the issues, not in partisan and divisive ways, but in uplifting and educational ways. You can disagree without being disagreeable.
- The surprising secret of true confidence, according to Christine Lagarde, is "love." When you value the people you're addressing, you can operate from a place of warmth. In all your mannerisms, speech, and conduct, you lead with compassion and truly value people.

THE COMMUNITY THAT RAISED A BOY

One of Eric's favorite quotes is from Martin Luther King Jr., who wrote that we are all a part of an "inescapable network of mutuality, tied in a single garment of destiny. Whatever affects one directly, affects all indirectly."[3]

Madison Park, where Eric grew up, proved to be that inescapable network of mutuality. It's a historically Black community situated some fifteen minutes north of downtown Montgomery. The *Washington Post* describes it as "a little enclave on the rural edge of this history-drenched city."[4]

A group of fourteen freed slaves had founded Madison Park back in 1880. They'd sought to create a place where they could live, work, worship, and thrive together, all while building a better life for themselves and their children. And they wanted to do it together, and yet by themselves, to demonstrate self-reliance.

This communitarian ethos of a shared responsibility, of being your brother's keeper, was planted deep by its founders. The earliest residents farmed and operated a sawmill, gristmill, and cotton gin.[5] They were proud of the community they were making, and in time, they set aside twenty-five acres to build a park, planting oak trees around its perimeter to give shade for their descendants. The park was soon named after two of the community's founders, Eli and Frances Madison,[6] who propagated the belief that neighbors have more in common than not, and that those neighbors can manifest their shared values in thoughts, words, and deeds. The name of the park came to be used for the entire community.

When Eric was growing up in Madison Park, the community was a hub of generosity and determination. Lawn mowers were shared between neighbors. Vegetable plots were deliberately planted generously so gardeners could give away the excess produce. If someone's roof leaked, an impromptu band of neighbors gathered on Saturday morning and fixed it for free. Child-rearing was seen as a shared responsibility. Community members took it upon themselves to build character, determination, and principles into the next generation. All sorts of area residents participated in Eric's upbringing.

Early in first grade, Eric brought home a letter from his teacher, mentioning that his reading level had slipped. He'd been demoted from the "Rabbits" reading group to the "Turtles." Alarmed, Eric's grandmother phoned her neighbor and good friend Emma Madison Bell, who everybody called "Aunt Shine." Eric remembers Aunt Shine as "muscular in faith and physique," and she came over to the house immediately and informed Eric, in no uncertain terms, that if he was ever going to college, his reading performance needed to improve. Eric nodded his head.

Aunt Shine decided they needed even more help. The next Sunday in church, Aunt Shine stood, informed the congregation they had a serious problem with one of the community's bright young scholars, and that they all needed to pitch in and help. Learning was taken seriously in Madison Park, and the community responded. Neighbors brought additional books to the Motleys' house. Aunt Shine formed a committee of six retired teachers. For months, they rotated daily through Eric's house in groups of two to coach and quiz him in reading and comprehension. Aunt Shine required Eric to memorize the preambles to the Declaration of Independence and the Constitution of the United States. More than once, Aunt Shine said to Eric, "We are doing this because we believe you have potential. We are also doing this because we expect you to do something big in life." Then she would quote a Bible verse: "To whom much is given, much is required."[7] By spring, Eric was restored to Rabbit reading group status.

Another community mentor was Dr. John H. Winston Jr., the Motleys' family doctor. Dr. Winston had grown up in Madison Park, then moved to Nashville where he'd graduated in 1956 from Meharry Medical College School of Medicine. He'd returned to Alabama, becoming Montgomery's first board-certified Black surgeon.[8] Regularly, after finishing his work in downtown Montgomery for the day, Dr. Winston made house calls in Madison Park, providing medical services to low-income residents, often accepting no pay. He and his wife went to the same church as the Motleys. They took it upon themselves to have a hand in Eric's upbringing. Eric told us:

> I have lived a mentored life. It took a lot of people in a small town to mentor me. Both Dr. Winston and his wife, Bertha, recognized the richness of love and care that my grandparents had given me. But they also recognized a poverty of my grandparents' life—their lack of education and resources. So the doctor and his wife took me under their wings.
>
> Mrs. Winston was a highly educated woman who provided administrative support for her husband's practice. Even as young as I was, she believed I had a special gift of speech. Every week, she'd pull up in front of our house in her 1974 Cougar. She'd bring me a new book to read, and I would sit in her car with her so I wouldn't be distracted in the house. She would give me elocution lessons and help me with grammar. She'd give me a list of words to repeat over and over again.
>
> Dr. Winston also brought me books and took an interest in my mind. He became the first role model for me, because he captured what a life of the mind and curiosity could lead to.
>
> He was extremely influential in my life.

INTRODUCTIONS TO A LARGER WORLD

Eric never forgot the lessons learned in Madison Park. After graduating from high school, Eric left the community that had banded together to help him, but his journey ahead would be replete with additional mentors who would pick up where the townspeople of Madison Park had left off. He attended Samford University in Birmingham, earning his bachelor's in political science, and graduating with high honors. Dr. Thomas Corts, president of Samford, helped him along the way. The president had begun to mentor Eric his freshman year. Eric told us:

Dr. Corts introduced me to everything that made my life more expansive. He inspired me to read writers and poets such as T. S. Eliot, W. H. Auden, James Boswell, and George Eliot. He awakened my curiosity to philosophy, so much so that I ended up minoring in it. He encouraged me to take astronomy because he wanted me to have a sense of the vastness of interstellar space. He inspired my interest in classical Greek and Latin. He also helped me start understanding the art and science of collecting, and due to his influence, I eventually began collecting rare books.

He was a quintessential Renaissance man, and he wanted me to have an interior life of mind that transcended learning and extended to the cultivation of my soul and sensibilities. He introduced me to spiritual mystics such as St. Teresa of Avila, and the African American theologian Howard Thurman, helping me to center myself more fully in the spiritual laws of the natural world. With that came the full awareness of my own place and lineage within the universe. He edited a great many of my papers and bled over them with red ink, constantly encouraging me to perfect my work.

He taught me how to edit out the excesses and to be economical, both in my writing and in the manner in which I conducted life. We tend to embellish our lifestyles with a constant appetite for more. But he taught me the power of limitation and simplicity—how in silence, listening, and hearing, there is power. You temper out the things of life that are not needed. You realize that the strength of who you are and what you have lies not in abundance but in careful selectivity.

Some time after he died in 2010, his wife sent me three boxes of items that included the letters I had sent to him over the years. He had kept each one. He had also kept every editorial note on each essay I'd written. He'd sent me notes when I'd written my book, and he'd kept those notes. All in all, he'd kept about one hundred items. I am deeply humbled by the thoughtfulness he demonstrated in this action, and I am continually grateful for the role Dr. Corts had in my life.

Eric continued with his education at the prestigious University of St. Andrews in Scotland, where he earned both a master's degree and a PhD in international relations. When Eric matriculated from Samford, Dr. Corts had, unbeknownst to him, written a letter of introduction for Eric to the president of St. Andrews, the Scottish molecular biologist and chemist Struther Arnott, and he became a mentor too. Eric said:

> Dr. Arnott introduced me to new levels of thought and learning. He encouraged me to stay on at St. Andrews and do my PhD, and the mentoring relationship lasted the entire time I was there. He and his wife would take me to London at least once a year for theaters and lectures.
>
> He was immensely influential in my life.

Eric was honored to be asked to give the eulogies for all three of these mentors: Dr. Winston, Dr. Corts, and Dr. Arnott.

Following the completion of Eric's doctorate, he joined the White House staff at age twenty-seven, the youngest appointee in the George W. Bush administration,[9] where he worked closely with Dina in the presidential personnel office. There, Clay Johnson, the director of presidential personnel and later deputy director for management in the Office of Management and Budget, became Eric's mentor.

Clay realized that I was no longer in the confines of Madison Park and the towering spires of learning. I was now beginning my professional life, my first real job, and he helped me think about how I could take the support I'd received from Madison Park and the intellectual rigor I'd received in university and apply those things pragmatically in the working world. Clay and his wife, Anne, made room for me at their dining room table, with their two sons, and included me in special gatherings with people in the upper echelons of Washington life that I would have never met, given my rank and file in government. And what impressed me most was his consistent way of demonstrating both self-awareness and humility. He would often remind White House staff, who by the very nature of the place they work tend to feel a sense of self-importance, "Remember, none of us are important; the work we do is important. We are here to serve the president and a cause that is much greater than all of us."

I also worked closely with Dina Powell McCormick, whom I consider a mentor as well. Clay and Dina began taking me into the Oval Office, allowing me to make presentations directly to the president. Years later, when I made my transition to the State Department, I was very happy to be reunited with Dina, who was then serving as the assistant secretary of state for Educational and Cultural Affairs.

WHEN BENEFITS EXTEND BOTH WAYS

Two more people became important mentors of Eric's in the working world, one of whom may have been an unlikely figure—at least early in the process. The first was Walter Isaacson, profiled in chapter 2. After Eric's experiences at the White House and the State Department, he was recruited to join the Aspen Institute, as a vice president, when Walter was the president and CEO. He moved Eric's office two doors down from his, and the two became close professional collaborators and, with time, friends. The learning aspects of the relationship turned reciprocal. Eric told us:

There was no shortage of times that I often found myself in Walter's office sitting with some Fortune 500 CEO, head of state, or public intellectual, realizing that the only reason I was there was because Walter wanted to expose me to some of the most innovative thinkers of the day and in turn would invite me to engage in the conversation.

I remember on two specific occasions Walter sharing with me the excitement of ideas that captivated him. He'd met with Dr. Francis Collins [director of the National Institutes of Health], and later with Steve Jobs during the period that Walter was writing his biography. On both occasions, Walter came into my office, sat down, and shared with me the ideas that had been inspired by those conversations. On another occasion, after Walter came back from Windsor Castle, where he studied the queen's drawings by Leonardo da Vinci, he couldn't wait to show me some of the very detailed and elaborate drawings that he captured on his iPhone, revealing his fascination with all the intricacies of science and form. Over the decade that we worked together, I came to appreciate how he brought his journalistic instincts and keen investigative mind to bear on every idea that confronted him. For him, it was always about clarity and answering the simple questions of why, how, and when. Creativity and storytelling are foundational to how he communicates and interacts with the world.

Walter urged me to write my memoir, then he read the manuscript prior to publication and offered some critiques. He introduced me to editors and then wrote the foreword. Walter often told me that the purpose of a true mentoring relationship is to create a corridor of learning. You become so comfortable in the relationship that the conversations become informative for both of you. The exchange of ideas becomes so profoundly impactful that the relationship becomes a two-way street. The genius of mentoring is to be eventually mentored by your mentee. An equity of benefit is shared. That became manifest to me after I had written the book.

Walter phoned me one day on a Sunday afternoon, while traveling from DC to New Orleans. I picked up the phone, and he responded, "Where are you?" I replied that I was in New York for the weekend, and he asked, "Can you guess where I am?" After some back-and-forth conversation, he provided me with a clue: "I just texted you a few photos. Look at them." It was Walter in Madison Park, standing on the steps of the house that I grew up in. I scrolled to the next photo. He's at my grandparents' gravesite. I scrolled again. Walter's standing in front of the church that my grandfather had built.

As he and his wife, Cathy, were leaving DC and driving to New Orleans, they'd decided to take a detour. But what a detour it is to go all the way to Montgomery, Alabama, because they'd wanted to visit the place of my beginning! That's when the mentor not only wants to understand how you think, but the origin of your thoughts.

The final mentor Eric told us about was Ruth Bader Ginsburg, the famed associate justice who was appointed to the Supreme Court by President Bill Clinton. Eric and Ruth met in 2002 at a dinner party in Georgetown, when Eric was still working for the Bush administration. They struck up a conversation about music and reading. Following the party, they corresponded regularly, and often met for dinner or to attend concerts. She became good friends with Eric's then-fiancée, now-wife, Hannah, as well, and offered to marry them, which they planned to take her up on, although she passed away before being able to perform the ceremony.

I (David) was at a dinner once at the Library of Congress where I sat next to Justice Ginsburg. She told me about her friendship with Eric and how much she adored him. We'll let Eric tell a piece of this story in his own words from an op-ed that he wrote for the *New York Times* upon her passing:

> While many of the topics we discussed touched on the political, we never spoke of politics in a partisan fashion; rather, we spoke of ideas that underlie political theories and ways of thinking. We never reduced the complexity of ideas to partisan labels. We always discussed issues, even potentially divisive ones, from a cultural and historical perspective, more nuanced than the Democratic versus Republican dichotomy allows. As it so often turned out, our views on those ideas were not as far apart as our nominal party affiliations might have suggested.
>
> I would often sit quietly like a student at the feet of a master teacher when she would suddenly say in her quiet way, Eric, what are you thinking? We are friends, and I hope you know that you can say whatever you want.
>
> She was a friend in all seasons, and [often reminded] me that friendship mattered most.[10]

When Justice Ginsburg died in September 2020, her family sent Eric a letter and a small box of mementos. He still keeps in touch with her son and daughter-in-law. Eric told us, "I think, in many quiet ways, she became one of the mentors who never officially became a mentor, but who kind of quietly sank into my life in very profound ways. The relationship was about two people who loved ideas and valued the deep friendship they shared."

THE TOTAL COMMUNITY IN ACTION

Eric's story serves as an important reminder that transformative mentors can shape individuals in powerful ways for good. Through mentoring, Eric became his best self. The mentoring he received has been felt in the people he influences and inspires today. In Eric's case, he was shaped by mentors in his family, hometown community, church, educational institutions, and work. Some of his mentors were more traditional types. One was even an unlikely mentor.

His story also points to the importance of church as one of the central institutions of mentorship and cultural life, a concept we've touched upon in various places in this book. As Eric grew up, church was not solely a place to worship; it was the hub of his community. For Eric, church was where the support for his studies came from, and where his relationship to the doctor was established. In many communities today, the church knits together values and commitment and allows the formation of transformative relationships.

But church membership is declining, which can only have a detrimental effect upon mentoring. Gallup representatives first measured church attendance in America in 1937. Some 73 percent of all Americans regularly attended church then—a figure that hovered near 70 percent for the next six decades. But beginning in 2000, attendance started to rapidly decline. In 2018, only about half of all Americans were attending church, and in 2020, even before the COVID-19 lockdowns radically affected church services nationwide, the figure dipped below half for the first time. Today, the lack of church participation is particularly noted among millennials, of whom only 36 percent attend church.[11]

This is a trend we'd like to see reversed among all age groups. Church can help people not only experience a sense of the transcendent but also discover a place of belonging, encouragement, and growth. The best churches uplift and challenge us intellectually and spiritually and ultimately help us find and employ the deeper purposes of our lives.

Overall, as you've seen, Eric's story is about hope, and in many ways, he has achieved the essence of the American dream. People can be lifted from humble beginnings. They can be inspired to create goals and then work to achieve those goals. In the end, they can live purposeful, altruistic, and noble lives—not distinguished by rank or title but exalted by character and excellence.

Advancing that constructive spirit and practice has been the main goal with this book, and we realize that ours is a radical hope. We have not wished merely to restore mentoring to a position of prominence or discuss how mentoring is generally a good thing in communities and businesses. Rather, we have hoped to redefine and elevate mentoring for a new era, helping to establish transformative mentoring as a vital building block of American community and culture. We have done that because we want the best for this nation. We want to see the United States on a consistent, admirable track.

With transformative mentoring, trust can be rebuilt.

PRAGMATIC NEXT STEPS

Think back over the many stories presented in this book. We have asked some of the country's best and brightest leaders how they became successful, and we have heard story after story about how they all had good mentors. We want to see many more stories such as these come to reality. Imagine if every one of us had a genuine impact on somebody's life in a transformational way and helped them find their purpose. Is there a greater gift any of us could give someone else beyond helping them find their true purpose and calling and realize their full potential?

That's what each of us can do. A few people can indeed start a revolution and change the course of history. Working together, we can help make the world a better place. We can create a new generation of admirable and highly proficient leaders—dedicated, trustworthy, and caring people who not only realize their full potential as individuals but also see their place in a united country and on a global playing field. All of us, together, can resolve to build not only good businesses and organizations but stronger, healthier communities that produce leaders who lead well.

Practically, what can each of us do?

1. We can start by dedicating ourselves to becoming transformative mentors, no matter how busy we are. We can commit to the concept and practice of investing time and resources to help someone find their purpose, reach their full potential, and become their best self. We keep in mind, always, that our mentoring can have a compounding effect on our nation. When we help one person, and then encourage that person to help another person, our mentoring efforts can be magnified exponentially.

2. When the time is right, we can identify a specific person, and assess whether there is an opportunity to serve as a mentor. All it takes is a simple statement that starts a conversation—something like, "I see real promise in you, and I want to help you unlock it. Would you like my help?"

3. We can then undertake the process of mentoring. As you've seen in this book, there is no one way to mentor everyone, but you and your mentee will find the best practices that work for you.

4. As part of the mentoring process, we can realize that our commitment extends to the whole person. We are not merely mentoring to impart job skills or help a person get ahead in their career. We are mentoring to help guide a mentee's life and shape their worldview. We are there to help develop mental strength and a heroic mindset in another person. That's how we can help unite the nation.

5.   We can help build confidence in our mentee and help them find a voice as we communicate to our mentee that "You belong here," "You have good things to say," and "You are capable of giving much to the world." We can encourage our mentee to undertake new and difficult challenges, and while we want to set high standards and expect commitment and growth from our mentee, we cannot demand perfection.

6.   While mentoring, we don't need to talk only about work. We can talk about all of life, as the relationship authentically progresses. We can ask questions and listen. We can learn from our mentees, just as they learn from us. We can commit to staying present and available for our mentee. We can decide not to hold tightly to them in the interest of job retention, but can encourage them on the career path that's best for them.

7.   We can mentor across gender lines and cultural lines, being wise, prudent, and respectful in our approach. We can listen and learn more than we speak, and we can note that not all people have the same challenges, experiences, and opportunities that we have had.

8.   We can mentor people in different industries, paying close attention to those who have different economic and educational levels than us, noting that some of the best mentor-mentee relationships will seem the most unlikely at first. Our research saw the prevalence of mentorship increase as education and income levels increased, indicating a possible mentoring gap within certain segments of the population.[12] We can work to bridge those gaps.

9.   We don't need to stick with a mentee forever. If the relationship has run its course, the arrangement can be politely and professionally concluded or fade away with time.

10.   Ultimately, we can mentor people well when we adopt the mindset of genuinely valuing people. In all our mannerisms, speech, and conduct, we can choose to lead with compassion and humanity. We truly do want what's best for other people and our country.

EVERYBODY'S HONOR
IS ON THE LINE

It will take a collective effort to build this new culture of trustworthiness in our country, yet when we build better leaders, we create a wiser America, both now and for future generations. With trustworthy leaders, we can skillfully navigate the social ills that befall our nation.

What might this collective effort look like? It begins with a simple commitment to care, and already we have great hope for this endeavor. Two writers, Jordan Blashek (who is also president of America's Frontier Fund and a former Marine) and Christopher Haugh (a former speechwriter in the US Department of State's Policy Planning staff), recently traveled across forty-four states and "saw firsthand how Americans are more empathetic and less dogmatic than many are inclined to believe. Beneath the polarized rhetoric, people care about their fellow citizens, are bewildered by the hostility all around them, and want many of the same things out of our democracy."[13]

A recent survey held up the two writers' findings. It showed that the majority of Americans today do not position themselves on the polarizing extreme of any spectrum. Rather, some 67 percent of our nation's citizens comprise what the institute is now terming "the exhausted majority." This majority does not have an "us-versus-them" mindset. We are simply tired of feeling like everything is a fight. We are "eager to find common ground" and believe that "our differences aren't so great that we can't work together."[14] Americans do believe in interdependence; our shared values and commitment to unity are more intertwined and connected than we think. An important caveat is in order here. Some people on the Right and the Left believe we're in a battle of ideals for the soul of our society. They see a risk of simply "getting along" while the country erodes. The key then, in this conflict of ideals, is not to lose our commonality, our humanity, and our love for America.

A story from Calvin Theological Seminary professor Dr. Gary Burge provides a telling image of interconnectedness and honor. For years, he has been deeply invested in the study of cooperative cultures,[15] and he notes that plenty of people view their surroundings through shared lenses and subsequently live with that perspective. A single person is important, but so is an entire family, tribe, or people group. Americans believe this too. As much as we are a country of rugged individualists, we are also a community. The concept of honor, for instance, can be valued and felt not only by an individual but by a team, a business, an organization, and a community as a whole.

While on a trip to Cairo, Dr. Burge made plans to visit a child that he and his wife sponsor through a global humanitarian organization that seeks to eradicate poverty, illiteracy, and injustice. His handler took him by taxi into an impoverished neighborhood where the child lived with her family in an apartment building. There was no elevator, so Dr. Burge and his handler climbed the stairs to the fifth floor where the child's father warmly welcomed them into their home. Greetings and small gifts were exchanged. The father thanked the professor for partnering with the family and aiding the child's development and education. Then he disappeared behind a corner into the kitchen and returned, proud and smiling, with a gift he evidently viewed as climactic to the visit: an entire case of ice-cold American soda pop in glass bottles.

Dr. Burge smiled outwardly but inwardly hesitated. A health enthusi-ast, he has a strong aversion to sugared drinks. But the handler whispered in Dr. Burge's ear that it would be highly disrespectful if he refused the gift. The professor was obliged to drink at least one bottle. Perhaps more than one. So Dr. Burge drank.

When the meeting was over and the goodbyes were said, Dr. Burge and the handler descended the stairs and hailed another taxi. On the way out, the professor was surprised to see that not only did the family follow him to the taxi, but all the people in the apartment block came out to watch and wave. On the ride back to the hotel, Dr. Burge asked the han-dler why everyone had turned out.

The handler explained that the professor was the first Westerner to come to their apartment building. Hospitality is greatly valued through-out the region and subculture, and everybody's honor was on the line. The case of pop had been so costly in that impoverished area that the entire building had needed to pool their resources. Seven families had shared what little they had to present the man with a valuable gift.[16]

THE NOBLE QUEST

When it comes to America today, everybody's honor is on the line. The challenges we face as a nation are great, yet we can band together to present valuable gifts to this and the next generation. These gifts might be costly. Mentoring requires the investment of time and resources, and when are leaders ever not busy? Yet transformative mentoring is the gift we must give.

It's far too easy to complain about the ills of America today. We are in the midst of a grievance season, and many people are wearied by the challenges and disputes. But instead of venting our frustrations, our hope is that we can all focus our energies on fostering positive change. That's what our founders and forebears did about the problems of their era. They knew then what we can remind ourselves of today; in the words of

Theodore Roosevelt, "It is not the critic who counts. The credit belongs to the man who is actually in the arena, who spends himself in a worthy cause."[17] In other words, a nation will reach its goals only if citizens are willing to take the steps and move forward on the path.

What if all Americans, in each individual's unique way, made it their collective aim to invest in this and the next generation by producing an abundance of admirable, principled, and highly proficient leaders? If we all invest together in that common purpose, then our young democracy will stand a much better chance of staying on the path toward a more perfect union. Imagine a large contingent of Americans united within the fabric of transformative mentoring, each person making it their ambition to positively impact another person's life. The growth that results will be exponential.

America is not a perfect country by any means, but we do believe it is an "exceptional" country, to use French political theorist Alexis de Tocqueville's idea.[18] By this, we do not mean that Americans are superior to any of the rest of the world's citizens, but that our country is unique in its style of and commitment to liberty. We are steadfastly resolved to throw off the yoke of any tyranny, even that of our own making, and when it comes to elevating our core social building blocks, America has the right stuff. As Condoleezza Rice stated to the world leader in the story in chapter 3, "In America, we possess strength because our strength comes from our people."

Picture again with us that image we provided in the opening chapter, although in our vision it's a day when the despairing statistics are reversed. That's what this book humbly works toward. Envision a renewed America where we've regained our trust for every type of leader and their institutions because they have earned our trust. Imagine business executives who lead with vision and wisdom. Journalists who report accurately and impartially. Educators who teach well and truthfully. Clergy who shepherd their flock and do not ignore sin and injustice within their own ranks. Law enforcement and judges and attorneys and state officials and politicians who have regained our public trust. A country where we trust our leaders because they have been mentored to be trustworthy, and now they display that trustworthiness in how and who they lead.

That's why building more trustworthy leadership is not merely a good idea; it's also a patriotic duty. We must undertake it for the people around us, and also for our entire country. We have to reconcile the very real problems we see in America today with the faith and hope we have for America's future. The challenges we face in America today do not need to defeat us. Rather, those ills can be turned around for good. The power of transformative mentoring raises people up and helps them become the leaders that our nation so desperately needs.

We are not naïve to believe that transformative mentoring solves every problem we face today. But in the effort to rebuild trust in American society, transformative mentoring is an important and needful solution. It's part of the overall mosaic of answers, and it's a way we can all contribute to a better America. Transformative mentoring offers the pathway to solving the fundamental deficit of trust in the United States. This kind of mentoring helps people reach their full potential, which in turn results in significant, positive impact on our nation.

We hope that you will join us on this noble quest.

KEY TAKEAWAYS

- Transformative mentoring works. In this book, we've seen how many people became effective leaders because others believed in them and positively impacted their lives.

- The first step is to commit yourself to becoming a transformative mentor. When the time is right, and a person is identified, you can ask them if they want your help in achieving their potential through mentorship. Characterize the relationship with authenticity, empathy, and the transference of wisdom.

- Transformative mentoring can help America today. Imagine a large contingent of Americans united within the fabric of transformative mentoring, each person making it their ambition to positively impact another person's life. The growth that results will be exponential, and will be an important part of rekindling the American dream.

NOTES

YOUR INVITATION

1. The quote refers to a 1974 *Los Angeles Times* story referenced in Deanne Barkley's 2013 obituary. See Elaine Woo, "Deanne Barkley Dies at 82; Pioneering TV Executive," *Los Angeles Times*, April 11, 2013, https://www.latimes.com/local /obituaries/la-xpm-2013-apr-11-la-me-deanne-barkley-20130412-story.html.

CHAPTER 1

1. "Those with High Personal Trust Have Higher Confidence in Key Leadership Groups," Pew Research Center, July 18, 2019, https://www.pewresearch.org /politics/2019/07/22/trust-and-distrust-in-america/.
2. David Brooks, "America Is Having a Moral Convulsion," *The Atlantic*, October 5, 2020, https://www.theatlantic.com/ideas/archive/2020/10/collapsing-levels -trust-are-devastating-america/616581/.
3. Bright Line Watch, June 2021 survey, https://brightlinewatch.org/still-miles -apart-americans-and-the-state-of-u-s-democracy-half-a-year-into-the-biden -presidency/. See also Adam Barnes, "Shocking Poll Finds Many Americans Now Want to Secede from the United States," Changing America, July 15, 2021, https://thehill.com/changing-america/enrichment/arts-culture/563221 -shocking-poll-finds-many-americans-now-want-to.
4. Ian Bremmer, "The U.S. Capitol Riot Was Years in the Making. Here's Why America Is So Divided," *TIME*, January 16, 2021, https://time.com/5929978 /the-u-s-capitol-riot-was-years-in-the-making-heres-why-america-is-so-divided/.
5. Timothy P. Carney, *Alienated America: Why Some Places Thrive While Others Collapse* (New York: Harper, 2020), 91.
6. Robert D. Putman, *The Upswing: How America Came Together a Century Ago, and How We Can Do It Again* (New York: Simon and Schuster, 2020), 158.
7. Dr. John Hillen, "Restoring Trust and Leadership in a Vacuous Age," *Law & Liberty*, April 27, 2021, https://lawliberty.org/restoring-trust-and-leadership-in -a-vacuous-age/.
8. Sissela Bok, *Lying: Moral Choice in Private and Public Life* (New York: Pantheon Books, 1978), 31.
9. The term "transformational leadership" (or "transformative mentoring") was coined by James MacGregor Burns in 1978, https://www.businessballs.com /leadership-styles/transformational-and-transactional-leadership/. See also

James MacGregor Burns, *Transforming Leadership* (Washington, DC: Atlantic Monthly Press, 2003), 24–25.

10. See also Robert Nisbet, *The Quest for Community* (Wilmington, DE: ISI Books, [1953] 2019).

11. PwC Workforce Pulse Survey, June 15, 2020, https://www.pwc.com/us/en /library/covid-19/what-employees-need-to-be-confident-2.html.

12. Yuvrah Malik and Aditya Soni. "Melinda Gates to Exit Gates Foundation with $12.5 Billion for Own Charity Work," Reuters, May 13. 2024, https://www .reuters.com/business/melinda-gates-step-down-co-chair-bill-melinda-gates -foundation-2024-05-13/.

13. Marquis, Christopher, V. Kasturi Rangan, and Cathy Ross, "Goldman Sachs: The 10,000 Women Initiative," Harvard Business School Case 509-042, June 2009 (revised July 2010), https://www.hbs.edu/faculty/Pages/item. aspx?num=37423.

14. Goldman Sachs, "One Million Black Women," https://www.goldmansachs .com/our-commitments/sustainability/one-million-black-women.

15. Bloomberg Philanthropies, "Goldman Sachs 10,000 Small Businesses," https:// www.bloomberg.org/founders-projects/goldman-sachs-10000-small-businesses.

CHAPTER 2

1. Walter Isaacson, "Walker Percy's Theory of Hurricanes," August 4, 2015, *New York Times*, https://www.nytimes.com/2015/08/09/books/review/walker -percys-theory-of-hurricanes.html.

2. David Marquet, "The Original Mentor Failed—What Went Wrong," *Forbes*, January 23, 2017, https://www.forbes.com/sites/davidmarquet/2017/01/23 /the-original-mentor-failed-what-went-wrong/?sh=2d78f91d9e48.

3. Kim Wise, "Famous Mentors/Mentees—Dynamics Duos That Made Their Mark in History," Mentor Resources, May 21, 2020, https://www. mentorresources.com/mentoring-blog/famous-mentors/mentees-dynamic -duos-that-made-their-mark-in-history.

4. Ion Soteropoulos, "Aristotle's Influence on Alexander the Great's Political Thought," Apeiron Centre, https://apeironcentre.org/aristotles-influence-on -alexander-the-greats-political-thought/.

5. Barnabas, John Mark, and Paul, see Acts 13:13, 15:36–41. Jack Zavada, "John Mark—Author of the Gospel of Mark," *Learn Religions*, April 9, 2019, https:// www.learnreligions.com/john-mark-author-of-the-gospel-of-mark-701085.

6. Rev. David Rogers, "The Difference Between the Four Gospels," *Carlsbad Current Argus*, January 26, 2019.

7. For more information on Leonardo da Vinci, see Walter Isaacson's book *Leonardo da Vinci* (New York: Simon & Schuster, 2017).

8. American Foundation for the Blind, "The Miracle Worker," https://www.afb .org/about-afb/history/online-museums/anne-sullivan-miracle-worker.

9. "Mays, Benjamin Elijah," Stanford, the Martin Luther King, Jr., Research and Education Institute, https://kinginstitute.stanford.edu/encyclopedia/mays -benjamin-elijah.

10. Gerald Roche, "Much Ado About Mentors," *Harvard Business Review*, January 1979, https://hbr.org/1979/01/much-ado-about-mentors.
11. Daniel J. Levinson (with C. N. Darrow, E. B. Klein, M. H. Levinson, and B. McKee), *The Seasons of a Man's Life* (New York: Knopf, 1978).

SPOTLIGHT ON MENTORING: A CONVERSATION WITH GENERAL H. R. MCMASTER

1. Gal Perl Finkel, "US National Security Adviser Faces Challenges at Home and Abroad," *Jerusalem Post*, February 22, 2017, https://www.jpost.com/Opinion/US-national-security-adviser-faces-challenges-at-home-and-abroad-482328.
2. H. R. McMaster, "What We Learned: From the Battle of 73 Easting," HistoryNet, https://www.historynet.com/learned-battle-73-easting.htm.
3. Brian Adam Jones, "As a Young Captain, McMaster Commanded One of the Most Epic Tank Battles in History," Task & Purpose, February 24, 2017, https://taskandpurpose.com/history/young-captain-mcmaster-commanded-one-epic-tank-battles-history/.
4. The full story of the battle is described in this forty-seven-minute documentary: "Battle of 73 Easting: the Tank War to Topple Saddam Hussein," Timeline—World History Documentaries, Breakthrough Entertainment, Little Dot Studios, https://www.youtube.com/watch?v=WKZn-vT9CRE.

CHAPTER 3

1. Smithsonian, National Museum of American History, "Separate Is Not Equal," https://americanhistory.si.edu/brown/history/1-segregated/jim-crow.html.
2. Tatiana Serafin, "#1 Condoleezza Rice. The World's 100 Most Powerful Women," *Forbes*, 2005, https://images.forbes.com/lists/2005/11/MTNG.html.
3. K. E. Kram, *Mentoring at Work: Developmental Relationships in Organizational Life* (Glenview, IL: Scott Foresman, 1983). Cf. K. E. Kram, "Improving the Mentoring Process," *Training & Development Journal* 39, no. 4 (1985): 40–43.
4. Kram, "Improving the Mentoring Process," 32.
5. James MacGregor Burns, *Transforming Leadership* (Washington, DC: Atlantic Monthly Press, 2003), 24–25.
6. U.S. Department of State. Bureau of Educational and Cultural Affairs Exchange Programs. https://exchanges.state.gov/non-us/program/fortune-us-department-state-global-womens-mentoring-partnership.
7. Journey to Lead. https://www.journeytolead.org/how-it-works/.
8. Maria L. La Ganga, "In Face for White House, the 'Cult of Condi' Plays Growing Role," *Los Angeles Times*, May 28, 2000, https://www.latimes.com/archives/la-xpm-2000-may-28-mn-35018-story.html.
9. Gregory Clay, "Mentors Don't Have to Look Like You," *Inside Sources*, September 18, 2017, https://insidesources.com/mentors-dont-have-to-look-like-you/.

CHAPTER 4

1. Tunku Varadarajan, "The Smearing of Nikki Haley," *Wall Street Journal*, August 27, 2020, https://www.wsj.com/articles/the-smearing-of-nikki-haley -11598549001.
2. Chiara Vercellone, "Fact Check: Nikki Haley Didn't 'White-Wash' Her Name. It's Punjabi," *USA Today*, May 7, 2021, https://www.usatoday.com/story/news /factcheck/2021/05/05/fact-check-haley-didnt-white-wash-her-name-nikki -punjabi/4928061001/.
3. For instance, Eby et al. conducted a meta-analysis composed of 112 individual research studies and found that mentoring indeed has noteworthy behavioral, attitudinal, health-related, relational, motivational, and career benefits. Moreover, positive protégé perceptions were most strongly associated with greater similarity in attitudes, values, beliefs, and personality with their mentors. Where protégés perceived greater instrumental support and stronger relationship quality with their mentors, associations with enhanced social capital were primarily noted. Additionally, greater psychosocial support was most readily associated with interaction frequency. In regard to consequences, protégé perceptions of greater instrumental support and stronger relationship quality were most strongly associated with situational satisfaction, and perceptions of psychosocial support were most highly associated with a sense of affiliation. Comparisons between academic and workplace mentoring generally revealed differences in magnitude, rather than direction, of the obtained effects. L.T.d.T. Eby, T. D. Allen, B. J. Hoffman, L. E. Baranik, J. B. Sauer, S. Baldwin, M. A. Morrison, K. M. Kinkade, C. P. Maher, S. Curtis, and S. C. Evans, "An Interdisciplinary Meta-analysis of the Potential Antecedents, Correlates, and Consequences of Protégé Perceptions of Mentoring," *Psychological Bulletin* 139, no. 2 (2013): 441–76.
4. Amy Morin, medically reviewed by Rachel Goldman, PhD, "6 Ways to Build Your Self Confidence," *Very Well Mind*, April 20, 2021, https://www .verywellmind.com/how-to-boost-your-self-confidence-4163098.
5. Dan Merica, "Trump, Working with Ivanka, to Push Expanded Apprenticeship Programs," CNN, June 15, 2017.
6. Tim Alberta, "Nikki Haley's Time for Choosing," *Politico*, 2021, https://www .politico.com/interactives/2021/magazine-nikki-haleys-choice/.

SPOTLIGHT ON MENTORING:
A CONVERSATION WITH SARAH HUCKABEE SANDERS

1. "President Trump Visits U.S. Troops in Iraq," ABC News, December 26, 2018, https://www.youtube.com/watch?v=quRHFKAGRyY.
2. "Sarah Huckabee Sanders for Governor," SarahForGovernor.com, January 24, 2021, https://www.youtube.com/watch?v=opbMn-n76AQ.
3. Scott Neuman, "Sarah Sanders Reportedly to Get Temporary Secret Service Protection," NPR, June 27, 2018, https://www.npr.org/2018/06/27/623779273 /sarah-sanders-reportedly-to-get-temporary-secret-service-protection.

4.   Maya Salam, "Peter Fonda Apologizes for Barron Trump Tweet; Secret
     Service Is 'Aware,'" *New York Times,* June 20, 2018, https://www.foxbusiness
     .com/politics/peter-fonda-committed-a-crime-and-should-be-arrested-mike
     -huckabee.
5.   Avi Selk and Sarah Murray, "The Owner of the Red Hen Explains Why She
     Asked Sarah Huckabee Sanders to Leave," *Washington Post,* June 25, 2018,
     https://www.washingtonpost.com/news/local/wp/2018/06/23/why-a-small
     -town-restaurant-owner-asked-sarah-huckabee-sanders-to-leave-and-would-do
     -it-again/.
6.   Sonia Rao, "Did the Red Hen Violate Sarah Huckabee Sanders's Rights
     When It Kicked Her Out?" *Washington Post,* June 25, 2018, https://www
     .washingtonpost.com/news/food/wp/2018/06/25/was-sarah-huckabee
     -sanders-denied-public-accommodation-when-a-restaurant-kicked-her-out/.
7.   Rex Nelson, "Remembering Bill Downs," Ouachita Baptist University (blog),
     April 24, 2019, https://obu.edu/stories/blog/2019/04/remembering-bill-downs.
     php.

CHAPTER 5

1.   See Sandra C. Burt and Linda Perlis, *Parents as Mentors* (New York: Prima
     Lifestyles, 1999).
2.   Julia Link Roberts, "Parents Can Be Mentors, Too!" *Gifted Child Today* 15, no. 3
     (1992): 36–38, https://journals.sagepub.com/doi/10.1177/1076217592015
     00310.
3.   Matthew Continetti, "American Decline Is Not Fated—Unless Our Leaders
     Make It So," *Washington Free Beacon*, October 8, 2021, https://freebeacon.com
     /columns/the-leadership-deficit-doom-loop/.
4.   Ioana Lupu, "Your Feelings About Work-Life Balance Are Shaped by What You
     Saw Your Parents Do," *Harvard Business Review*, October 20, 2017, https://hbr
     .org/2017/10/your-feelings-about-work-life-balance-are-shaped-by-what-you
     -saw-your-parents-do.
5.   "Employment Characteristics of Families—2020," Bureau of Labor Statistics,
     April 21, 2021, https://www.bls.gov/news.release/archives/famee_04212021
     .pdf.
6.   Amy Morin, "The Five Things Successful Working Parents Give Up to Reach a
     Work-Life Balance," *Forbes*, January 20, 2014, https://www.forbes.com/sites
     /amymorin/2014/01/20/the-five-things-successful-working-parents-give-up-to
     -reach-a-work-life-balance/?sh=288028a557ea.
7.   Cara Birnbaum, "Is Work-Life Balance for Moms Total BS?" *Parents*,
     September 19, 2019.

SPOTLIGHT ON MENTORING: A CONVERSATION WITH ALEX GORSKY

1. Jordan Valinsky, "Johnson & Johnson Is Breaking Up Band-Aids and Pharmaceuticals," CNN Business, November 12, 2021, https://www.cnn.com/2021/11/12/investing/johnson-johnson-split/index.html.
2. Robert F. Kennedy Human Rights, "Alex Gorsky," https://rfkhumanrights.org/who-we-are/our-people/alex-gorsky.

CHAPTER 6

1. Rhonda Walker, "How Detroit Native Rosaline 'Roz' Brewer Is Breaking Barriers," Click on Detroit, May 5, 2021, https://www.clickondetroit.com/news/local/2021/05/05/how-detroit-native-rosalind-roz-brewer-is-breaking-barriers/.
2. Emma Hinchliffe, "The Female CEOs on This Year's Fortune 500 Just Broke Three All-Time Records," *Fortune*, June 2, 2021, https://fortune.com/2021/06/02/female-ceos-fortune-500-2021-women-ceo-list-roz-brewer-walgreens-karen-lynch-cvs-thasunda-brown-duckett-tiaa/.
3. Amelia Lucas, Melissa Repko, Marc Gilbert, and Christina Cheddar Berk, "Walgreens Taps Starbucks Operating Chief Roz Brewer as Its Next CEO," CNBC, January 26, 2021, https://www.cnbc.com/2021/01/26/starbucks-coo-roz-brewer-leaving-to-become-ceo-of-publicly-traded-company.html; and Jeanne Sahadi, "Thasunda Brown Duckett to Helm TIAA, Making Her the Second Black Woman to Be Named Fortune 500 CEO This Year," CNN, February 25, 2021, https://www.cnn.com/2021/02/25/success/tiaa-thasunda-brown-duckett-ceo/index.html.
4. Chauncey Alcorn, "Rosalind Brewer Officially Takes the Helm at Walgreens, Becoming the Only Black Woman Fortune 500 CEO," CNN, March 15, 2021, https://www.cnn.com/2021/03/15/business/rosalind-brewer-walgreens/index.html.
5. Jennifer Warnick, "Glass Ceiling Slayer Roz Brewer Dubs Grads 'Generation Quest,'" *Starbucks Stories and News*, May 21, 2018.
6. "Rosalind Brewer: Find Your Voice and Don't Be Silent," Interview by Joy Huang for Stanford Graduate School of Business, June 23, 2021, https://www.gsb.stanford.edu/insights/rosalind-brewer-find-your-voice-dont-be-silent.
7. David Gergen, *Hearts Touched with Fire: How Great Leaders Are Made* (New York: Simon & Schuster, 2022). Quote found at: Mike Allen, "First Look: David Gergen's Playbook for Young Leaders," Axios, October 21, 2021, https://www.axios.com/david-gergen-book-leadership-27755c14-31a1-4822-a844-f97b44e21144.html.
8. Veronica M. Fruiht and Laura Wray-Lake, "The Role of Mentor Type and Timing in Predicting Educational Attainment," *Journal of Youth and Adolescence* 42, no. 9 (2013): 3 and 5, https://www.researchgate.net/publication/230797846_The_Role_of_Mentor_Type_and_Timing_in_Predicting_Educational_Attainment.

9. Ros Hill and Peter Reddy, "Undergraduate Peer Mentoring: An Investigation into Processes, Activities and Outcomes," *Psychology Learning and Teaching* 6, no. 2 (2007): 98–103, https://journals.sagepub.com/toc/plj/6/2.
10. See Alyza Sebenius, "The Importance of High School Mentors," *The Atlantic*, January 13, 2016, https://www.theatlantic.com/education/archive/2016/01/mentorship-in-public-schools/423945/. See also Valoris's video: "Why Public Schools Should Reinvent Mentorship," YouTube, https://www.youtube.com/watch?v=BlX4neUClbo&t=114s. See also https://www.linkedin.com/in/jessica-valoris-658a3b39.
11. "Who Mentored Walter Cronkite," Harvard School of Public Health.
12. Jim Bell, "Remembering Walter Cronkite," *Houston Public Media*, July 20, 2009, https://www.houstonpublicmedia.org/articles/news/2009/07/20/16184/remembering-walter-cronkite/.
13. Walter Cronkite, *A Reporter's Life* (New York: Knopf, 1996).
14. "Walter Cronkite," *Kansas City Star*, https://www.legacy.com/us/obituaries/kansascity/name/walter-cronkite-obituary?pid=129897979.
15. David Folkenflik, "Walter Cronkite, America's 'Most Trusted Man,'" *NPR*, July 18, 2009, https://www.npr.org/templates/story/story.php?storyId=106770499.
16. David Folkenflik, "Walter Cronkite, America's 'Most Trusted Man.'"
17. Lindsey Bever, "Sam's Club CEP Called 'Racist' for Remarks on Diversity," *Washington Post*, December 15, 2015, https://www.washingtonpost.com/news/morning-mix/wp/2015/12/15/sams-club-ceo-called-racist-for-remarks-on-diversity/.
18. Lindsey Bever, "Sam's Club CEP Called 'Racist' for Remarks on Diversity."
19. Sara Ashley O'Brien, "Sam's Club CEO Takes Heat for Comments," CNN Business, December 16, 2015.
20. Bobbi Booker and Phillip Jackson, "Starbucks Apologizes, Calls Arrests 'Reprehensible,'" *Philadelphia Tribune*, April 17, 2018, https://www.phillytrib.com/news/starbucks-apologizes-calls-arrests-reprehensible/article_6f2a561a-0ef2-503b-81ef-e0f9fdd35c71.html.
21. "Starbucks to Close All Stores Nationwide for Racial-Bias Education on May 20." *Starbucks Stories & News*, https://stories.starbucks.com/press/2018/starbucks-to-close-stores-nationwide-for-racial-bias-education-may-29/.
22. Amelia Lucas, "Starbucks Pledges to Have 30 Percent of Corporate Workforce Identify as a Minority by 2025," CNBC, October 14, 2020, https://www.cnbc.com/2020/10/14/starbucks-to-have-30percent-of-corporate-staff-identify-as-a-minority-by-2025.html.
23. Makoto Fujimura, *Art and Faith: A Theology of Making* (Yale University Press, 2020), 118.

**SPOTLIGHT ON MENTORING:
A CONVERSATION WITH STEPHEN A. SCHWARZMAN**

1. See "Our People: Steven A. Schwarzman," Blackstone, https://www.blackstone.com/people/stephen-a-schwarzman-2/.

2. See No Guarantees, https://www.noguarantees.com/.
3. Barbara Kiviat, "Builders & Titans: Stephen Schwarzman," *TIME*, May 3, 2007, https://content.time.com/time/specials/2007/time100/article/0,28804 ,1595326_1615737_1616000,00.html.
4. Nathan Vardi, "Money Masters: The Most Powerful People in the Financial World," *Forbes*, May 11, 2016, https://www.forbes.com/sites/nathanvardi/2016 /05/11/money-masters-the-most-powerful-people-in-the-financial-world/?sh =584726a12792.
5. "Profile: Stephen Schwarzman," *Forbes*, https://www.forbes.com/profile /stephen-schwarzman/?sh=68486d18234a.

CHAPTER 7

1. Todd Bishop, "Microsoft Adds 23k Employees in One Year, Growing 14% Despite Pandemic and Tight Labor Market," *GeekWire*, October 27, 2021, https://www.geekwire.com/2021/microsoft-adds-23k-employees-one-year -growing-14-despite-pandemic-tight-labor-market/. See also "Facts About Microsoft," Microsoft, https://news.microsoft.com/facts-about-microsoft /#EmploymentInfo.
2. Shanhong Liu, "Operating Systems Market Share of Desktop PCs 2013–2021, by Month," *Statista*, September 10, 2021, https://www.statista.com/statistics /218089/global-market-share-of-windows-7/.
3. Nicole Goodkind and Elisabeth Buchwald, "Microsoft Is Worth More Than $3 trillion. It's the Second Company to Ever Break That Threshold," CNN, January 24, 2024, https://www.cnn.com/2024/01/24/investing/microsoft -three-trillion-market-value/index.html. Confirmed at: "Market capitalization of Microsoft (MSFT)," CompaniesMarketCap, https://companiesmarketcap .com/microsoft/marketcap/.
4. "Satya Nadella Says Microsoft's Old Mission Statement Is Obsolete," *Media Marketing*, February 24, 2017, https://www.media-marketing.com/en/news /satya-nadella-says-microsofts-old-mission-statement-is-obsolete/.
5. Eugene Kim, "Microsoft Has a Strange New Mission Statement," *Insider*, June 25, 2015, https://www.businessinsider.com/microsoft-ceo-satya-nadella -new-company-mission-internal-email-2015-6.
6. Alex Konrad, "Exclusive CEO Interview: Satya Nadella Reveals How Microsoft Got Its Groove Back," *Forbes*, December 10, 2018, https://www.forbes .com/sites/alexkonrad/2018/12/10/exclusive-ceo-interview-satya-nadella -reveals-how-microsoft-got-its-groove-back/?sh=4b90ac0b7acb.
7. Ruchira Chaudhary, "How Satya Nadella Brought a Growth Mindset to Microsoft," *Mint*, March 5, 2021, https://www.livemint.com/news/business-of -life/how-satya-nadella-brought-a-growth-mindset-to-microsoft-11614874643362 .html.
8. Ruchira Chaudhary, "How Satya Nadella Brought a Growth Mindset to Microsoft."

9. Nicola Cronin, "Mentoring Statistics: The Research You Need to Know," *Guider*, February 3, 2020, https://www.guider-ai.com/blog/mentoring-statistics -the-research-you-need-to-know.

10. Vince Scalia, "The Basic Anatomy of All Corporate Mentorship Programs," *Gloo* (blog), December 3, 2018, https://blog.gloo.us/anatomy-corporate -mentorship-programs.

11. Cue Ball, https://cueball.com/home/.

12. Anthony Tjan, "What the Best Mentors Do," *Harvard Business Review*, February 27, 2017, https://hbr.org/2017/02/what-the-best-mentors-do.

13. Anthony Tjan, "What the Best Mentors Do."

14. Belle Rose Ragins, "From the Ordinary to the Extraordinary: High-Quality Mentoring Relationships at Work," *Organizational Dynamics* 45, no. 3 (July– September 2016): 4.

15. Belle Rose Ragins, "From the Ordinary to the Extraordinary," 5.

16. Nadine El-Bawab, "Reese Witherspoon's Hello Sunshine to Be Sold to Blackstone-Backed Media Company for $900 Million," CNBC, August 2, 2021, https://www.cnbc.com/amp/2021/08/02/reese-witherspoons-hello-sunshine -to-be-sold-for-900-million.html.

17. "A Happy Warrior: Mellody Hobson on Mentorship, Diversity, and Feedback," McKinsey & Company, June 18. 2020, https://www.mckinsey.com/featured -insights/diversity-and-inclusion/a-happy-warrior-mellody-hobson-on -mentorship-diversity-and-feedback.

18. Richard Waters, "Satya Nadella Brought Microsoft Back from the Brink of Irrelevance," *Los Angeles Times*, December 21, 2019, https://www.latimes.com /business/technology/story/2019-12-21/satya-nadella-reinvigorated-microsoft.

19. Note that 600 percent reflects the share at the time this book was researched and written. See Jordan Novet, "Microsoft Closes Above $2 Trillion Market Cap for the First Time," CNBC, June 4, 2021, https://www.cnbc.com/2021 /06/24/microsoft-closes-above-2-trillion-market-cap-for-the-first-time.html.

CHAPTER 8

1. Tory Burch LLC is a privately owned company. As such, the company's financials are not disclosed. Various media sources offer estimations of its multibillion-dollar valuation. See Teresa Novellino, "Tory Burch Sitting Pretty—and Privately—on $3.5B Company," Biz Journals, February 2, 2015, https://www.bizjournals.com/bizjournals/news/2015/02/02/tory-burch-llc -now-valued-at-3-point-five-billion.html. Her lifestyle brand was expected to sell $1.5 worth of product in 2021. "#31 Tory Burch: 2021 America's Self-Made Women Net Worth," *Forbes*, August 4, 2021, https://www.forbes.com/profile /tory-burch/?sh=4b6cb3323dfb.

2. "Tory Burch on How She Built a Fashion Empire from the Ground Up," *Glamour*, October 8, 2014, https://www.youtube.com/watch?v=3I8niXFJmag.

3. "Buddy Values," https://www.toryburch.com/en-us/about-us/.

4. Maria Katsarou, "Women and the Leadership Labyrinth, Howard vs Heidi," drmariakatsarou.blog.

5. Kristin Faulkner, "Tory Burch Restyles the Art of Mentoring with Frankness and Scale," *Forbes*, July 23, 2019, https://www.forbes.com/sites/kristifaulkner /2019/07/16/tory-burch-restyles-the-art-of-mentoring-with-frankness-and -scale/.

6. Judith Warner, Nora Ellmann, and Diana Boesch, "The Women's Leadership Gap," *Center for American Progress*, November 20, 2018, https://www .americanprogress.org/issues/women/reports/2018/11/20/461273/womens -leadership-gap-2/.

7. "The State of the Gender Pay Gap in 2021, Executive Summary," *Pay Scale*, https://www.payscale.com/research-and-insights/gender-pay-gap/.

8. "The Women's Leadership Gap," https://www.americanprogress.org/issues /women/reports/2018/11/20/461273/womens-leadership-gap-2/.

9. Areva Martin, "It's 2021—Women Reaching the C-Suite Shouldn't Be Historic," *Chief Executive*, September 22, 2021, https://chiefexecutive.netits -2021-women-reaching-the-c-suite-shouldnt-be-historic/.

10. In our survey, we found that, due to mentoring, 40 percent of men received new professional opportunities, while just 24 percent of women did.

11. Michael Shnayerson, "An Empire of Her Own," *Vanity Fair*, February 26, 2007, https://www.vanityfair.com/news/2007/02/tory-burch-200702.

12. Marguerite Ward, "Self-Made Millionaire Tory Burch Shares the Best Career Advice Anna Wintour Gave Her," CNBC, March 13, 2017, https://www.cnbc .com/2017/03/13/self-made-millionaire-tory-burch-shares-the-best-career -advice-anna-wintour-gave-her.html.

13. Dr. Pragya Agarwal, "In the Era of #MeToo Are Men Scared of Mentoring Women?" *Forbes*, February 18, 2019, https://www.forbes.com/sites /pragyaagarwaleurope/2019/02/18/in-the-era-of-metoo-are-men-scared-of -mentoring-women/?sh=4495141c7d0d.

14. Dr. Pragya Agarwal, "In the Era of #MeToo Are Men Scared of Mentoring Women?"

15. Billy Graham, "What's the Billy Graham Rule?" Billy Graham Evangelistic Organization, July 23, 2019, https://billygraham.org/story/the-modesto -manifesto-a-declaration-of-biblical-integrity/.

16. Andrew Exum, "Mike Pence and the 'Billy Graham Rule,'" *The Atlantic*, March 30, 2017, https://www.theatlantic.com/politics/archive/2017/03/mike -pence-and-the-sexism-of-the-billy-graham-rule/521328/.

17. Ruth Graham, "What the Pence Rule Looks Like in Practice," *Slate*, March 31, 2017, https://slate.com/human-interest/2017/03/the-pence-billy-graham-rule -isnt-that-weird-in-practice.html.

18. Danielle Kurtzleben, "Beyond the Mike Pence Misogyny Debate, the 3 'Billy Graham Rules' You Haven't Read," NPR, April 2, 2017, https://www.npr .org/2017/04/02/522247794/beyond-the-mike-pence-misogyny-debate-the-3 -billy-graham-rules-you-havent-read.

19. Andrew Exum, "Mike Pence and the 'Billy Graham Rule,'" *The Atlantic*, https://www.theatlantic.com/politics/archive/2017/03/mike-pence-and-the -sexism-of-the-billy-graham-rule/521328/.

20. Wayne and Kristi Northup, "A Ministry Couple Looks at the Billy Graham Rule," July 15, 2019, *Influence Magazine,* https://influencemagazine.com /Practice/A-Ministry-Couple-Looks-at-the-Billy-Graham-Rule.

21. Joe Tamborello, "After Weinstein, Mike Pence's 'Billy Graham Rule' Gains Traction—and Criticism," *IndyStar,* November 17, 2017, https://www.indystar .com/story/news/politics/2017/11/17/after-weinstein-mike-pences-billy-graham -rule-gains-traction-and-criticism/874460001/.

22. Ray Kimball, "Broadening Your Horizons Through Cross-Gender Mentoring," *Medium,* July 29, 2020, https://medium.com/leadership-counts/broadening -your-horizons-through-cross-gender-mentoring-95f647dd0eec.

23. Katelyn Beaty, "A Christian Case Against the Pence Rule," *New York Times,* November 15, 2017, https://www.nytimes.com/2017/11/15/opinion/pence-rule -christian-graham.html.

24. Anna Marie Valerio and Katina B. Sawyer, "The Men Who Mentor Women," *Harvard Business Review,* December 7, 2016, https://hbr.org/2016/12/the-men -who-mentor-women.

CHAPTER 9

1. "David Chang Discusses Edible Bugs, Robot-Made Pizza, and the Future of Food," *New Yorker,* October 30, 2021, https://www.newyorker.com/culture /culture-desk/david-chang-discusses-edible-bugs-robot-made-pizza-and-the -future-of-food.

2. Maura Judkis, "Ramen, Noise and Rebellion," *Washington Post,* September 19, 2019, https://www.washingtonpost.com/graphics/2019/lifestyle/food/david -chang/.

3. Maura Judkis, "Ramen, Noise and Rebellion."

4. Sam Dean, "Momofuku, the Most Important Restaurant in America," *Bon Appetit,* February 13, 2013, https://www.bonappetit.com/restaurants-travel /article/video-5.

5. "Our Restaurants," https://momofuku.com/.

6. "About Ko," https://ko.momofuku.com/about-us/.

7. Justina Huddleston and Joel Stice, "The Untold Truth of David Chang," Mashed, July 2, 2018, https://www.mashed.com/127640/the-untold-truth-of-david-chang/.

8. "Chef David Chang of Momofuku," StarChefs, May 2012, https://www .starchefsarchive.com/cook/chefs/bio/david-chang.

9. Pete Wells, "Why David Chang Matters," *New York Times,* August 28, 2018, https://www.nytimes.com/2018/08/28/dining/david-chang-kojin-toronto.html.

10. See, for instance, Scott Simon, "David Chang Discusses Mental Health and His New Memoir," NPR, September 5, 2020, https://www.npr.org/2020/09/05 /909969011/david-chang-discusses-mental-health-and-his-new-memoir; "'A Very Powerful Carrot': Celebrity Chef David Chang on How His Workaholism Fueled a Mental Health Crisis," CBC Radio, December 2, 2020, https://www .cbc.ca/radio/q/thursday-dec-3-2020-david-chang-katy-perry-and-more-1 .5816071/a-very-powerful-carrot-celebrity-chef-david-chang-on-how-his

-workaholism-fueled-a-mental-health-crisis-1.5816079; and Ana Calderone, "Chef David Chang Opens Up About Bipolar I Disorder in New Memoir: 'It Has Shaped Me in So Many Ways,'" *People*, August 26, 2020, https://people .com/food/david-chang-opens-up-bipolar-disorder-new-memoir/.

11. Claire Williamson, "Life in David Chang's Kitchen Isn't Always Peachy," *Japan Times*, January 9, 2021, https://www.japantimes.co.jp/culture/2021/01/09 /books/david-chang-eat-a-peach/.

12. "Joe Chang (1942–2020)," *The Dave Chang Show*, podcast, MP3 audio, June 16, 2020, https://podcasts.apple.com/us/podcast/the-dave-chang-show/ id1375877915.

13. David Chang (@davidchang), Twitter, June 16, 2020, 3:19 p.m., https://twitter .com/davidchang/status/1272972010008784899.

14. Larissa MacFarquhar, "Chef on the Edge," *New Yorker*, July 24, 2008, https:// www.newyorker.com/magazine/2008/03/24/chef-on-the-edge.

15. See Oxford Reference, "Via Negativa," https://www.oxfordreference.com /view/10.1093/oi/authority.20110803115625575; and Sayyed Haider Hassan, "The Case for Via Negativa," *Yale Daily News*, May 5, 2021, https:// yaledailynews.com/blog/2021/05/05/hassan-the-case-for-via-negativa/.

16. Lee Tran Lam, "Momofuku's David Chang Reveals How His 'Openness to Failure' Led to Success," *Special Broadcasting Service*, October 15, 2020, https:// www.sbs.com.au/food/article/2020/10/15/momofukus-david-chang-reveals -how-his-openness-failure-led-success.

17. Jeff Gordinier, "2004, the Year That Changed How We Dine," *New York Times*, December 13, 2013, https://www.nytimes.com/2014/01/01/dining/2004-the -year-that-changed-how-we-dine.html.

18. Joelle Jay, "How to Know If You Have a Mentor or Tormentor," *Forbes Coaches Council*, July 22, 2021, https://www.forbes.com/sites/forbescoachescouncil/2021 /07/22/how-to-know-if-you-have-a-mentor-or-tormentor/?sh=15a6d2d376f0.

19. Meryl Moss, "Mentor Versus Tormentor: 5 Characteristics to Finding the Psychic Bond," *Inc.* https://www.inc.com/meryl-moss/mentor-versus-tormentor -5-characteristics-to-finding-the-psychic-bond.html.

20. Carolyn O-Hara, "How to Break Up with Your Mentor," *Harvard Business Review*, May 29, 2014, https://hbr.org/2014/05/how-to-break-up-with-your-mentor.

21. Toni Feldstein, "How to Pick Up the Pieces When Our Mentors Fail Us," *Huffington Post*, May 11, 2011, https://www.huffpost.com/entry/how-to-pick-up -the-pieces_b_853470.

22. "Text of Draft Proposal for Bailout Plan," *New York Times*, September 20, 2008, https://www.nytimes.com/2008/09/21/business/21draftcnd.html.

23. Justin Fox, "Runners-Up: Henry Paulson," *TIME*, December 17, 2008.

24. Roger Baylor, "Anthony Bourdain's Genius Was Not in the Kitchen. His Genius Was in Knowing Which Side He Was On," Food and Dine, June 25, 2020, https://foodanddine.com/anthony-bourdains-genius-was-not-in-the-kitchen-his -genius-was-in-knowing-which-side-he-was-on/.

25. Felix Behr, "The Truth About Anthony Bourdain's Relationship with David Chang," Mashed, July 18, 2021, https://www.mashed.com/464078/the-truth -about-anthony-bourdains-relationship-with-david-chang/.

26. Brian Stelter, "CNN's Anthony Bourdain Dead at 61," CNN, June 8, 2018, https://www.cnn.com/2018/06/08/us/anthony-bourdain-obit/index.html.

27. Kim Severson, Matthew Haag, and Julia Moskin, "Anthony Bourdain, Renegade Chef Who Reported from the World's Tables, Is Dead at 61," *New York Times*, June 8, 2018, https://www.nytimes.com/2018/06/08/business /media/anthony-bourdain-dead.html.

CHAPTER 10

1. For instance, see Vicky McKeever, "ECB's Lagarde Says a Rate Hike Unlikely for 2022; Euro Slides," CNBC, November 19, 2021, https://www.cnbc.com /2021/11/19/ecbs-lagarde-says-a-rate-hike-unlikely-for-2022.html.

2. In 2019, 2020, and 2021, *Forbes* ranked her the second most powerful woman.

3. Russia was in the group from 1998 to 2014, and during that time it was called the G-8. Silvia Amaro, "Five Things to Know About Christine Lagarde, the First Woman to Lead the European Central Bank," *CNBC News*, July 11, 2019, https://www.cnbc.com/2019/07/11/who-is-christine-lagarde-the-new-ecb -president.html.

4. Adi Ignatius, "Pathbreaking Leadership," *Harvard Business Review*, November 13, 2013, https://hbr.org/2013/11/pathbreaking-leadership.

5. European Central Bank, "About," https://www.ecb.europa.eu/ecb/html/index .en.html.

6. "Eurozone Countries 2021," World Population Review, https:// worldpopulationreview.com/country-rankings/eurozone-countries.

7. "Projected GDP 2021," *Statistics Times*, https://statisticstimes.com/economy /projected-world-gdp-ranking.php.

8. "Euro Zone GDP—Gross Domestic Product," Country Economy, https:// countryeconomy.com/gdp/euro-zone.

9. See Kimberly Amadeo, "Largest Economies in the World," Reviewed by Thomas J. Catalano, *The Balance*, May 5, 2021, https://www.thebalance.com /world-s-largest-economy-3306044. See also "Projected GDP Ranking," *Statistics Times*, October 26, 2021, https://statisticstimes.com/economy /projected-world-gdp-ranking.php.

10. "GDP Ranked by Country 2021," *World Population Review*, https:// worldpopulationreview.com/countries/countries-by-gdp.

11. John Dickerson, "Christine Lagarde on the Global Economy: We Are All in This Together," *60 Minutes, CBS News*, October 20, 2019, https://www.cbsnews .com/news/international-monetary-fund-european-central-bank-head-christine -lagarde-60-minutes-interview-2019-10-20/.

12. Uwe Hessler, "Christine Lagarde Will Need All Her Skills to Steer ECB Through Trying Times," *Deutsche Welle*, January 11, 2019, https://www.dw.com /en/christine-lagarde-will-need-all-her-skills-to-steer-ecb-through-trying-times /a-51046045.

13. David Lawder, "IMF's Lagarde Warns Trade Conflicts Dimming Global Growth Outlook," Reuters, October 1, 2018, https://www.reuters.com/article /us-imf-g20-lagarde/imfs-lagarde-warns-trade-conflicts-dimming-global

-growth-outlook-idUSKCN1MB32L. See the full text of Christine Lagarde's speech, "How Global Trade Can Promote Growth for All," at https://www.imf .org/en/News/Articles/2018/10/09/sp101018-md-trade-conference-opening -remarks.

14. Silvia Amaro, "'I Was Expecting Something More Quiet,' Lagarde Admits on Her ECB Top Job," CNBC, September 24, 2021, https://www.cnbc.com/2021 /09/24/ecb-lagarde-on-her-president-role-was-expecting-something-more-quiet .html.

15. Katie Hope, "Christine Lagarde: The 'Rock Star' of Finance," *BBC News*, July 2, 2019, https://www.bbc.com/news/business-48847473.

16. See, for instance, Alison Smale and Jack Ewing, "Christine Lagarde on Her Plans for the European Central Bank," *New York Times*, November 17, 2020, https://www.nytimes.com/2020/11/17/business/christine-lagarde-european -central-bank.html; and "Christine Lagarde and Klaus Schwab Discuss How to Overcome the World's Greatest Challenges," *TIME*, September 1, 2021, https://time.com/6094159/klaus-schwab-christine-lagarde-dialogue/.

17. Laura D'Angelo, "Going Where No Woman Has Gone Before: Christine Lagarde," *The Edge, a Leader's Magazine*, June 1, 2020, https://theedgeleaders .com/christine-lagarde/.

18. "Financial Times," Media Bias Fact Check, Last updated April 13, 2021, https://mediabiasfactcheck.com/financial-times/.

19. Ralph Atkins, Andrew Whiffin, and FT reporters, "FT Ranking of EU Finance Ministers," *Financial Times*, November 16, 2019.

20. David Gelles, "Red Brands and Blue Brands: Is Hyper-Partisanship Coming for Corporate America?" *New York Times*, November 23, 2021, https://www .nytimes.com/2021/11/23/business/dealbook/companies-politics-partisan .html.

21. Amelia Lucas, "After Calls to Boycott Coca-Cola, CEO Says the Company Has Always Opposed New Georgia Voting Law," CNBC, March 31, 2021, https:// www.cnbc.com/2021/03/31/coca-cola-ceo-says-the-company-has-always -opposed-new-georgia-voting-law.html.

22. "Opinion: A Majority of Americans Think US Democracy Is Broken. Here Are 12 Ideas for Repairing It," CNN, October 14, 2022. See the subhead "Yuval Levin: Make Congress Actually . . . Work," https://www.cnn.com/2022/10/14 /opinions/american-democracy-broken-solutions-roundup.

23. Cassella M. Slater, "Effects of Mentorship on Empathy Development and Civility in an Upper School Community," St. Catherine University, 2019, https://sophia.stkate.edu/cgi/viewcontent.cgi?article=1325&context=maed.

24. Rick Woolworth, "Great Mentors Focus on the Whole Person, Not Just Their Career," *Harvard Business Review*, August 9, 2019, https://hbr.org/2019/08/great -mentors-focus-on-the-whole-person-not-just-their-career.

SPOTLIGHT ON MENTORING:
A CONVERSATION WITH CESAR CONDE

1. Sara Fischer, "Exclusive: NBC News Adding 200+ Jobs as Part of Major Streaming Push," Axios, July 27, 2021, https://www.axios.com/exclusive-nbc-news-adding-200-jobs-as-part-of-major-streaming-push-e59ae042-6a79-4412-adf9-292b2f0917d3.html.

CHAPTER 11

1. Eric L. Motley, *Madison Park: A Place of Hope* (Grand Rapids, MI: Zondervan/HarperCollins, 2017), 22.
2. Eric L. Motley, *Madison Park: A Place of Hope*, 51.
3. Martin Luther King Jr., *Letter from the Birmingham Jail* (San Francisco: Harper San Francisco, 1994).
4. Wil Haygood, "A Path All His Own," *Washington Post,* June 11, 2006, https://www.washingtonpost.com/wp-dyn/content/article/2006/06/10/AR2006061001040.html.
5. "The Place the Freed Slaves Made," interview by John van Sloten, *Christianity Today*, February 6, 2018, https://www.christianitytoday.com/ct/2018/january-web-only/place-freed-slaves-made.html.
6. "Eli Madison, 1840–1916," tribute at Find a Grave, https://www.findagrave.com/memorial/210058862/eli-madison.
7. Luke 12:48.
8. Madison Winston, "The Fabulous Life of Dr. John Henry Winston, Jr.," https://www.smhall.org/uploaded/documents/News_Events/The_Fabulous_Life_of_Dr._John_Henry_Winston_Jr_by_Madison_W.pdf.
9. Wil Haygood, "A Path All His Own," *Washington Post,* June 11, 2006, https://www.washingtonpost.com/wp-dyn/content/article/2006/06/10/AR2006061001040.html.
10. Eric Motley, "My Unlikely Friendship with Ruth Bader Ginsburg," *New York Times*, September 21, 2002, https://www.nytimes.com/2020/09/21/opinion/ruth-bader-ginsburg-friendship.html.
11. Jeffrey Jones, "US Church Membership Falls Below Majority for First Time," Gallup News, March 29, 2021, https://news.gallup.com/poll/341963/church-membership-falls-below-majority-first-time.aspx.
12. For instance, when we asked all people of all ages and demographics if they had experienced a significant mentoring relationship at some time in their life, the number was slightly higher for men than women (58 percent to 57 percent). Yet we saw a larger discrepancy when we broke it down by education level—71 percent of graduate students said yes to having had a mentor, and 60 percent of people whose highest level of education was a bachelor's degree said yes, but only 55 percent of people with no degree said yes. We also saw this discrepancy with income level—69 percent of people making more than $100K per year said yes, 56 percent of people making $50K–$100K said yes, and 56 percent of people making under $50K said yes.

13.   Jordan Blashek and Christopher Haugh, "Americans Appear to Be Deeply Divided. But We Found a Different Story Traveling the U.S.," *USA Today*, August 6, 2020, https://www.usatoday.com/story/opinion/2020/08/06/americans-more-united-than-our-political-rhetoric-indicates-column/3297493001/.

14.   Dan Vallone, Stephen Hawkins, Dr. Noelle Malvar, Paul Oshinski, Taran Raghuram, and Daniel Yudkin, *Two Stories of Distrust in America* (New York: More in Common, 2021), 12. See also "The Hidden Tribes of America," Hidden Tribes, 2018, https://hiddentribes.us/.

15.   "Gary M. Burge," Professor Profiles, Calvin Theological Seminary, https://www.calvinseminary.edu/profile/gary-m-burge.

16.   Dr. Gary M. Burge, *Jesus, The Middle Eastern Storyteller: Ancient Context, Ancient Faith* (Grand Rapids, MI: Zondervan, 2009), 36–37.

17.   "The Man in the Arena: Citizenship in a Republic," speech by Theodore Roosevelt, University of Paris, April 23, 1910.

18.   "Alexis de Tocqueville," History, https://www.history.com/topics/france/alexis-de-tocqueville. See also Alexis de Tocqueville, *Democracy in America*, vol. 1, translated by Henry Reeve (London, Saunders and Otley: 1835).

APPENDIX

As part of our quantitative research we conducted three surveys:

- Survey **1 | 79** Yale School of Management **MBA students** conducted by Yale research team.
- Survey **2+3 | 2,200** members of the **general US population** and 147 **C-Suite Executives** conducted by Morning Consult.

Survey **snapshot:**

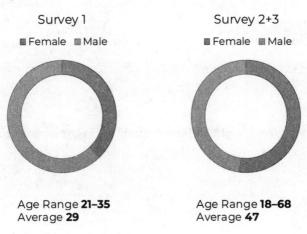

Survey 1	Survey 2+3
■ Female ■ Male	■ Female ■ Male
Age Range **21–35**	Age Range **18–68**
Average **29**	Average **47**

Who had a **mentor?**

78%
of MBA students

<

72%
of C-suite executives

<

57%
of general population

The **younger** the respondent, the **greater** the likelihood of having a mentor...

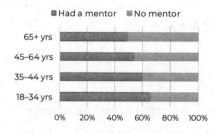

... and the **higher educational** attainment translated into a **greater** likelihood of having a mentor

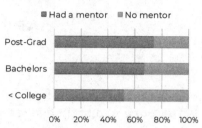

Those **earning $100K+** indicated a **greater** likelihood of having a mentor versus those earning **<$100K**...

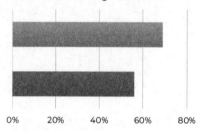

... and **men** had a **greater** likelihood of having a mentor than **women**

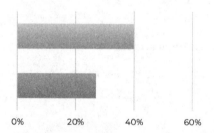

Men and women sought different qualities in their mentors...

men were more likely to seek: **power**   **prominence**

women were more likely to seek: **authenticity**   **good listener**

& AMONG PROFESSIONS, THOSE IN **GOVERNMENT** WERE **MOST LIKELY** TO HAVE A MENTOR

70%

of those working in the government sector had a mentor

Across all survey respondents, three actions, were cited as critical during the mentoring relationship:

1. Encouragement to think more broadly

2. Building confidence

3. Serving as a teacher, coach, or advisor

> C-suite professionals discussed a broader variety of personal and professional topics with mentors compared to other respondents

> For less educated, more diverse, or lower income respondents, mentors had a greater impact in swaying life decisions but less so with professional opportunities

57% of MBAs... | **33%** of General Population... | **40%** of C-suite...

... received a new professional opportunity

52% of MBAs... | **16%** of General Population... | **13%** of C-suite...

... pursued their first or additional degree

24% of MBAs... | **40%** of General Population... | **34%** of C-suite...

... made a different life decision

Across Black, White, and Hispanic survey respondents, we found the following:

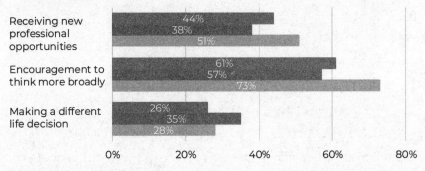

Receiving new professional opportunities
- 44%
- 38%
- 51%

Encouragement to think more broadly
- 61%
- 57%
- 73%

Making a different life decision
- 26%
- 35%
- 28%

0%   20%   40%   60%   80%

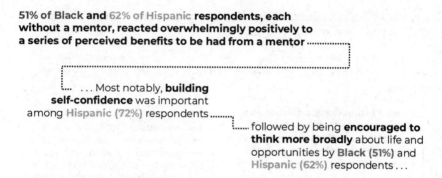

51% of Black and 62% of Hispanic **respondents, each without a mentor, reacted overwhelmingly positively to a series of perceived benefits to be had from a mentor** ⋯⋯⋯⋯⋯

⋯ . . . Most notably, **building self-confidence** was important among Hispanic (72%) respondents ⋯⋯⋯⋯⋯

⋯⋯ followed by being **encouraged to think more broadly** about life and opportunities by **Black (51%)** and Hispanic (62%) respondents . . .

. . . Finally, **formalizing the relationship** (e.g., establishing goals or committing to regular meeting times) was a strong commonality among all survey respondents, with an **increased likelihood for Black and** Hispanic **respondents**

ACKNOWLEDGMENTS

We are fortunate to have had terrific support from a number of friends and colleagues for this project. Thank you to Matt Baugher, Tim Burgard, and the entire team at HarperCollins Leadership, and our literary agents, Cait Hoyt and Mollie Glick. Thank you, also, to our friend and CAA president Richard Lovett. We are also indebted to our research team, Dr. Jeffrey Sonnenfeld, Dr. Elise Walton, Stephanie Posner, and Stephen Henriques, who brought original research and insight to our questions about mentorship. Alan Fleischmann helped shape the idea of this book from the very beginning, and our writing partner Marcus Brotherton did an exceptional job of bringing our research and these remarkable stories of mentorship to life. We also want to thank our mentors without whom neither of us would be where we are today. We're also so very grateful for our six daughters, who are the inspiration for this book. As our daughters choose their paths in life, we hope they and their generation are as fortunate to have the kinds of mentors we had, and we hope theirs is a generation that invests in transformational mentoring. Finally, we thank the extraordinary leaders who agreed to be interviewed for this book. We are inspired by their stories and the stories of the giants on whose shoulders they stand.

INDEX

ABOUT THE AUTHORS

Dina Powell McCormick is vice chairman, president, and global head of client services of BDT & MSD Partners, a leading merchant bank for founders and strategic investors.

She has helped build some of the largest mentoring programs in the world, including 10,000 Women, 10,000 Small Businesses, and One Million Black Women. Her programs have provided female entrepreneurs around the world with business and management education, mentoring and networking, and access to capital.

Dina previously worked at Goldman Sachs for sixteen years where she was global head of the sovereign business, global head of sustainability and inclusive growth, and served on the firm's Management Committee. While at Goldman Sachs, Dina led and worked with the teams that created signature inclusive growth and economic initiatives.

Earlier in her career, Dina served in the U.S. government for more than a dozen years, including as assistant to the president for Presidential Personnel and assistant secretary of state for Public Affairs and Public Diplomacy. In 2017, she rejoined the government as deputy national security advisor where she worked on a broad range of national security initiatives, including President Trump's historic visits to Saudi Arabia and China, as well as the foundations that led to the creation of the Abraham Accords.

Dina is currently chairman of the board of the Robin Hood Foundation and a trustee of the National Geographic Society, the Lincoln Center for the Performing Arts, Mount Sinai Hospital, and the Atlantic Council. She is also a member of the board of the ExxonMobil Corporation.

An essay and oil painting of Dina is featured in George W. Bush's bestselling book, *Out of Many, One: Portraits of America's Immigrants.*

❖　❖　❖

David McCormick is the recently elected United States senator from the commonwealth of Pennsylvania. Prior to that, he was the CEO of Bridgewater Associates, one of the world's largest and most successful investment firms.

Dave grew up in rural Pennsylvania and attended West Point where he was cocaptain of the Army wrestling team. After completing West Point, he graduated from the U.S. Army Ranger school and joined the 82nd Airborne Division. He served as a combat engineer officer in Iraq during the Gulf War. He retired from the Army in 1992 and went on to earn a PhD at Princeton University's School of Public and International Affairs.

David's career has included a wide range of positions in business and government, including as CEO and then president of two publicly traded software companies based in Pittsburgh, and roles at the National Security Council and the Department of Commerce. He served as President Bush's undersecretary of the Treasury for International Affairs during the global financial crisis of 2007–2008, acting as America's leading international economic diplomat.

David has served as a trustee on several nonprofit boards, including the United Service Organizations (USO), the Hospital for Special Surgery, and Carnegie Mellon University.

He is author of two books, and his essays have appeared in the *Wall Street Journal, New York Times, Washington Post, Financial Times, Fast Company*, and other notable publications.

Dave and his wife, Dina Powell McCormick, live in Pittsburgh and have six daughters between them.